How to Do *Everything* with

eBay

Greg Holden

McGraw-Hill/Osborne

New York   Chicago   San Francisco   Lisbon
London   Madrid   Mexico City   Milan   New Delhi
San Juan   Seoul   Singapore   Sydney   Toronto

The McGraw·Hill Companies

McGraw-Hill/Osborne
2100 Powell Street, 10th Floor
Emeryville, California 94608
U.S.A.

To arrange bulk purchase discounts for sales promotions, premiums, or fund-raisers, please contact **McGraw-Hill**/Osborne at the above address. For information on translations or book distributors outside the U.S.A., please see the International Contact Information page located on page xiv of this book.

How to Do Everything with eBay®

1234567890 FGR FGR 01987654

ISBN 0-07-225426-2

Publisher:	Brandon A. Nordin
Vice President &	
Associate Publisher	Scott Rogers
Senior Acquisitions Editor	Jane Brownlow
Project Editor	Elizabeth Seymour
Acquisitions Coordinator	Athena Honore
Technical Editor	Amy Hoy
Copy Editor	Mike McGee
Proofreader	John Gildersleeve
Composition	Apollo Publishing Services
Illustrator	Melinda Lytle
Series Design	Mickey Galicia
Cover Series Design	Dodie Shoemaker
Cover Illustration	Tom Willis

This book was composed with Corel VENTURA™ Publisher.

About the Author

For much of his adult life, Greg Holden has been hunting down and reselling collectibles, oddball items, and antiques of all sorts. In his younger days, he assembled an old sports car from pieces of three different sports cars. He bought and restored a century-old townhouse. Now, he hunts down fountain pens, watches, and other items online. Greg has written more than 20 books on computers and the Internet, including *How to Do Everything With Your eBay Business,* also by McGraw Hill/Osborne, and *Internet Auctions for Dummies* and *Cliff's Notes Guide to Buying and Selling on eBay*, both published by Hungry Minds. His lifelong interests in literature and writing and the history of Chicago recently culminated in the book *Literary Chicago: A Book Lover's Tour of the Windy City*, published by Lake Claremont Press. He lives in Chicago in the house he restored along with his two daughters and an assortment of pets.

Acknowledgments

Whether you only buy on eBay occasionally or sell there on a full-time basis, much of your work seems to be done at home, by yourself. But the truth is that, whenever you post a message, place a bid, leave feedback, or put an item up for sale, you are participating in a community activity. Any transaction sale on eBay depends on help and cooperation from lots of people. Trust and cooperation make online auctions work.

In the same way, writing a book about eBay depends a community of individuals you might never meet face to face. First, I want to thank the eBay sellers who took the time to talk to me either on the phone or by e-mail and share their knowledge. Thanks go to Lori Baboulis, Jill Featherston, Jennifer Karpin-Hobbs, Christoph Marx, Shannon Miller, Roni Neal, Suzanne Niesche, Wally Rockawin, Emily Sabako, and Tom and Betty Carroll.

I have been impressed with the enthusiasm and encouragement I have received from all the folks at Osborne-McGraw Hill, starting with Jane Brownlow, who got the ball rolling (and kept it rolling smoothly); Agatha Kim, who served as project editor; technical editors Amy Hoy and Michael Bellomo; project editor Elizabeth Seymour; and publicity manager Bettina Faltermeier.

Thanks also to my agent Neil Salkind and everyone at Studio B Productions. Also thanks to Ann Lindner, my intrepid assistant, who helped me with this. Last but not least, thanks to my mother and father, who instilled the love of giving new life to someone else's castoffs-a practice that carries over perfectly to the new electronic flea market, eBay. Bargain hunting is an art I'm now passing down to my two daughters, Zosia and Lucy, as their sharp eyes are becoming ever more skilled at finding just what they're looking for at thrift shops and garage sales. Sharing so many adventures with them puts fun in my life, especially when they allow me to share their ever-widening circle of loving friends and pets.

Contents

Introduction

The American business landscape is littered with victims, many having fallen after the dot-com bubble burst in 2001. Yet eBay continues to weather all of the recent economic storms. It thrives because it was founded on time-honored American traditions such as free enterprise, individual entrepreneurship, and the desire to continually search for something better. Thrifty Ben Franklin would applaud the way eBay enables people to save money. But even more impressive is the fact that eBay has helped thousands of sellers change their lives by giving them new careers.

If you haven't started buying on eBay yet, this book will give you a user-friendly introduction to the world's most popular marketplace. If you've done a few searches on eBay for long-lost toys from your childhood, this book will help you round out your collection s by showing you how to purchase more safely. And, whether you need to clear out your garage or want a new source of regular income, this book will provide the know-how to sell on eBay.

You don't have to take just my word for any of it, either. This book includes tips and advice from folks who have successfully used eBay—both as buyers and sellers, some from the U.S. and others who live abroad, both male and female, young and old. Whether I was asking how to make the most of a sales listings or how to find a bargain, I was overwhelmed by their spirit of generosity. In fact, it is that eagerness to share with others that has helped make eBay a true community.

Okay, as in any neighborhood, not every resident of eBay is a good citizen. There are a few who get distracted and don't follow through with transactions and even some who actively try to swindle other people. Accordingly, the experienced members who are featured in this book's Voices of the Community sidebars tell you how to stay out of trouble, too.

But most of the aspects of the free market that eBay has inherited are good. And through the years it has become more reliable and easier to use. So, whether you're a casual computer user or have been surfing the Internet for awhile, this book will have you buying and selling on eBay in no time.

The only assumptions this book makes about you, the reader, is that you have some familiarity with the Web and the Internet and that you want to use eBay successfully. Part I starts at the beginning—explaining how eBay works, how to find your way around the site, and how to become a registered user. You also get suggestions for how to win some auctions and make some purchases, and examples of things you can do on eBay that go beyond simply buying. As you'll soon find out, eBay can become a way of life and a social venue.

Part II, "Find Everything You Want and Shop Safely," seeks to take you beyond being a casual eBay user. In Chapter 4, you learn the importance of building an initial positive feedback rating to build your credibility, and to check other members' feedback. In Chapter 5, you get some tips on bidding strategies designed to increase your chances of winning auctions. In Chapter 6, you learn how to deal with the common sorts of difficulties that eBay sellers occasionally confront. Some of these are commonsense approaches, while others take advantage of various problem-solving mechanisms that eBay has put in place for individuals just like you.

Part III, "Selling on eBay," focuses on how to start selling and generating some income on eBay. Chapter 7 describes the basics: putting up items for sale, choosing what forms of payment to accept, and providing good customer service. You also learn how to sell merchandise at fixed price in an eBay Store. In Chapter 8, you explore the ins and outs of one of the most important ways to attract bids: providing good images of your merchandise. Chapter 9 focuses on finalizing sales: accepting payments, packing your merchandise to protect it from damage, and choosing an economical and dependable shipper.

Part IV, "Advanced Selling," takes a look at the "back end," indispensable business operations that can take your eBay sales business to a new level. Chapter 10 focuses different options for managing your eBay sales: adding information, answering questions, or re-listing items when you need to. Chapter 11 presents some tips for maximizing your sales success: selling your items at the price you want while giving your customers secure ways to transfer payment. Chapter 12, you learn about the special issues involved in operating a full-time business on eBay: how to purchase what you want to resell, and how to use auction software and services that can streamline the process of getting sales online and storing images, and provide you with records that are sure to come in handy at tax time.

eBay has quickly become a part of everyday life in America rather than a novelty enjoyed by an elite few. Chances are you've heard about eBay in the news, either by viewing its own commercials or (more likely) hearing about bizarre and noteworthy sales that have attracted the attention of the media. Accordingly, this book's special insert commemorates some of the most famous—and infamous—sales ever conducted on the site.

I didn't write this book with the expectation that you would read it from beginning to end like a story. Like the Web itself, you should feel free to skip around from chapter to chapter to find the information you need to get down to business immediately. Here are some special elements that will help you get the most out of the book:

- How to...   These boxes explain, in a nutshell, how to accomplish essential tasks. Read them to focus on key points covered in each chapter.

- Did You Know...   These short sections provide you with extra information so that you can better understand eBay or a particular way you might want to use the site.

- Notes   These spotlight basics that will give you an immediate grasp of a particular topic.

- Tips   These tell you how to do something smarter or faster.

- Cautions   These point out potential pitfalls that you need to steer around so you can keep operating smoothly.

- Sidebars   Here I address topics that are related to the subject at hand and that illuminate it in a new way.

Within the text, you also find words in special formatting. New terms are in italics, while specific commands you need to choose or type yourself are in boldface.

Along the way, you'll read comments and tips by individuals who sell on eBay on a daily basis, and who have been generous enough to share their expertise with you. The information in this book has been compiled by me with the help of other online "experts." Don't get upset if a Web page or a piece of software isn't exactly where it's described in the book. eBay's site changes all the time, as does the rest of the Web. That's part of the fun of doing business online. I wish you happy buying and selling on eBay. Please relax, have fun, and enjoy being a member of the community. And why not keep the ball rolling by telling me about your own experiences and whether this book has helped you? Please drop me a line at greg@gregholden.com. Either on eBay or via e-mail, I look forward to seeing you around.

INTERNATIONAL CONTACT INFORMATION

AUSTRALIA
McGraw-Hill Book Company
Australia Pty. Ltd.
TEL +61-2-9900-1800
FAX +61-2-9878-8881
http://www.mcgraw-hill.com.au
books-it_sydney@mcgraw-hill.com

CANADA
McGraw-Hill Ryerson Ltd.
TEL +905-430-5000
FAX +905-430-5020
http://www.mcgraw-hill.ca

**GREECE, MIDDLE EAST, & AFRICA
(Excluding South Africa)**
McGraw-Hill Hellas
TEL +30-210-6560-990
TEL +30-210-6560-993
TEL +30-210-6560-994
FAX +30-210-6545-525

MEXICO (Also serving Latin America)
McGraw-Hill Interamericana Editores
S.A. de C.V.
TEL +525-1500-5108
FAX +525-117-1589
http://www.mcgraw-hill.com.mx
carlos_ruiz@mcgraw-hill.com

SINGAPORE (Serving Asia)
McGraw-Hill Book Company
TEL +65-6863-1580
FAX +65-6862-3354
http://www.mcgraw-hill.com.sg
mghasia@mcgraw-hill.com

SOUTH AFRICA
McGraw-Hill South Africa
TEL +27-11-622-7512
FAX +27-11-622-9045
robyn_swanepoel@mcgraw-hill.com

SPAIN
McGraw-Hill/
Interamericana de España, S.A.U.
TEL +34-91-180-3000
FAX +34-91-372-8513
http://www.mcgraw-hill.es
professional@mcgraw-hill.es

**UNITED KINGDOM, NORTHERN,
EASTERN, & CENTRAL EUROPE**
McGraw-Hill Education Europe
TEL +44-1-628-502500
FAX +44-1-628-770224
http://www.mcgraw-hill.co.uk
emea_queries@mcgraw-hill.com

ALL OTHER INQUIRIES Contact:
McGraw-Hill/Osborne
TEL +1-510-420-7700
FAX +1-510-420-7703
http://www.osborne.com
omg_international@mcgraw-hill.com

Chapter 1

Get Online and Start the Bidding!

How to...

- Get acquainted with eBay and find out why it is so popular
- Start navigating the eBay web site
- Choose your User ID and password and create your own user account
- Understand eBay's auction and fixed-price sales
- Learn from eBay's experienced sellers
- Become a smart shopper by researching sales items as well as sellers

In the late nineteenth century, mail-order catalogs changed the way people shopped. Suddenly, everyone from city dwellers to farm families could buy the same household goods without ever leaving the comfort of their homes. In the late twentieth century, a web site initially called AuctionWeb, later renamed eBay, brought about another revolution. Now, without ever leaving the comfort of their homes, everyone with a computer and a connection to the Internet could shop for the same things. The difference was that the merchants doing the selling were individual people, and the merchandise was chosen by those individuals.

Everybody loves a bargain. Shoppers love to find them. Sellers love to give shoppers the feeling that they are getting them. Due to these tendencies, eBay has become a bargain-hunter's paradise. It's also become a way of life for anyone who wants to find collectibles or scarce and valuable merchandise of all sorts. More than that, eBay has changed people's lives, as you'll learn when you read the profiles of the members who took the time to help newcomers like you by providing tips and talking about their experiences on the world's most popular auction site. This chapter provides you with an overview of the most important features you need to be familiar with, whether you intend to buy or sell on eBay.

What Is eBay?

eBay is a web site that gives anyone who can connect to it with a web browser the ability to make purchases or sell merchandise. It's an online marketplace that is built around auction sales. But over the years, it has expanded to enable sellers to open up their own web sites called eBay Stores, where they sell catalog merchandise at fixed prices.

The World's Most Exciting Marketplace

The rather dry description doesn't describe how business is actually transacted on eBay. It doesn't convey how exciting it can be to bid at auction or, if you are a seller, to watch bidders compete for what you are selling and often pay far more than you ever anticipated. Although stores and fixed-price sales are taking on more and more importance on eBay, auctions were what originally made eBay so popular, and today they remain the most popular types of transactions held online.

If you are at all familiar with the kinds of traditional auctions held by antiques dealers, liquidation sellers, and others, you can understand eBay better by comparing how traditional auctions work to how virtual auctions work on eBay. Table 1-1 describes some differences.

Difference	Traditional Auctions	eBay Auctions
Location	The auction takes place at a given time and place. Everyone bids together either in person, over the phone, or online.	Sellers and buyers may be located around the world, but the sale is presented on eBay.
Timing	The sale is generally over in a matter of minutes.	Sales last one, three, five, seven, or ten days and end at a specific date and time. This makes last-minute or last-second bids critical.
Inspection	You can inspect the merchandise in person if you go to the auction location before the sale.	Unless you live near the seller, you can't touch the merchandise in person. You rely on the seller's description and photos of the objects being sold.
Appraisal and worth	Expert appraisers are often available to describe sales items and tell both buyers and sellers what they are worth.	It's up to both buyers and sellers to do their homework and determine what an item is worth.
Seller reputation	Both buyers and sellers depend on the reputation of the organization conducting the sale to handle things honestly.	A feedback system rewards honest behavior. A member's feedback rating (a numeric value assigned to positive and negative feedback), as well as comments left by others who have done business with the person, can be reviewed.

TABLE 1-1   Differences Between eBay and Traditional Auctions

TIP

Many of the aspects of traditional auctions are integral to the sales conducted on eBay Live Auctions. You can find out more about this area of eBay in Chapter 3.

Another thing that makes eBay so popular and exciting for both buyers and sellers is the fact that so many people use it. eBay has said that it has as many as 69 million members. Every day, an estimated two million new items are being offered for sale either on the main eBay site in the United States or in other versions of eBay around the globe. With that kind of volume, shoppers are bound to find just about anything up for sale on eBay sooner or later. If you are a seller, you gain the ability to place your sales items before the eyes of prospective customers around the world.

NOTE

The figures about eBay's membership are taken from an eBay Radio show conducted in early 2004, as well as an interview with an eBay spokesman on the Web Talk Guys site, www.webtalkguys.com/article-ebay.shtml, in summer 2003. eBay Radio is a weekly show presented on the Internet live every Tuesday. You can read instructions on how to listen in at www.wsradio.com/ebayradio.

A Place Where New Careers Are Born

The figures mentioned in the preceding section don't reflect the fact that, by eBay's estimate, as many as 165,000 people have become so proficient at selling on eBay that they do it full-time. It doesn't describe the personal connections that develop in eBay's discussion areas and user groups. That's something you have to experience for yourself. Join in on some discussions or watch the way longtime users greet one another in eBay's chat rooms (see Chapter 4 for more on these and other types of community venues).

It's not an exaggeration to say that eBay has the potential to change people's lives. Most members turn to eBay at holiday time, or when they have a few items they want to clean out of their basement or garage. They are casual users. But others have found eBay to be full of surprising experiences.

While I was writing this book, a school district in the heart of Kansas decided to sell off one of its buildings due to declining enrollment. It would have been happy to sell the building for $5000 (or even one dollar), but when the building was listed on eBay (see Figure 1-1), it received bids and inquiries from all over the world.

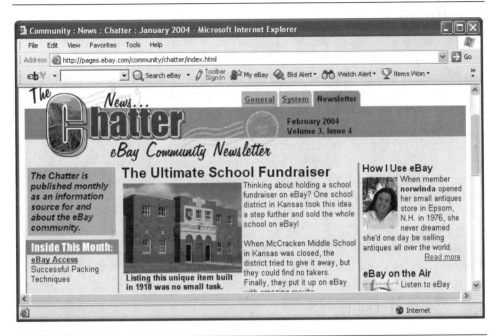

FIGURE 1-1 eBay helps sellers find buyers, even for old school buildings like this.

The building eventually sold for $49,500, and the school district was overjoyed. But that's not the whole story. The buyers turned out to be city dwellers and longtime eBay sellers who decided to move to Kansas and use the building as a distribution center—for their thriving business selling on eBay.

Navigating eBay

You don't need any special software to connect to eBay. One of the reasons why the site is so popular is that it's so easy to get started using it. First of all, it's free to shop on eBay. If you are only going to shop on eBay, you can do so with your existing Internet connection and web browser. Before you can buy something, you'll need to register with eBay. The process of navigating eBay's voluminous site and becoming a registered user is described in the sections that follow.

NOTE *If you plan to sell on eBay, you may need to purchase a digital camera or scanner in order to obtain digital images of your merchandise. See Chapter 8 for more on adding images to your sales listings.*

The Home Page

eBay's home page is one of the most popular locations on the Internet, a site visited by millions of people each day. It's the logical place to start exploring eBay. But you may not realize that the version of the home that you see differs depending on whether or not eBay "recognizes" you as a registered user. A registered user of eBay is someone who has created an account that tells eBay who you are.

When you first register (a process described in the section "Becoming a Registered User" later in this chapter), you submit your real name, address, and other personal information to eBay. You also choose a User ID, a name by which you will be publicly known when you trade or post messages on the site, and, finally, a password—a series of characters you keep secret and that protects your identity on the site.

If you haven't yet registered (or if you are a registered user but you haven't yet signed in, or if eBay has not placed a cookie on your computer as described in the following sidebar), you'll see the version of eBay's home page shown in Figure 1-2. Try it yourself: connect to the Internet, start up your web browser, and connect to the home page URL, www.ebay.com.

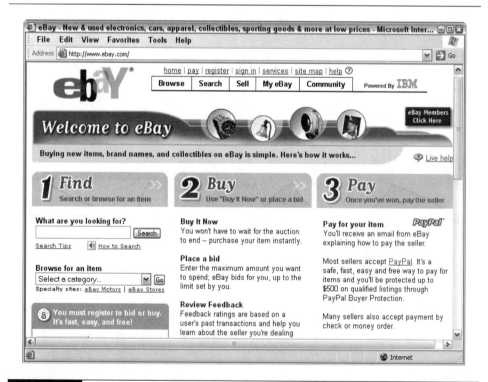

FIGURE 1-2   This version of eBay's home page appears to new users.

The Welcome to eBay version of the home page encourages you to register. You can become a registered user by clicking the Register Now button in column 1. But you don't *have* to register in order to shop on the site. You can shop for items currently up for sale on eBay in one of two ways:

- Enter a keyword or phrase in the box labeled "What are you looking for?" and click Search to search eBay's site for merchandise. You'll be presented with a list of auctions that have your specified search term(s) in their title.

- Click the drop-down list arrow on the right side of the box labeled Browse for an Item. Choose a category from the drop-down list, and then click Go to look through items currently up for sale in that category.

Once you are on a category page or on a page of search results, you can navigate eBay's site much the same as any registered user. But you can't place bids on anything until you register yourself. Once you are registered, if you are signed in, you see the version of the home page shown in Figure 1-3.

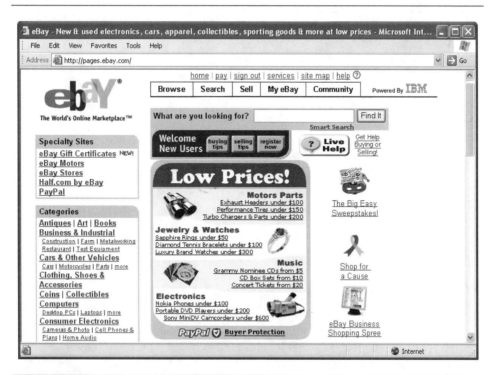

FIGURE 1-3   If you have signed in previously and eBay "recognizes" you, you see this version of the home page.

 **Sign In and Sign Out**

When you become a registered user (a process described later in this chapter), you identify yourself to eBay. You assign yourself a User ID and password that you use to place bids and access different services on eBay's web site. The process of signing in is one you'll have to get used to. You are frequently asked to sign in, whether you want to search through eBay's database of completed sales, place a bid, or access your My eBay page (a special page eBay provides you, which you can use to keep track of your purchasing and sales activities).

To sign in, click the Sign In link in the row of links at the top of the eBay navigation bar. You are asked to provide your username and password. Take notice of the check box labeled Keep Me Signed In on this Computer Unless I Sign Out. It's just beneath the Password box, and shown in the following illustration.

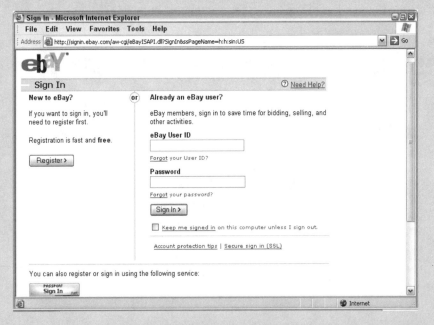

If you check the "Keep me signed in..." box, eBay "remembers" you when you visit parts of the site. It does this by placing a tiny bit of digital information called a *cookie* on your computer. You won't need to sign in again so often if you have checked this box—that is, until you sign out. Once you have signed in, the link usually labeled Sign In at the top of the navigation bar changes to Sign Out. Click the Sign Out link to sign out from eBay's site.

You might well wonder why you should ever sign out, since it's so convenient to remain signed in. One answer is security: you don't want your kids, coworkers, or other unauthorized users to place bids while you are signed in. Another is that, like many eBay members, you may want to create multiple eBay accounts. Some members use separate accounts for buying and selling on eBay, for instance. In order to switch from one account to another, you need to sign out of the first account and then sign in again using the second User ID and password.

You'll also notice at the bottom of the eBay Sign In page another button that enables you to sign in or sign out of eBay. This button uses an identification system created by Microsoft Corporation called Microsoft Passport. A Passport is an e-mail address and password that you use to access a variety of services, such as Microsoft's popular Hotmail e-mail service, and its Microsoft bCentral web hosting service. When you click the Passport Sign In button, your browser displays a different sign-in form (see Figure 1-4) that you can use to access services on eBay.

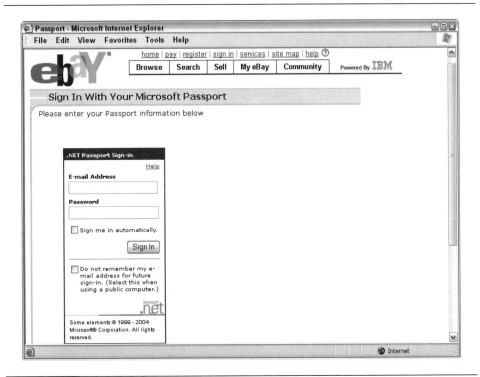

FIGURE 1-4   You can sign in to eBay using your eBay account or your Microsoft Passport ID information, if you have a Passport.

The Navigation Bar

When you board an elevator, you press a button that determines where you want to go. (If you're feeling mischievous, of course, you can push multiple buttons.) Similarly, eBay includes a set of buttons at the top of nearly all pages on the site. It's called a navigation bar (see Figure 1-5), and it leads you to the most popular areas of the site.

The main part of the navigation bar contains five boxes. Clicking any one of the boxes takes you to a different part of eBay. For example, if you click Browse, you go to a page containing all of eBay's categories so you can browse through the ones of your choice. If you click Search, you go to the Basic Search page. At the same time, a new second set of subcategories drops down beneath the Search main navigation category after you click that main category.

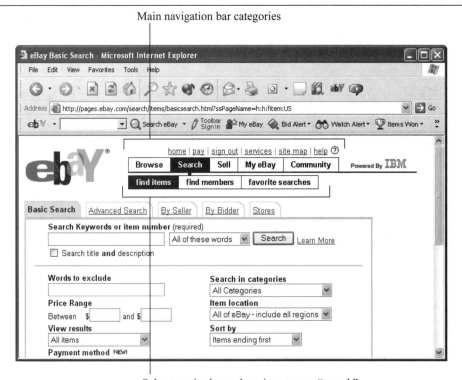

FIGURE 1-5   eBay's navigation bar is nearly always present and helps you move from one part of eBay to another.

Above the main row of buttons, there are six links that also point you to important locations or get you started with important tasks. These six links and the five main buttons and their functions are described in Table 1-2.

Link	Where It Takes You	What You Can Do There
Home	eBay's home page	View featured auctions, get Live Help, or browse categories
Pay	Sign In, then the Pay for Items I've Won page	Pay for sales you have made or leave feedback for sellers from whom you have purchased items
Sign In/Sign Out	Sign In takes you to the Sign In page; Sign Out automatically signs you out and takes you to the Home page.	Sign In enables you to browse and access services with your User ID; Sign Out lets you sign back in with a second account if you have one.
Services	Services page	Access a wide variety of resources relating to trust, safety, selling, and buying on eBay
Site Map	Site Map page	Get an overview of most of the category and other links on eBay
Help	eBay Help page	Search for a term you don't understand, contact eBay, or get answers to questions about using eBay
Browse	Buy Everything on eBay page	Links to all of the top-level categories on eBay, with numbers representing the number of items in each one
Search	Basic Search	Search eBay by keyword; click Advanced Search for more options, By Seller to find an individual's sales, By Bidder to find someone's bids, and Stores to find an eBay Store.
Sell	The Sell Your Item form	Put up an item for sale on eBay
My eBay	Your own My eBay page	Track your buying and selling activities, watch sales, and change your preferences
Community	Community Hub Overview	Links to eBay's Discussion Boards, Chat Rooms, the Answer Center, Workshops, eBay Groups, and other ways to meet eBay members

TABLE 1-2   eBay Navigation Bar links

 *eBay provides you with another way to search the site quickly and access popular locations within it. You can install eBay Toolbar, which is added to your browser's set of toolbars and lets you connect to eBay no matter what web site is currently displayed in your browser window. See Chapter 5 for more on using the eBay toolbar.*

The Site Map

eBay has one of the most extensive web sites around; if you count each one of the user-created auction listings or sales descriptions as a part of its site, you have millions of pages to navigate. After years of scouring through the site, I still have trouble finding certain pages easily. It's impossible to gather links to every one of those pages in one location. But the Site Map attempts to gather all of the links to all of the site's main areas.

The Site Map link in the row of links at the top of the navigation bar takes you to the Site Map page shown in Figure 1-6. Having looked through this page extensively over the years, I can tell you that it doesn't list every single eBay resource. But I can also tell you that it is a good place to go if you can't find what you're looking

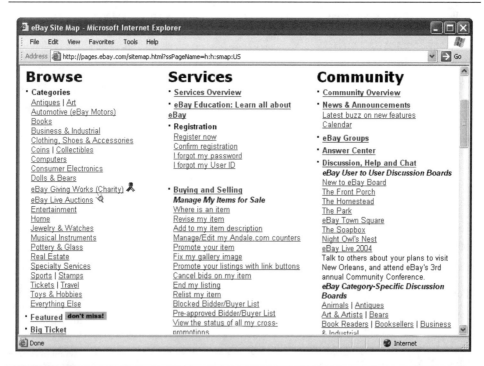

FIGURE 1-6   The Site Map page contains links to most of eBay's important areas for buyers and sellers.

for any other way. Even if you don't find the specific page you want, you'll find links that eventually lead to it.

If you have some time on your hands or need to take a break between browsing or selling activities, scan the Site Map and do some exploring. Click the Specialty Services link, and you get an overview of all categories. Click Regions, and you go to a page that lets you search for items currently up for sale on eBay in various countries and American cities. Click Suggestion Box, and you discover a page that lets you send a suggestion directly to eBay.

Some of the "hidden areas" within the Site Map are described in Chapter 3. So are some parts of eBay that enable buyers to purchase merchandise at a fixed price, Half.com and eBay Stores, for example, as well as eBay Motors and eBay Live Auctions.

Becoming a Registered User

Browsing the site map and shopping through the many categories on eBay's web site only takes you so far. Sooner or later, you'll want to actively participate by placing a bid, making a purchase, or putting something up for sale. In order to be a full participant on eBay, you need to become a registered user.

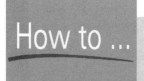

How to ... Create an eBay User Account

The process of registering with eBay is easy. Just keep in mind that you must be age 18 or older to register, and you must give eBay your real name and address as well as a telephone number and other personal information. A few minutes later, you can be trading on eBay yourself. Just follow these steps:

1. Go to the eBay Home page. Click the Register Now button.

2. When the Registration: Enter Information page appears, enter your name, address, phone number, and e-mail address in the appropriate text boxes. Also enter a User ID and password, a secret question, and your date of birth. Take care when you select your User ID and password; you'll be entering them frequently when you use eBay in the future. In particular, your User ID will represent your "public identity" on eBay. See the "What's in a User name?" section later in this chapter for more information.

3. Click Continue. One of two things happen:

■ If your User ID is available, you move to the next Enter Information page.

■ If your preferred User ID is not available, you will see the page shown in Figure 1-7. You can either fill in three of your favorite things (hobby, person, color, animal, food, and so on) on the left side of the screen and then click Suggest Some User IDs, or enter another User ID in the box on the right-hand side of the page and then click Create Another User ID. In either case, don't be discouraged. eBay has 69 million registered members, and more than 69 million User IDs have been created (many of those members have more than one account). Your first choice (or second, or third) may already belong to someone.

4. When you have chosen a unique User ID, your browser will next display a second page entitled Enter Information. Here, the information you are asked to enter is your credit card number. Why do you need to enter a credit card number even before you have taken part in a single transaction on eBay? Don't worry: it's for identification purposes only. And you don't have to provide a credit card number at all (unless you plan to register to sell as well as buy. Alternatively, you can also enter a second e-mail address from an Internet service provider, such as America Online (AOL), if you have one.

5. After your identification information has been accepted, the Registration: Agree to Terms page appears. Read the User Agreement and check the two boxes at the bottom of this page: I am 18+ years old, and I understand that I can choose not to receive communications from eBay.

6. Click I Agree to These Terms.

7. You're now asked to check your e-mail inbox. Look for a message from eBay that contains a special number that lets you confirm your registration. When you receive the e-mail message, click the Confirmation Registration Form link on the Registration - Step 1 Complete page. Enter the number and click the Complete Your Registration button.

When you have completed the process, a web page appears confirming that you have successfully registered with eBay. You can now move on to placing some bids or making some instant purchases by clicking a Buy It Now button when it is available.

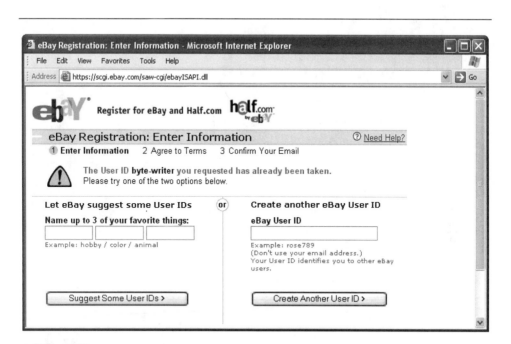

FIGURE 1-7   On this page, eBay helps you find a User ID.

Be sure to select a secure password when you create your eBay account. A secure password is one that is difficult for someone to guess. Many passwords are "cracked" by unauthorized users simply because they are obvious. They may be the same as the User ID, the word "password" itself, part of the owner's real name, or a recognizable word in the dictionary. Simply avoiding one of these common mistakes makes your eBay password more secure. See the "Picking a Good Password" section in Chapter 6 for some suggestions.

TIP   *If you ever lose or forget your password, you can go to a special Forget Your Password? page (http://cgi3.ebay.com/aw-cgi/ eBayISAPI.dll?ForgotYourPasswordShow) and eBay will send you an e-mail so you can choose a new one.*

You're Never too Old to Start with eBay

The twilight years are a time for many seniors to start sorting through their worldly goods. But what to do with unwanted items, many of them never used? eBay turns out to be the perfect solution. Plus, age is not a barrier to becoming a member of eBay—nor to learning to use your first computer, for that matter. Consider Tom and Betty Carroll of Fort Wayne, Indiana. The Carrolls are both age 85 and sell actively on eBay.

Tom and Betty Carroll

"After we got a computer about four years ago, one of the first things we did was go on eBay. I sold some of my 'Heirlooms of Tomorrow' (small porcelain art objects) and the lady we sold them to was delightful and she really got us started. We have since disposed of many items we've had for years; everything from antique sleigh bells for a horse for $125, and an old leopard coat we were just ready to give to the Goodwill for $140, a campground membership for $1000, old watches (around the house for 50 years or more) for $50 to $100, and an early issue of Sports Illustrated for $175.

"We have always gotten our payment and positive feedbacks, except for one person who didn't reply. We send the item immediately and give the buyers a good feedback. We try to treat our buyers like we would like to be treated. We have had a lot of fun and made some money. We've also successfully resisted friends wanting us to put their items on for them."

Besides the monetary benefits, selling on eBay has added a new dimension to the Carrolls' life. "You meet wonderful people doing this. eBay has really added a big amount of interest—and suspense—to our lives."

What's in a Username?

If you have surfed the Web for even a little while, you know the value of domain names that are easy to remember and that tell you something about the content of a web site. (A domain name is the "microsoft.com" or "whitehouse.gov" part of a URL.) You enter such names in your web browser's Address box, as well as the rest of the URL, when you visit a web site. My children find it easy to remember domain names like barbie.com and neopets.com.

When you create an account with eBay, you should take some time picking a user ID. Your own shoppers shouldn't be left scratching their heads if they want to do a search for your current sales or send you an e-mail message using eBay's contact system. In that system, if you want to reach a member, you don't send a message directly to the person's e-mail address unless you have already obtained that address from the member during a transaction or another communication. Rather, you use the User ID to contact the person, and eBay relays your message to the member using its own communication system. It's another reason why picking a good User ID is so important.

> **NOTE** *eBay puts itself "in the middle" in order to maintain its members' privacy. If real, legitimate e-mail addresses were published on eBay, the e-mail marketers who specialize in sending unsolicited commercial e-mail or "spam" would have a field day. Often, marketers use computer programs that scour the content of web pages looking for e-mail addresses. In its early days, eBay let members use their e-mail addresses as their User IDs. Those members (including me) were soon overrun by spam e-mail. Now, eBay prohibits members from using e-mail addresses as User IDs.*

What's an ideal User ID? First of all, make sure you choose a User ID that meets eBay's requirements. You already know you can't use an e-mail address, but here are some other rules to follow:

- Don't use a URL as your User ID.

- Don't use the word "eBay" as part of the User ID.

- Don't use any blank spaces; you can use the underline (_) or hyphen (-) character if you need to separate words.

- Don't use obscene or offensive words.

You *can* use letters, numbers, and symbols on the keyboard, except for & and @, that is. If you plan to sell, consider a User ID that refers to your business, or to something you know well. Some of the successful sellers profiled in this book have User IDs that refer to their business name.

The two women who run Venus Rising Limited have the User ID venusrisinglimited, for instance; the proprietor of Morning Glorious Collectibles uses the User ID morning-glorious. If you don't have a business or business name, just choose something that reflects upon you in a positive and professional way and is easy for others—and for you—to remember.

Learning the Lingo of eBay

Every marketplace has its own terminology and its own ways of doing business. Some stores conduct "Blue Light Specials." Others have "rollbacks," markdowns, and seasonal sales. eBay, too, has its own ways of doing business. In order to find the bargains you want, or make the money you want by selling, you have to know how to play the game. This section gives you an introduction to eBay's auctions and fixed-price sales so you know what your options are when you want to do some shopping.

Auction Types

Auctions are the types of sales that pop into people's heads when they first think about eBay. But auctions on eBay are not all created equal. As a seller, the type of auction you choose for your merchandise can have a direct impact on the number of bids you receive. As a bidder, you need to know how long the auction lasts, and whether there are special features like reserve prices or Buy It Now options involved, so you can decide when and how much to bid.

Auctions on eBay can last one, three, five, seven, or ten days. The seller chooses how long the auction can last. The auction's ending time is determined by the time it appears on eBay: if a sale goes on eBay at 10:05 A.M. PST on a Sunday and the seller chooses a length of seven days, the sale will end at 10:05 A.M. the following Sunday. The seller can choose to end the sale early, but this does not happen often, because doing so can damage the seller's reputation. The sale can also end before the specified time if the seller has added a Buy It Now price. If a Buy It Now price is available, a buyer can click the Buy It Now button and purchase the item immediately.

Standard Auctions

A standard auction is the simplest type of auction on eBay. The bidding goes up by increments, and the winner is the high bidder at the time the sale ends. The seller specifies a starting bid—a bid that is placed initially to get the bidding started. Sometimes, sellers specify a starting bid that represents the minimum amount they want to receive for an object.

For instance, if someone is selling a set of china and wants to receive at least $300 for it, the seller might place a starting bid of $300. That way, in order to become the high bidder, someone would have to place a bid of at least $300 in order to be the high bidder and have a chance of winning.

Most starting bids are kept low by sellers. Many start the bidding at $1 or at $9.99. If a seller wants to guarantee that he or she receives a minimum bid for something in order to avoid a loss, he or she can specify a reserve price as described in the following section.

Reserve Auctions

A reserve auction is the same as a standard auction, with one difference. When the sales description is created, the seller specifies a reserve price. Bids placed on the item must meet or exceed the reserve in order for the seller to be obligated to sell it. When a reserve price is present, bidders initially see the message "Reserve not yet met" next to the current high bid. The reserve price itself is kept secret until someone's bid meets the reserve. When that happens, the message changes to "Reserve met."

Reserve prices are usually known only to the seller so that bidding can potentially go higher than the reserve amount. A few sellers make the reserve known in their item descriptions, but this is not common. If bids fail to meet the reserve when the sale ends, the seller is not obligated to sell the item. (However, some sellers may negotiate with the high bidder after the sale to see if the high bidder will meet the reserve.)

Multiple-Item Auctions

A multiple-item auction, also known as a Dutch auction, is used to auction multiple, identical items at the same time. The seller specifies a starting bid and the number of items that are available. Potential bidders can bid at, or above, the minimum for one or more of the objects being offered. At the close of the auction, all winning bidders pay the lowest successful price (that is, the lowest bid that is still above the minimum price). Dutch auctions and the concept of "successful price" can be hard to understand. An example can help clarify this type of sale:

Suppose you uncover a box full of ten Chuckles-the-Cat Bean Bag Babies at a garage sale. You put all ten up for sale at the same time in a single Dutch auction. You specify a minimum bid of $20 for each cat. Eighteen separate bidders place bids: One bids $30, two bid $25, three bid $24, two bid $22, two bid $21, and the rest bid $20. The ten highest bidders win: these are the individuals who bid $30, $25, $24, $22, and $21, respectively. However—and this is the confusing part—in a Dutch auction, they all purchase at the *lowest* successful price, which is $21. Those who bid $20 lose out because there are no more than ten cats available.

Fixed-Price Sales

As eBay expands and businesses both small and large sell on the site, you see more and more fixed-price sales: items that the seller is offering for a set value. Fixed-price sales have attractive options for both buyers and sellers. Buyers who discover something they really want and who don't want to run the risk of being outbid by other collectors can click the Buy It Now button, if it is available, and buy it immediately at that fixed price. They might pay a little more than they would through the bidding process, but they also have the certainty that the item will soon be theirs.

For sellers, fixed-price sales bring convenience: sales can end quickly, which means they can get paid faster. Since sellers should specify a Buy It Now price that represents what they really want to be paid for the merchandise, they should be happy if someone makes the purchase. On the other hand, sellers can never be sure that they are getting the best possible price for their offerings; bidders could have bid more than the specified fixed price.

Buy It Now

Sellers can offer a fixed Buy It Now price (commonly abbreviated as BIN) in several situations on eBay. Often, the BIN price is the only option offered. The many items sold in eBay Stores are all offered with BIN prices, for instance. But BIN prices can be offered as an option in auction sales, too.

Sometimes, you'll see auctions that have a high bid price as well as a BIN price. Other times, you'll see an auction that has a reserve price as well as a BIN option. As indicated in Figure 1-8, you can either place a bid or buy the item by clicking the Buy It Now button.

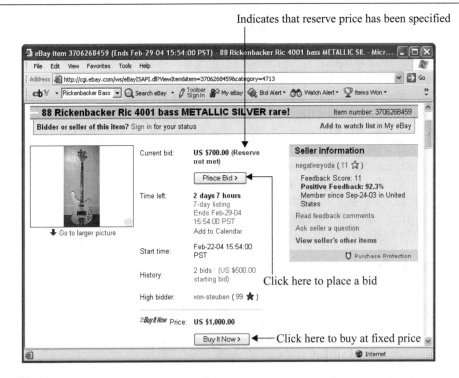

FIGURE 1-8   Buy It Now fixed prices are often combined with auction bids to give buyers options.

If you see a BIN price along with a Place Bid button on an item, you have to keep a couple of important rules in mind. Suppose you see a standard auction item with a Buy It Now price. Chances are, the BIN price won't be there long. In such cases, the BIN price disappears as soon as the first bid is placed. However, in a reserve auction with a BIN price, the BIN price remains until the reserve price is met.

Some crafty bidders are "BIN killers." They place a low bid on a standard auction item that has a BIN price just to eliminate the BIN option. They can then wait until the end of the auction to swoop in and hopefully win the item at a bargain. It's just one of several bidding strategies described in Chapter 2.

eBay Stores

An eBay Store is a place on eBay's site where experienced sellers offer merchandise at a fixed price. It's a little like setting up shop in a shopping mall or a strip mall in the real, brick-and-mortar business world. Sellers organized their wares by category, and they are able to keep sales items online for as long as 30 days, compared with the maximum ten days available with auction sales. Jennifer Karpin-Hobbs, who runs a store called Morning Glorious Collectibles, is able to sell time at the Vermont bed-and-breakfast she runs with her husband, as shown in Figure 1-9.

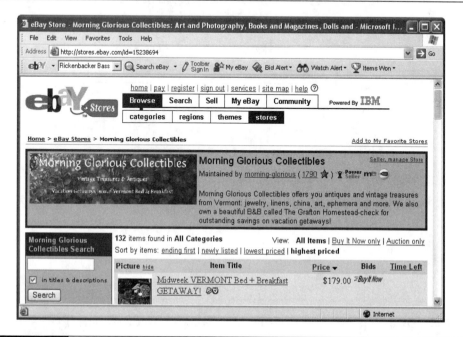

FIGURE 1-9   eBay Stores give experienced eBay sellers another sales venue for their wares.

eBay Stores give you a place to buy merchandise from sellers with whom you have already done business. If you like their auction items, you'll probably like what they have to offer in their store.

When it comes to finding an eBay Store, you have several options:

■ Sellers who create auction listings have a note at the bottom of the Seller Information box that appears with their description: "Visit this Seller's eBay Store!" followed by the name of the store.

■ You can click the eBay Stores icon next to the User ID of someone who operates a store and your browser will connect to the store's Home page.

■ You can do a search for someone's current sales by clicking the By Seller tab in Basic Search or Advanced Search and, at the top of the list of sales, click the icon Visit this Seller's eBay Store.

■ You can go to the eBay Stores home page (http://stores.ebay.com, shown in Figure 1-10), enter all or part of the store's name in the Search for Stores box, click the button next to Store name and description, and click Search.

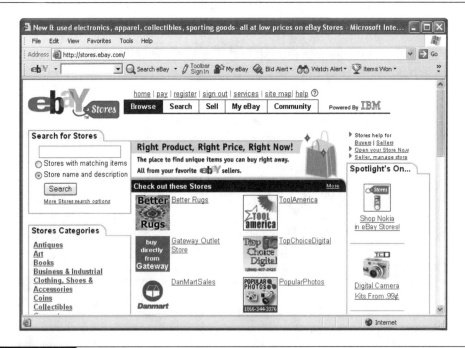

FIGURE 1-10   eBay Stores let you shop for fixed-price items offered by experienced sellers.

You can also search for fixed-price items being offered in eBay Stores by clicking Stores with matching items, entering a keyword that describes what you are looking for, and then clicking Search.

Learning from eBay's PowerSellers

Throughout this book, you will read profiles and get tips from real-life eBay sellers. The sellers I interviewed have been particularly successful. Many have a coveted designation called PowerSeller that eBay only bestows upon its most successful sellers. People in the PowerSellers program get a variety of benefits, not the least of which is group health insurance.

For PowerSellers, and for many other longtime sellers who visit eBay on a daily basis, the marketplace has become an integral part of their lives. They visit with old friends they meet in the message boards. They learn how to provide good customer service, process payments, and fulfill orders just like longtime businesspeople. They discover how to promote themselves and solve problems. Get to know the people with the PowerSeller icon after their User ID; they exemplify the rewards for honest dealing and helpful service that keep eBay going and make it so popular.

One Good Deed Leads to Another, eBay Seller Discovers

Roni Neal is committed to doing the right thing. For example, Neal (whose User ID is roniheart) is a dutiful daughter who left a thriving business in Colorado she had owned for 12 years. "I relocated to the Nashville, Tennessee area in 2002 to help care for my elderly father who is disabled with a serious heart condition," she explains. But one good turn leads to another, as Neal discovered when her father suggested she become a full-time seller on eBay.

"I needed to find something that would allow me the freedom to care for my father and help him with his pets, housework, acres of land, hospital visits, shopping, and so on. After several job interviews, all of which I turned down for one reason or another, but mostly because of the time factor and pay, my

Father said to me, 'What about eBay?' He knew of another woman who was selling on the site. I registered on December 15, 2002 and began selling seriously in January of 2003. I had previously listed a few auctions on December 26, 2002 on the free listing day.

"Already licensed from my previous business, I set out buying and selling to see what I could do. Within a month or two, I felt that I was on my way to selling enough to make a living. By June, I made the PowerSellers program. Now, eBay is my full-time career. eBay has been a blessing for me; it gives me the income I need and the time I need. I find it very ironic that I relocated here to help my Father and he is the one who sent me to eBay."

Neal holds herself to high professional standards as an eBay seller. She has developed a following of repeat customers. "Occasionally everyone will get an unhappy customer," she points out. "I treat all people the way I wish to be treated, with respect. I am open to their points of view even if I do not agree with them. I offer a solution and try to resolve problems promptly, attentively, and with kindness."

Running a business on eBay is a full-time job for Neal. "I believe that you must be serious about it, the same as you would any other full-time position. It takes some time, research, customer-service skills, and self-discipline. I am readily available to answer e-mails in a timely manner. I believe in shipping in a timely manner as well. I ship packages usually within one day after payment is received and I ship at the Post Office six days a week. It is my belief that anytime there is an exchange of money, retail, wholesale, or eBay, the seller should show due care for the service and product they are providing. If they do this, they will succeed."

In one eBay Group she particularly enjoys, Neal finds other female sellers who are also interested in benefiting the less fortunate. "PowerChicks is a private group for women who actively sell on eBay. We have one group leader, four moderators, and approximately 100 members. The group is currently accepting new members by referral only. This private group is a network for women to find and give support, and to share their hopes and dreams, joys and sorrows, triumphs and defeats, all in a safe environment. The PowerChicks are all different in their backgrounds, education, and so on, but they all share the same active goal: selling on eBay. Our group is currently organizing 'PowerChicks Philanthropy,' and we are planning charity auctions, donations, and a PowerChicks cookbook to benefit the needs of others.

"I realize that I am still a small seller compared to many, but I also believe that I have made improvements from when I first began selling. I believe eBay provides a wonderful opportunity for anyone who has a desire to succeed."

Finding What You Want

Once you've become a registered eBay user and have learned the basics of using the site, you can begin to do some shopping and start placing your first bids. Bidding on an item is easy—so easy that I urge you to take some time and do some research before you start opening your checkbook or credit card account. Don't bid on anything for the first day or two. Search for items that you collect yourself and that you know well. See how many items are being offered for sale and watch how the bidding proceeds. The sections that follow suggest some smart shopping techniques you can pursue before you try out the smart bidding techniques described in Chapter 3.

Investigating Sales Descriptions

Auctions on eBay typically remain online for several days. This gives you plenty of time to do your homework about what's being sold as well as who is selling it. Remember, much of the freedom of using eBay comes from the fact that you, the user, are in charge. That means you need to be well informed; it's up to you and the seller to determine how much something is worth.

A good sales description is the key to placing a reasonable bid on an item. Each sales listing on eBay appears on its own web page. The description is located in the middle of the page, followed by photos of the item in question. A minority of the items put up for sale on eBay do not include photos at all, only textual descriptions. But because of the increasing ease with which digital photos can be captured and added to auction listings, photos are now a part of most sales listings on the site. Not only that, but sellers frequently add three, four, or even more photos to their descriptions, providing a variety of views of their items.

The photos and descriptions should tell you a lot about what's being sold. Make sure you learn the following:

- What is the condition of the item? Is it new? Are there cracks, stains, or other flaws? Most honest sellers will specifically photograph the parts of the item that are damaged. This prevents buyers from claiming that they didn't know about the problems before they bid, and it cuts down on disputes that sometimes occur after an item is shipped.

- Is the item new, almost new, refurbished, or rebuilt? Is it in its original condition? Does it include its original box or case (or any box or case)?

- What's the size and model number? Is there an identifying serial number that would help date the item?

If you don't find the answers to such questions in the body of the description or in the photos, ask the seller for more information, and possibly more photos as well. Reputable and helpful sellers will be happy to answer the questions and provide more photos if requested.

Stop, Lurk, and Listen

Pick one or two items you are interested in. Don't bid, but note the eBay item numbers of the items as well as the ending time for the sale. By all means, connect on a Saturday or Sunday when many sales end. If you can be present at the end of a sale, you can connect to the sale's web page and click your browser's Refresh or Reload button to keep updating the high bid information. When the sale ends, you can immediately see who won and what was paid.

But you don't have to actually be present at the end of a sale to view the final sales information. Just follow these steps:

1. After the sale ends, click Search in the eBay navigation bar to go to the Basic Search page.

2. Click Advanced Search.

3. When the Advanced Search tab moves to the front, click the box next to Completed Items Only.

4. Enter the item number of the item in the search box. Then click Search.

5. When the sales description appears in your browser window, you can immediately view the high bid price.

6. Click the link that tells you the number of bids next to History (for instance, "History: 4 bids") to see who placed the bids and when.

The other part of the sale to research is the seller. What kinds of comments have been left for the seller as part of previous transactions? You can find out by scanning the Seller Information box at the top of the description (see Figure 1-11).

The Seller information box shown in the preceding figure contains links that can tell you a great deal about this seller if you do some research. First, you can click the User ID (in this case, tradrmom) to ask the seller a question. You can click the feedback score (1104) to read feedback comments. This way, you'll learn what

FIGURE 1-11   The Seller Information box gives you many clues to the seller's identity and reputation.

percentage of the seller's feedback is positive, and how long the person has been an eBay member. You can click the "me" icon to view the seller's About Me page. You can visit the seller's eBay Store and view other items the seller has for sale.

It's always a good idea to ask the seller a question, even if you already think you know everything you need to know about an item. Asking a question can tell you something about the seller. If the seller is slow to respond, curt, and impatient, this could either indicate that the seller is having a bad day, or that the seller isn't committed to giving good customer service (or both). If the seller responds quickly and courteously, inviting you to bid and thanking you for interest, this can, and should, produce a feeling of trust. (You should always back up this trust by checking the seller's feedback, too.)

Being Prepared for Trouble

One of my goals in this book is to help you become a smart eBay user and keep you out of trouble. I don't want to suggest that everyone on eBay runs into problems using the site. I also don't want to discourage you from using eBay by mentioning possible pitfalls in the very first chapter. However, it's a fact of life that, due to its very popularity, eBay presents criminals with a tempting target. But you can avoid trouble simply by being aware of what can happen and what not to do. Here are some examples:

■ Don't answer e-mail messages claiming to be from eBay and asking you to give out your personal information. Such messages may ask to verify your account information, or warn you that your registration is in jeopardy for some reason. Don't be fooled: such messages are scams that try to fool gullible individuals into giving out credit card numbers, checking account numbers, and the like. eBay will never ask you for such information by e-mail.

■ Don't click links embedded in e-mail messages that take you to web pages that look like they are part of eBay. They, too, are cleverly created spoofs.

■ Don't give in to sellers who ask you to pay by wire-transferring your money to an overseas location.

■ Don't give in to members who try to get you to bid on their items by sending you e-mail messages asking you to do so.

If you receive an e-mail message that appears to be fraudulent, forward it to spoof@ebay.com. See Chapter 6 for more information about how to avoid common problems with eBay.

Where to Find It

Web Site	Address	What's There
eBay Radio	www.wsradio.com/ebayradio	A weekly live show "streamed" online and saved in archived versions that you can listen to at any time
eBay's home page	www.ebay.com or http://pages.ebay.com	eBay's welcome page for new or current users
Forget Your Password?	http://cgi3.ebay.com/aw-cgi/ eBayISAPI.dll?ForgotYourPasswordShow	A page containing a short form you can fill out to have eBay e-mail your password in case you have forgotten it
eBay Stores	http://stores.ebay.com	A welcome page for eBay Stores: online storefronts from which sellers offer fixed-price items

Chapter 2

Insiders' Tips: Bidding and Winning

How to…

- Take advantage of the feedback system for rating buyers and sellers
- Place your first bid or make your first purchase
- Synchronize your shopping and bidding with eBay's schedule
- Make sure you have all the information you need about an item
- Pick the right bidding strategy for your needs
- Do comparison shopping and research to make sure you get a bargain
- Customize the way you use eBay through My eBay

Simply exploring the extensive eBay site, including the discussion boards where members socialize and the About Me pages that members create to describe themselves, is an enjoyable activity. But that, of course, is not why you're learning how to do everything with eBay. You want to learn how to find some bargains and make some extra money by selling what you have on the site.

Buying on eBay is easy. You can put a sale online in a matter of minutes; you can place bids with just a few mouse clicks. Without taking the time to do some research and investigate what's being sold, however—as well as who is selling it—you can easily end up with things you don't want. Worse, you might run into sellers who fail to keep up their end of the bargain.

This chapter will have you bidding and buying the smart way right from the start. You'll learn how to find bargains, ensure that the sellers you deal with have good reputations, and make sure you know everything you need to know about an item's good points as well as its flaws. That way, you'll get the most out of your bids and fixed-price purchases. You'll also get a rundown of the basic strategies eBay buyers typically use, and thus choose the one that not only fits your temperament but that enables your bid to win.

Falling Back on Feedback and Other Indicators

Any marketplace has to observe certain rules in order to function smoothly. One of the fundamental rules is to treat others with respect and trust. For sellers, it means giving buyers a good price and following through with a sale by shipping the product in a timely fashion. For buyers, it means communicating clearly and paying both in full and on time. When buyers and sellers treat others fairly, they develop a good reputation. eBay takes advantage of this natural and time-honored way of rewarding good business through its feedback system.

Understanding Feedback

Once you have registered with eBay and begun to search and browse the site, you should familiarize yourself with the feedback system. Feedback is a rating system that attaches a numeric value to the trust and level of satisfaction eBay members have developed. Each member has a feedback rating that "follows" them through the site. The feedback rating appears next to the individual's User ID. The feedback rating goes up or down depending on the comments left by those who have conducted transactions with that individual. Each member is encouraged to leave a positive feedback comment for a buyer or seller after concluding the transaction.

- **Positive comments**   These indicate that the buyer or seller behaved well and is trustworthy.

- **Negative comments**   These indicate that the buyer didn't pay up, the seller didn't ship, or that something else happened in the transaction that was unsatisfactory.

- **Neutral comments**   These don't indicate that the buyer or seller did anything wrong, just that they didn't provide the desired level of service— for instance, the buyer didn't pay quickly, or the seller took a long time to ship what was purchased.

Interpreting the Feedback Rating

Feedback is an important part of membership in the eBay community. At a recent eBay Live annual gathering, eBay's Chairman Meg Whitman reportedly asked those members in attendance with a certain feedback rating to stand up. She asked those with feedback ratings of more than 1000, 5000, and finally 10,000 to remain standing. At the end, those with the highest feedback ratings received great applause.

Members take pride in their feedback rating—as well they should. Sellers have their feedback rating posted right on the auction description page, at the very top of the listing where everyone can check it out. The feedback rating for a young German seller named Christoph Marx, who provides some comments in the Voices of the Community feature later in this chapter, is shown in Figure 2-1.

The visual form of "applause" for high feedback ratings on eBay takes the form of stars. Members with feedback ratings of 10 or more get a star next to their names. The color of the star changes as more positive comments are left by other

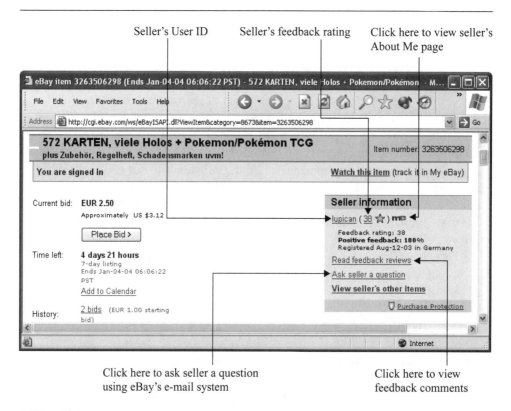

Seller's User ID   Seller's feedback rating   Click here to view seller's About Me page

Click here to ask seller a question using eBay's e-mail system

Click here to view feedback comments

FIGURE 2-1 Research a seller's feedback before you decide to bid or buy.

members. Those with the highest feedback ratings are called shooting stars. You can see the full set of star colors if you click the star itself, as shown in the chart in Figure 2-2.

Whenever you want to research someone's feedback, you need only click the feedback rating number. This works if you have the buyer or seller's User ID displayed on a web page. What if you have written down the User ID, or someone has sent it to you in an e-mail message? In that case, you can look up feedback in one of two ways. Here's the first way: Go to the Find Members page (click Search, then click Find Members in the navigation bar) and enter the person's User ID in the Feedback Profile box at the top of the page (see Figure 2-3).

The second option for researching feedback gives you many more options. Go to the Feedback Forum page (http://pages.ebay.com/services/forum/feedback.html). A research box at the top of the page lets you enter the User ID of an eBay member

2

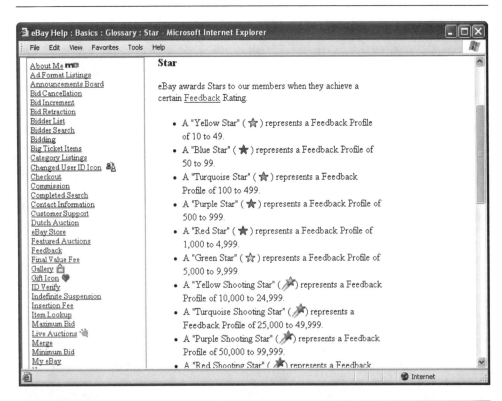

FIGURE 2-2   eBay's star listing visually indicates a member's feedback rating.

whose feedback you want to review. A series of links enabling you to perform common functions is presented near the top of the page. Click the link that corresponds to the kind of research you want to conduct. The following options are available:

- Leave feedback about an eBay user (use this when you want to make a general comment about someone that doesn't have to do with an actual transaction)

- Review and respond to feedback comments left for you

- Review and follow up on feedback you have left about others

- Hide your feedback. This enables your feedback to be private, so it can only be seen by you. You should avoid doing this unless you have some negative comments you don't want others to see. Hiding your feedback will likely cause other eBay members to avoid doing business with you.

FIGURE 2-3 The Find Members page lets you research other eBay buyers and sellers.

When you enter a User ID in the search box at the top of the page and click Search, you view the member's feedback summary as well as individual feedback comments left for that individual. If the person's feedback rating is high, you may gain access to pages and pages of feedback comments. You can view not only comments left for the member but comments the person has left for other eBay members. Viewing feedback left for others gives you a better picture of the individual's dealings with other buyers and sellers.

When you click one of the other links, you'll generally be asked to sign in with your User ID and password. You'll then go to a form where you can view feedback, leave feedback, or perform other functions. As you can see, you not only get the opportunity to leave feedback for someone, but to add your own comments in response to feedback that has been left for you. On occasion, members who lose their temper do leave angry and sometimes vulgar comments. You might want to add your own "rebuttal" or further explanation to clarify what's been said. See

Chapter 4 for more about how to use feedback and participate in the eBay community.

What sorts of "warning signs" or positive points should influence your decision on whether or not to buy from someone? A PowerSeller icon is someone who can definitely be trusted: such sellers have maintained a high number of sales and a 98-percent-plus feedback rating over a length of time. An ID Verify icon tells you that someone has paid $5 to have their identity verified, which tells you they aren't using a false or stolen eBay User ID. Feedback of 0 or –1 or less, or several negative comments warning users not to deal with someone, is a sign to keep shopping.

In between the PowerSellers and the users with negative feedback, it's up to you to decide what constitutes a trustworthy rating. Many sellers have told me that when they reach a feedback level of 1000 or 1200, their sales go up because buyers tend to trust them more. However, you shouldn't feel reluctant to buy from someone with a feedback rating of 10, either, if that person responds to your questions clearly, is up-front about any flaws, and provides multiple clear photos of auction items.

CAUTION   *It's important not to assume that a member's feedback rating tells you all you need to know about that person's history on eBay. Some members who have negative feedback take out a new User ID and start over; you can't tell from looking at the new User ID's feedback what they have done in the past. You can see how many User IDs an individual has had on eBay—and check out the feedback for each one—on the Find Members page (click Search and then Find Members in the navigation bar). Also take into account how the seller presents his or her sales, how well and how quickly he or she responds to your questions, and what kind of feedback they leave for others.*

ID Verify and Other Indicators

There are a number of other icons that can appear next to a buyer or seller's User ID that can tell you something about whether he or she is trustworthy. Each of these tells you something about the user.

- **ID Verify**   This icon tells you that the seller has paid a $5 fee to have a credit company verify his or her identity based on information such as social security numbers and driver's license numbers. The issue of stolen User IDs being misused by both buyers and sellers is a real one, and the ID Verify icon makes it very unlikely (nothing is impossible) that the individual is using a "stolen" identity.

■ **About Me** This tells you that the seller has taken the time to create a personal About Me home page on eBay's web site. Visit the page: it will tell you about the individual and what he or she sells. It might go into detail about the seller's qualifications or experience with the type of item being sold. You might even get personal information about who the seller is, where he or she lives, and possibly a link to a more extensive web site.

 ■ **PowerSeller** This tells you that the seller has maintained a 98-percent positive feedback rating for a length of time and has made a consistent number of sales on eBay. Generally, PowerSellers are reputable. But you should always use your personal judgment, even when deciding to do business with such highly experienced sellers. In some cases, even PowerSellers who have had a long record of good behavior have suddenly turned to fraudulent transactions in which other members lost money or merchandise. In some cases, PowerSellers were victims of identity theft, and criminals used their accounts to cheat other members.

 ■ **New User ID icon** The seller has just joined eBay. This doesn't mean that the person can't be trusted, of course. But establish personal contact so you can get an idea of whether the person is likely to provide good customer service throughout the sale.

 ■ **Changed User ID icon** This icon tells you that the User ID was created within the past 30 days. People change their User IDs for various reasons, so this may not be a warning sign. Use the Find Members page to track the seller's complete User ID history. You can view feedback for previous User IDs even after they change to a new ID; the feedback follows them from one ID to the next.

The ID Verify icon doesn't always "follow" one's User ID. For instance, Christoph Marx's ID Verify icon didn't appear in his auction listings. It only showed up when his full feedback rating and comments were viewed (see Figure 2-4).

How to Be a Smart Shopper

A friend of mine once told me she couldn't afford to go out to dinner. "I spent all my money on eBay," she explained. She proceeded to tell me about the wild flamenco hat (black, with little balls dangling from the brim) and the other things

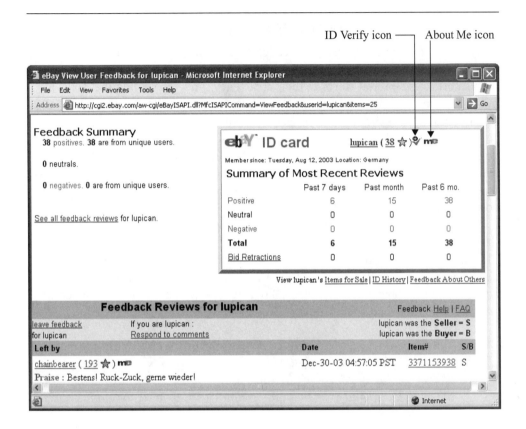

FIGURE 2-4   ID Verify and About Me icons let you know that you can trust a seller.

she had purchased. They now cluttered her apartment, and yet some of them she has no intention of ever using.

She had succumbed to impulse buying due to many of the things that make eBay an enjoyable place to shop such as the fact that you can buy some things instantly if a Buy It Now price is available, that you can compete for items by engaging in "bidding wars," and that you can find unusual or one-of-a-kind merchandise on the world's largest auction site. As you may have guessed, she was not a smart shopper. To help keep you from making similar mistakes, the following sections describe some "smart" ways to shop on eBay.

Knowing What Constitutes a Bargain

eBay has been around for nearly a decade. People tend to assume that the prices
they see on eBay are lower than they could ever find at one of the big retail outlets,
or even brick-and-mortar stores in their area. They think everything that sells on
eBay is a good buy. They also assume that because an item has received 20, 30,
or more bids, it must be "hot" or especially desirable.

Not true. eBay doesn't always have the lowest price around. It always pays to
do some shopping beforehand to determine what really constitutes a bargain. If you
can find a DVD player for $49 at a retail store, you'll know when to stop bidding
on eBay—perhaps around $40 or $45, because you always need to take shipping
costs into account as well as handling fees that some sellers add to their sales.

You can get comparison prices through the consumer search service Froogle
(http://froogle.google.com) or through PriceGrabber (www.pricegrabber.com).
The latter site takes your shipping and sales tax charges into account based on your
geographic location. It then finds the lowest prices for you. Some comparisons
between PriceGrabber.com prices and eBay Buy It Now prices from December 2003
are shown in Table 2-1.

*You don't always have to pay sales tax on eBay purchases. An Internet
sales tax, which has frequently been discussed by U.S. Congress, is not in
effect yet. You only have to pay sales tax if you and your eBay seller live in
the same state. And even then, some states and some sellers don't charge
tax on Internet purchases.*

Improving Your Search Ability

eBay wouldn't be as successful as it is if it wasn't so easy to search for—and
find—exactly what you're looking for. Shoppers on the Internet are in a hurry.
They don't want to browse through long lists of items for sale in categories and

Item	eBay Completed Items, High Bid	PriceGrabber.com Price
Canon PowerShot A70 digital camera	$280, $274.95	$246.95
Apple iPod 10GB MP3 player	$300, $405, $275	$294
Barbie Talking Townhouse	$99, $89.99	$54.88
The Lord of the Rings: The Two Towers DVD	$26, $12.50	$24.98

TABLE 2-1   eBay Is Not Always the Cheapest Shopping Source

subcategories. People who like to spend time surfing the Internet tend to like technical challenges—or at least they like to click links and explore resources online. eBay's extensive set of search utilities gives them just want they want. This section describes the different options, such as how to refine searches by entering multiple search terms, how to save searches, and other tricks.

> TIP   *People love searching on eBay so much that they even discuss the topic in two special discussion areas. Visit the Search discussion board (http:// forums.ebay.com/forum.jsp?forum=80) or the Search Question & Answer Board (http://answercenter.ebay.com/forum.jsp?forum=18) to learn about how longtime users conduct searches.*

Basic Searches

You probably already know that you can search for an item on almost any eBay page (except, curiously, an actual auction description page). You simply enter your search terms in a search box and click a button labeled Find It, Search, or something similar. If you click Search in the eBay navigation bar or the link Smart Search (see Figure 2-5), you'll be taken to the Basic Search page.

Click here to go to the Basic Search page for more search options

You can enter a maximum of 250 characters in this search box

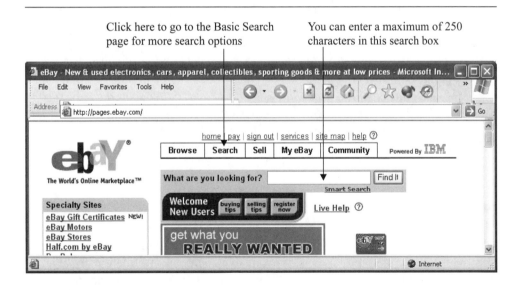

FIGURE 2-5   Search boxes like this are limited; Basic Search and Advanced Search contain more options.

The Basic Search page, shown in Figure 2-6, gives you many more options for finding what you want on eBay. You can search for items that accept PayPal, or search for an exact sequence of keywords by choosing Exact Phrase from the drop-down list. Other options of interest on the page include

- ■ **Price Range** If you are looking for a home in a certain price range, for example, you can enter the dollar amounts here.

- ■ **Item location** If you are looking for a home or other item in a certain part of the world, you can specify a U.S. state from this drop-down list. Otherwise, the default option is to search all U.S. states. (If you want to search for items available in other countries than your own, choose Advanced Search.)

- ■ **"Sort by" options** By default, Basic Search presents items that match your search terms and that end first. However, if you have already scanned a category thoroughly, you don't need to know what ends first; you need newly listed items, and you can get them from this drop-down list, along with items arranged by current high bid or Buy It Now price.

- ■ **Words to exclude** Enter any words that you do *not* want included in the search in this box. If you are searching for Volkswagen Passat cars but not the V6 models, type **V6** in Words to exclude.

NOTE *You may not know this, but there's a maximum number of characters you can enter when conducting a search. The search box on eBay's home page (www.ebay.com) lets you enter 250 characters. Other search boxes, such as those on the Basic search or Advanced Search pages, only let you enter 100 characters. Such limits only come into play if you are trying to conduct complex searches that combine different operators, as described later in this chapter in the section, "Adding Some Wildcards and Operators."*

Advanced Searches

Most people probably choose the Advanced Search tab for a single reason: they want to search for completed auctions. eBay's record of completed auctions, which only stays online for about 90 days, is a valuable source of information about how much particular merchandise is worth. If you're trying to evaluate an antique or figure out a maximum bid for an item, you can see what others have actually paid for it in past auctions.

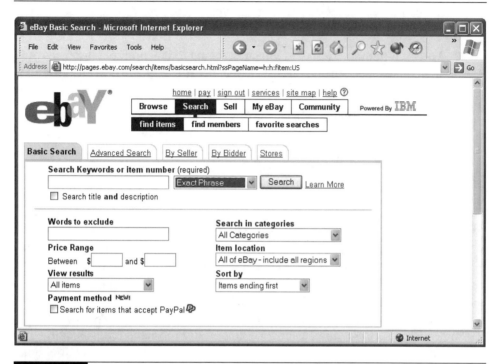

FIGURE 2-6   Basic Search lets you sort and filter search results.

Completed Items Only searches are one of the most important tools available to smart bidders. By searching for recent sales that have been completed and that resemble or exactly match what you want to buy, you get some real-world data about what the item sells for. The Advanced Search tab also lets you conduct the following kinds of searches, which aren't provided for in Basic Search:

■ **International sales**   The Location/International area of Advanced Search lets you find items offered in specific countries if you choose one of eBay's overseas locations from the Items Located In... drop-down list. You can find items available to specific countries by making a choice from the Items Available To... drop-down list. Sometimes, sellers in one country constrain their sales only to bidders in their own country or in neighboring regions; this option turns up sales that aren't restricted to the selected country.

■ **Currency**   You can constrain your search to items offered in U.S. dollars or Euros, for instance. (However, you can always convert the seller's currency by using eBay's currency converter at http://pages.ebay.com/services/buyandsell/ currencyconverter.html.)

- **Multiple-item auctions** If you are looking to buy multiple instances of something, check the box next to "Quantity greater than 1." This turns up sales that offer multiple items.

- **Fixed-price auctions** Check the box next to Buy It Now Items only if you want to find auction sales that have a fixed-price option, or fixed-price sales.

Basic Search and Advanced Search aren't the only places where you can do searches. eBay Stores (www.ebaystores.com) has its own search as well.

Adding Some Wildcards and Operators

When you're starting out, you search for items by entering a simple keyword or phrase in the search box: "Volkswagen Jetta" or "Pokemon cards," for instance. For many buyers, this is sufficient because eBay's search utilities tend to return such a rich selection of results. They never think of adding operators—symbols that a search program can interpret in order to make a search more inclusive or less specific.

Some eBay users are quite adept at adding groups of search terms in either the Basic Search or Advanced Search boxes. For instance, suppose you are looking for any souvenirs or collectibles that have to do with Los Angeles. eBay auction listings don't always use the exact term "Los Angeles" in the auction description. If you search for "Los Angeles" sales and someone has instead listed something with the term "L.A.," you won't find that sale. However, you could enter the following search terms, which would find these and other related terms:

```
("Los Angeles","L.A.","city of angels","hollywood","hollywood hills,")
```

In this search, the terms are all enclosed in parentheses. This tells eBay's search utility to look for all sales that include any of the enclosed terms. Each term is enclosed in quotation marks so the search utility will find the exact word or words. Each term is also separated from the next one by a comma and no blank spaces.

Another common sort of search uses a single term and adds other terms in parentheses to narrow it down. If you were to search for the term "Beatles," for instance, you would come up with all of the books, records, posters, tickets, and other things related to this famous rock band. However, if you are only interested in collecting music by the Beatles, you could enter the following:

```
beatles (45,album,LP,tape,CD)
```

Notice that "Beatles" doesn't have to be capitalized in order for the search to be accurate. Thus, the preceding example will search for all items with the word "beatles" and one or more of the following in the title: "45", "album", or "LP".

In the same way you use commas to add more search terms, you can use the minus sign (–) to exclude some terms. Some of the most common operators recognized by eBay's search utility include

- **Find one term AND another**   Do this by listing terms and putting a single blank space in between (term1 term 2).

- **Find one term OR another**   Do this by separating the terms with a comma and enclosing them in parentheses (term1,term2).

- **Find one term but NOT another**   Do this by inserting a minus sign before the term you don't want to find (term1 –term2). Be sure to separate the terms with a single blank space.

- **Use a wildcard character**   Do this by inserting an asterisk (*) in place of the characters you don't know. For instance, if you search for base*, eBay's search utility will find terms like bases, baseball, basement, and so on.

> **TIP**   *You can use operators and wildcards when you enter search terms in any of eBay's search boxes, such as the one on the home page—not just Basic Search or Advanced Search. You can also save your searches using My eBay, as described later in this chapter in the section "Tracking Sales with My eBay."*

Getting All the Information You Need

I ask at least one question of the seller before I bid on anything on eBay. It's not because I'm inquisitive (though I am). I always like to establish contact with a seller beforehand because:

- I get information if there's something I don't see in the description.

- I get a feel for the seller. If the seller's response to my inquiry is abrupt, that tells me to be wary. If the response is quick and forthcoming, that encourages me to trust the seller.

Some of the ways in which you can get such information are suggested in the sections that follow.

Asking to See More Photos

Once, I saw a Fender guitar (a well-known and desirable brand) available at auction without any bids having yet been placed on it. The reason? I thought it was simply because no photos were included with the listing. I thought I might have uncovered a bargain. When I e-mailed the seller to ask for a photo and received one in response, I saw an object that might have had a few Fender parts, but that was heavily beat up and didn't look anything like what I wanted.

That's an extreme example of why you need to see photos before you bid. Here is a more common scenario: You see a description of something—say, an automobile on eBay Motors—and it's been photographed from the front, back, and the driver's side. It looks terrific. You are interested. Should you bid? No. Instead, you should ask to see a photo of the passenger side. It's not at all uncommon for a seller to attempt to conceal damage on one side of a car by failing to provide photos of it. Sometimes, damage is not concealed, but it's not illustrated, either.

The Ford Cobra with 46,000 miles on it shown in Figure 2-7 has lots of photos. In the description, the seller states that "when I bought the car the rear bumper was scuffed by previous owner I never touched it b/c it is not that bad plus the paint is original and I didn't want to touch it." However, none of the photos supplied actually show the rear bumper.

If I was thinking of bidding on this car, I would certainly ask for a view of the scuffing on the rear bumper. A seller who wants to maximize the number of bids his or her merchandise receives, as well as maximizing positive feedback, won't be reluctant to take a photo and e-mail it to you. The same admonition applies to other items on eBay: if you need more photos or more details, ask for them.

Asking Questions

When you are shopping in a big electronics or sporting goods store, do you simply pick things off the shelf and throw them in your cart without a thought? Of course not. Chances are, you'll call an employee over and ask questions about what you see displayed. You should do the same with auctions you see on eBay. Retail stores might allow you to return and exchange items simply because you change your mind or they are not what you expected. eBay sellers don't have to do this, however. They'll accept returns if an item is broken or damaged or if it seems dramatically

FIGURE 2-7   Don't hesitate to ask for more photos if you are seriously interested.

different than what you saw or read about. But if you simply say, "I changed my mind," you're likely to get a negative response—and possibly some negative feedback.

It's your responsibility as a responsible member of the eBay community to know everything about an item before you purchase it. Don't hesitate to ask questions of the seller. Be sure to approach the seller early in the sale, if possible, to give the seller time to get back to you before the sale ends. You might ask questions about the following:

- **Condition**   Are there any cracks in the item? Any discoloration? Are all the pieces there or is anything missing?

- **Age**   How old is the item?

- **Identifying marks**   Is there a model number? Are there hallmarks, maker's marks, or other identifying symbols?

- **Box**   Did the item come in a box? Is the box available? If the box is included, what shape is it in? Is it in the *original* box or in a reproduction?

Perhaps the most important question is one you ask yourself: Do I really need this object? Will it add to my collection? Can I really afford to buy it now? Such questions might discourage you from making impulse purchases you come to regret later on.

If you purchase something on eBay and you or someone you bought it for simply isn't satisfied with it, you're better off reselling it on eBay yourself rather than asking the seller for a refund. You'll avoid negative feedback from the seller, and you might be able to sell it for more than you paid for it.

Placing Your First Bid

When you have done your shopping and research and are finally ready to place your first bid, you'll find that the process is easy—so easy, in fact, that it'll become apparent why impulse buying occurs so often on eBay. When you're ready to bid, click the Place Bid button. On Standard, Reserve, and Dutch auctions, the button appears both at the top of the description and farther down the page. It's a good idea to scroll down to the parts of the page labeled Payment Methods Accepted and Ready to Bid? (see Figure 2-8) because you get more information.

Payment Methods

The Payment Methods Accepted area describes what forms of payment a seller accepts. Not all sellers accept the same kinds of payments. Some sellers only take checks or money orders: You can send a personal check, but most sellers make you wait seven to ten days until it clears before they ship you the merchandise. If you go to the post office and get a postal money order, you pay a nominal fee, but sellers can cash them right away, so you're likely to get what you purchased much more quickly.

Many eBay buyers prefer to pay for merchandise with a credit card because all of the major credit card companies offer some form of "zero liability" buyer protection for purchases made online. In other words, if a seller defrauds them or someone steals their card number and makes a fraudulent purchase, they will not be charged.

PayPal (which is used by many eBay sellers) is displayed prominently in the Payment Methods Accepted area for a reason. PayPal is eBay's own payment system, and it's one that gives buyers and sellers an easy way to complete transactions using a credit card. In order to use PayPal, you need to become a member (go to the PayPal web site, www.paypal.com, for detailed instructions).

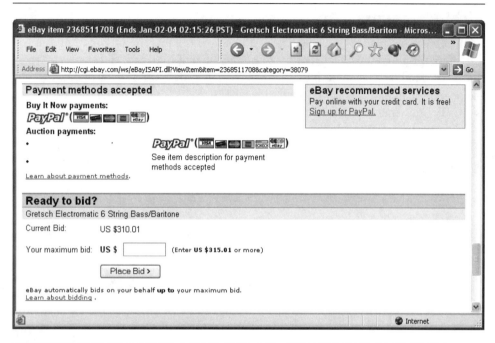

FIGURE 2-8   Read the payment terms and know how much you have to bid before you click the Place Bid button.

As part of the process of registering with PayPal, you identify a credit card that you want to use for making payments. You can then use PayPal to pay with that credit card; PayPal next transfers the funds to the seller using his or her PayPal account. One advantage of paying with a credit card is speed; it only takes a few seconds. The other, perhaps more important, advantage of paying with a credit card is the fraud protection that credit card companies provide: many hold you liable for $50 of the purchase price if someone steals your card and makes a fraudulent purchase with it.

Be aware, though, that PayPal's Buyer Complaint Policy User Agreement prohibits you from pursuing both a chargeback (you charge the loss back to the credit card company) and PayPal's buyer protection. You have to choose one or the other. In addition, PayPal buyer protection does not apply in cases when you receive an item and it was not as the seller described it. Read the policy carefully at www.paypal.com/cgi-bin/webscr?cmd=p/gen/ua/policy_buyer_complaint-outside.

Bid Increments

Each auction bid placed on eBay has an associated bid increment: the minimum amount a bid must increase in order to be the current high bid. Suppose you're thinking of bidding on something that has a current high bid of $75. In order to be the new high bidder, you have to bid at least $76. Why? Because the bid increment is $1. Bid increments on eBay are shown in Table 2-2.

 If a seller asks you to do a wire transfer using Western Union or another service, and offers you a discount if you agree to purchase immediately, before the auction is officially supposed to end, don't do it. This is a common scam being perpetrated by fraudulent sellers. Ending the auction early means you don't have eBay's fraud protection systems in place because the sale takes place outside of eBay's jurisdiction. If you transfer the funds, there's no guarantee the seller will ever ship you what you purchased— and probably won't. Play by eBay's rules and stick with credit card or PayPal payments whenever possible so you have at least some protection against fraud.

Learning to Work on eBay Time

Timing is everything when it comes to eBay. Standard and reserve auctions that don't have a Buy It Now option will end at a specific time. At this writing, eBay auctions are conducted in accordance with the time periods shown in Table 2-3.

Current High Bid	Bid Increment
$.01–$.99	$.05
$1.00–$4.99	$.25
$5.00–$24.99	$.50
$25.00–$99.99	$1.00
$100.00–$249.99	$2.50
$250.00–$499.99	$5.00
$500.00–$999.99	$10.00
$1000.00–$2499.99	$25.00
$2500.00–$4999.99	$50.00
$5000.00 and up	$100.00

TABLE 2-2   eBay Bid Increments

Type of Sale	Length of Time
Standard, Reserve, Dutch Auctions	one-, three-, five-, seven-, ten-day (ten-day sales cost the seller 10 cents)
Fixed-Price Sales	one-, three-, five-, seven-, ten-day
Real Estate Listings	30-day or 90-day
eBay Stores sales	30-, 60-, 90-, or 120-day

TABLE 2-3   Auction Time Spans

As you can see, fixed-price sales—sales that are offered at a Buy It Now price—are only online for a limited period of time. Anything with a Buy It Now price can be sold immediately, the moment a buyer clicks the Buy It Now button.

NOTE *There are exceptions to the official auction schedules listed earlier. Sellers can choose to end a sale early, as described in Chapter 10. eBay can choose to end a sale if something is put up for sale that it finds to be in violation of the user agreement. It has ended sales of children, entire families, and space shuttle debris, among other things. See this book's insert for more examples.*

Your first step, as a smart bidder, is to get synchronized with eBay. Doing something like setting your computer clock to eBay time is easy. It takes a little more effort to get used to the rhythm of sales on eBay. People who have been buying and selling on eBay for an extended length of time know that more sales go online at certain times.

The weeks before the Christmas-Hanukkah holiday season tend to see more sales than other times of year. Sunday night and Monday morning are good times to check for new listings, as many sellers put sales online on Sunday so they will end seven days later; Sunday is seen by many as a good day to attract bids from people who are home from work and have time to shop. Some suggestions for getting in schedule are presented in the sections that follow.

Setting Your Clock to eBay Time

Aside from the fact that they take place online, the biggest difference between auctions on eBay and traditional auctions that take place at Sotheby's, government surplus lots, and livestock markets is the way sales end. Traditional auctions end at the discretion of an auctioneer. If the auctioneer calls out "Going once, going twice..." and someone suddenly places a bid, the sale goes on until all bidding has stopped.

On eBay, Father Time is the auctioneer. The auction ends at the hour, minute, and second described in the auction description. This means that along with being the highest bidder, the winner also has to be the highest bidder *when the auction ends*. This has given risen to sniping—the popular practice of placing a bid at the last moment so no one has time to outbid you. Whether you snipe or not, it's important to get your computer clock synchronized with eBay time.

eBay time is the time during which auctions occur. Whether you do your buying and selling in the UK, Australia, or other parts of the world, auctions are scheduled according to the Pacific time zone (the time zone in which eBay's California headquarters is located). Your time zone may be different, but if you can track the end of the sale as closely as possible by being aware of the time difference and adjusting the minutes on your computer clock, you've got a better a chance at submitting a winning bid.

To change the clock on a Macintosh, click the time displayed on your screen, and then choose Date and Time from the shortcut menu. Change the settings in the Date & Time dialogue box that appears. On a Windows PC, double-click the time displayed in the system tray. Then change the settings in the Date/Time Properties dialog box. Try to get the minutes and even the seconds on your computer to match eBay time as closely as possible; the precise time comes into play if you try to snipe, as described later in this chapter.

eBay has a web page, shown in Figure 2-9, where it displays eBay time in relation to other parts of the U.S. (http://cgi3.ebay.com/aw-cgi/eBayISAPI.dll?TimeShow).

Keeping Track of Auction Schedules

Synchronizing your clock with eBay's is a one-time thing (unless your computer's clock, like mine, runs fast; in that case, adjust it periodically). You should also check eBay's sales on an ongoing basis. Sales activity fluctuates according to the time of week and the time of year. If you are looking for something that's hard to find, you are most likely to find what you're looking for around the end-of-the- year holidays, when many eBay sellers put sales online. You'll find less activity during the summer months—but that means you'll find less competition from other bidders, too.

If you're in the mood to win auctions, you'll notice that many of them end on weekends—especially on Sunday afternoon or evening. The reason is logical: this is when most people are home from work and sitting in front of their computers. Many sellers plan their sales so they'll end on Saturday or Sunday, when they are likely to get the most bids. On the other hand, some sellers like their sales to end during midweek, when there is less competition from other sellers.

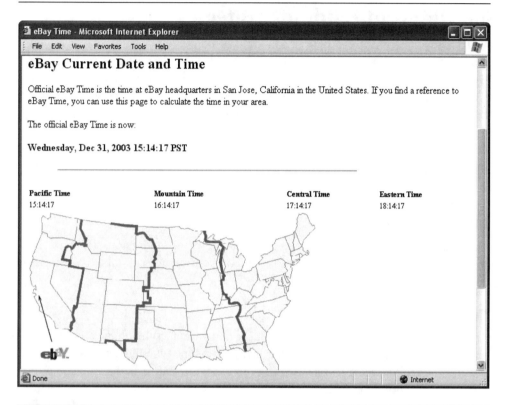

FIGURE 2-9   Make sure your computer matches eBay time so you know when sales end.

There are good and bad points to shopping and bidding at different times. Just be aware that you're likely to find sales ending if you check listings on a Friday night or a Saturday morning. And you'll get less competition from bidders if you look for sales that end during the week.

NOTE   *These are just generalizations; bidding software is available that enables buyers to place bids when they're not actually at their computers. Sniping software is configured to automatically place bids at the very end of auctions. eBay's own proxy bidding system is also designed to place counterbids until bidding reaches a maximum amount you have specified. So the truth is, you're likely to face competition at any time on eBay. You'll just find fewer people sitting in front of their computers placing bids at certain times of the week or year.*

Trying Different Bidding Strategies

You already know that the timing of a bid makes a difference when it comes to your chances of winning. The amount you bid also greatly affects your chances of success. By controlling when and how much you bid, you can make your shopping fit your temperament. For those who thrive on competition, few things can match the excitement of a "bidding war" that extends into the last few seconds of a sale.

If you shy away from counterbidding and outbidding and you can't take the heart-pounding thrill of it all as the remaining time dwindles away, you can take a less-stressful approach. Whatever you do, don't take things too seriously—just relax and, win or lose, have fun.

Low-Stress Bidding

There are probably as many bidding styles as there are bidders on eBay. But for those of us who shy away from crowds and competition, we can take the low-stress approaches described next.

Beating the Clock with Proxy Bids

In a traditional auction, sellers who can't (or don't want to) be physically present arrange to have a proxy bidder replace them—someone who places bids on their behalf. The real bidder instructs the proxy to bid up to a specified limit. The proxy bidder keeps bidding until he or she wins or the maximum is reached. In the same way, you can use eBay as your proxy bidder. The process works like this:

1. Suppose the current high bid is $50. You have done some research, and you've determined that you will spend a maximum of $125 for this item. You'll have eBay act as your proxy bidder.

2. Scroll down to the Ready to Bid? section of the auction description. In the box next to the Place Bid button, enter the amount of your maximum bid—in this case, $125. This is your proxy bid.

3. When you click Place Bid, the $125 proxy bid is placed. However, if you refresh your browser window, you won't see $125 as the current high bid. Instead, you'll see one of two things:

   a. If no one else has placed a proxy bid before you, you'll see the bid go up by the bid increment amount (see the "Bid Increments" section earlier in this chapter if you need refreshing on how increments work).

b. If someone else has placed a proxy bid that's between the current high bid and your proxy bid, you'll see the current high bid change to one increment above the other proxy bid. For example, if the other proxy bid was $75 and the increment is $5, the new high bid will be $80—and you'll be the high bidder.

c. If, on the other hand, someone else's proxy bid was higher than yours (say, $150) the next high bid will be one increment above yours—in this case, $130.

d. The beauty of proxy bidding is that you don't have to actually be present when the auction ends. You let eBay do the bidding and counterbidding for you.

Being a "Courteous" Bidder

A courteous bidder is someone who gives others a chance to get their last bids in by bidding, say, 10 or 15 minutes before the end of a sale. The courteous bidder bids the maximum amount and then walks away, so as not to worry about the end of the sale. If others want to outbid me, fine, says the bidder. I just won't worry about it. This strategy is relatively low stress: the bidder feels good, having bid the highest he or she is willing to pay.

Later, the bidder calmly checks the sale to see if he or she has won, or checks e-mail for an "outbid" notice. Usually such a notice appears—the courteous bidder preserves some sanity, but usually loses the sale to the more crafty snipers.

Crafty Bidding

The "crafty" bidder is the one who has usually learned by experience how to play the game to win. After losing sales to other bidders who place snipe bids, this person resolves to do the same. Sniping is only the best-known form of "crafty" bidding. Others you're likely to encounter on eBay include people who place bids in order to "kill" Buy It Now prices, and people who place small bids in order to draw out the competition and uncover reserve prices.

Bidding in Small Increments

The term "nibbler" or "lowballer" is eBay slang for a particular type of bidder: a timid yet crafty bidder, you might say. Suppose the current high bid is $155. There is a reserve amount on the item; the amount has not been met. Since the current

Teenage eBay Seller Impresses His Parents

Christoph Marx has been buying and selling on eBay in Cologne, Germany only since September, 2003. But then, he's only a teenager. He assures me he has his parents' permission to use eBay. "I started trading on eBay when my father opened a user account and allowed me to start buying and selling," he says. "To build some credibility, I encouraged my father to get his ID verified and bought some items to get positive feedback."

As far as bidding is concerned, Christoph is a committed sniper. "To win auctions, I never place my first bid earlier than two minutes before the auction ends, mostly even only seconds before," says Christoph. "With this strategy, other bidders have only a small chance to outbid me. The price stays lower and it also keeps me from getting involved in "bidding wars." To know exactly when to place my last-second bids, I've set a watch adjusted to eBay time."

He doesn't use automatic sniping software, however. It's not free, and "for me it's much more fun bidding personally." To track ongoing auctions he is conducting as well as items on which he has bid, Christoph uses My eBay. "As long as one doesn't sell more than five items a week, as I do, My eBay is probably the easiest program. But for research, I use a German program called 'Bay Wotch,' www.baywotch.de, which provides extensive statistics on auctions."

On the whole, Christoph reports, his parents are happy with him trading on eBay. "As I prepare all auctions, do the customer support and handle all transactions alone and under my name, my father has no problem, since his name only appears as the account holder. My father was amazed when I sold his eight-year-old computer monitor for about 76 EUROs ($95) yesterday. To me, it seems they are often quite impressed with my auction results."

high bid is $155, the bid increment is $2.50. There are two things the "nibbler" doesn't know and wants to find out:

- The high bidder's proxy bid, which is likely to be more than $155
- The seller's reserve price, which is certainly more than $155

In order to discover these things, the nibbler places bids that won't make him or her the high bidder: one bid might be $125, for example. The bidder positions him or herself in second place during the auction, and then swoops in with a winning bid at the end. More commonly, a nibbler bids over and over until the reserve price is met. Or, the nibbler consistently places bids that are the exact minimum necessary to win—in other words, one increment above the current high bid. In this case, a likely "nibble" bid would be $157.50. The nibbler keeps placing low bids until he or she is the high bidder. If this bid turns out to be the winner, the nibbler can take pride in the fact that he or she paid the least amount necessary to win the auction.

There are other advantages to nibbling. Sometimes, a "nibble" bid that matches the market value of an item will scare other bidders away. Suppose a new Barbie doll that retails for $29.95 is put up for auction. The nibbler bids increment by increment until the bid price plus shipping matches the market value—for instance, $24.95. The bidder may well scare off other bidders who are unwilling to pay more than the market value for the Barbie.

Nibble bids work well with Dutch auctions. Since the lowest qualifying bid is the winner, the nibbler can win one of the Dutch auction items and still be outbid by others. Nibbling has a number of disadvantages, however. Nibblers can be beaten by snipe bids. And if other nibblers show up, a bidding war can arise and the price will be driven up. It also requires a good deal of attention and energy to monitor the sale and keep placing nibble bids every time someone else moves into the lead.

> **TIP** *Don't place a nibble bid (or any other bid) that ends in a 0 or a 5. Most bidders place bids in familiar values such as 1.00, 25 cents, or 50 cents. Bid a couple cents more—for instance, 25.02 or $10.77—just in case the two-cent difference is enough to beat someone.*

Being a "BIN Killer"

You see something you really want on eBay. It's put up for auction with a starting price of only $1 and no reserve. That's great. But there's also a Buy It Now (BIN) price of $129. No bids have been placed as yet. Anyone who wants the item can instantly purchase it for $129. But you don't want to pay that much. eBay's policy is that, on auctions with no reserve, BIN prices disappear after the first bid is placed. (On reserve price auctions with a BIN option, the BIN price stays until the reserve is met.)

Some bidders, who are looking for a bargain, purposely place a bid in order to "kill" the BIN price. With the BIN option gone, the bidding can begin. The savvy bidder makes note of the original BIN price to make sure the bids don't reach or exceed it. If they do, the bidder who killed the BIN price will probably drop out, because he or she won't be getting the bargain that was desired.

Becoming a Sniper with Special Software

By now, sniping has been described several times, so you understand the most important distinguishing feature: the timing. The snipe bid is placed so close to the end of the auction that (the bidder hopes) no one will be able to refresh his or her browser window, type a new bid, and click the Place Bid button before the sale ends. Sniping is controversial; it angers many eBay bidders, who bombard the sniper with critical e-mails accusing them of being unfair.

By this time, sniping is so widespread that it's pretty much a way of life on eBay. It's true that the term "sniping" is not included in the A–Z Index that's part of eBay's Help files. But everyone who buys and sells on eBay knows that it's done and that it's an effective way to win auctions, so you should know as much as you can about it.

One thing you should know is that a snipe bid can also be a "nibble" or incremental bid, or it can be a proxy bid. Some snipers place purposely high proxy bids to win auctions, knowing that, because their bid is likely to be the last bid, it will only end up being one increment above the previous high proxy bid. Nibble bids can be placed at the last moment, but this can be risky: you never know if the previous high bid is actually a proxy bid, and if so, the proxy amount can beat the incremental bid.

The great disadvantage of sniping is that you only give yourself one bid at the end of an auction. Someone else who snipes you closer to the end can beat you. So can a proxy bid that is higher than your snipe proxy bid. Table 2-4 summarizes the pros and cons of the bidding approaches taken by many experienced eBay buyers.

When you snipe, be sure to set your computer up so you can do it effectively. If you have two computers available, each with its own monitor, you can use both. Otherwise, you can open up two browser windows on your single monitor. One browser window is used to monitor the time remaining and the current high bid. The other is used to actually place the bid. A possible setup is shown in Figure 2-10.

In the "bid" window, type your desired high bid and position the Place Bid button where you can reach it easily. In the "monitoring" window, keep refreshing the screen and watch the notice at the top of the auction description that tells you how much time is left: 1 minute 10 seconds...1 minute...50 seconds...when you are ready, switch to the other screen and place your snipe bid. Hopefully, you'll be the only "sniper" or, if other snipers are present, they won't outbid you.

Bidding Approach	Pro	Con
Sniping	Wins most auctions; it's very exciting	Once you place a snipe bid, you probably won't have time to place a second bid; you can be out-sniped and out-proxied.
High proxy bidding	Low stress. Can beat sniping occasionally, though not often.	Only wins auctions if competition is low
BIN Killer	Keeps someone from making a Buy It Now (BIN) purchase. You may be able to buy the item at a price that's much lower than the BIN price.	Opens up the possibility of a bidding war, sniping, and so on
Nibbling	You uncover the reserve price gradually, without having to place a proxy bid.	You can be beaten by sniping or by a high proxy bid, or fall into a bidding war.
Courteous	You bid 20 to 30 minutes before the end of an auction, then walk away.	You can be beaten by a sniper.

TABLE 2-4   eBay Bidding Strategies

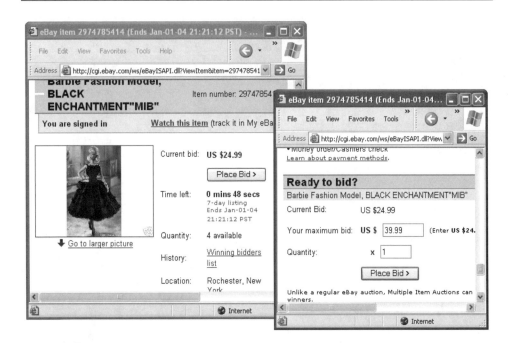

FIGURE 2-10   For quick snipe bidding, use two monitors or two browser windows.

Tracking Sales with My eBay

My eBay is one of the single most effective tools you have at your disposal. It enables you to control the way you use eBay, and to track your buying and selling activity. My eBay is a page you don't have to set up or configure yourself. eBay provides it for you automatically as a registered user. To access your My eBay page, click the My eBay button in the toolbar. If you haven't logged in as yet, you will be prompted to do so. If you have logged in, eBay uses the username and password you previously used to log in.

The My eBay page is divided into different "tabs," each with information about auctions you are tracking or want to track, auction sales you are conducting, auctions on which you have bid, and your own user preferences (see Figure 2-11).

One way to bid "smartly" on items is to track them while the sales are ongoing. It's not always a good idea to place a high bid early in the auction—it lets people know you are interested, and gives them an idea of how high you'll bid in the future. You can track sales from the Bidding/Watching tab on My eBay. This tab gives you a list of items on which you have bid recently (Items I'm Bidding On), auctions

FIGURE 2-11   My eBay enables you to track auctions and "watch" auctions you may want to bid on.

you have won recently (Items I've Won), and sales you want to keep an eye on so you can place a smart bid (Items You're Watching).

From the standpoint of savvy bidding, the Items You're Watching list is an indispensable tool. Whenever you spot a sale that you want to watch, click the Watch This Item link that appears near the upper right-hand corner of the auction description. When you do, the message at the top of the auction description changes to This Item Is Being Tracked In My eBay. At any time during the sale, you can go to the Bidding/Watching tab and see what the current high bid is. You can then decide whether or not you want to place a bid.

Where to Find It

Web Site	Address	What's There
eBay's Feedback Forum	http://pages.ebay.com/services/ forum/feedback.html	Links that enable you to view feedback, leave feedback, or respond to feedback comments left about you
eBay's Find Members page	http://cgi3.ebay.com/aw-cgi/ eBayISAPI.dll?MemberSearchShow	Links to a user's feedback history and User ID history
eBay Basic Search	http://pages.ebay.com/search/items/ basicsearch.html	Options for sorting and filtering searches
eBay Advanced Search	http://pages.ebay.com/search/items/ search_adv.html	Additional search options, including Completed Items
My eBay	Click My eBay in the navigation bar	Lists of items you have bid on, items you are selling, and items you are watching

Chapter 3

I Didn't Know You Could Do That on eBay!

How to...

■ Find anything you need on eBay's web site

■ Explore easily overlooked sales venues

■ Learn about amazing items that have been sold on eBay

■ Shop for big ticket items either through standard or live auctions

■ Make connections to eBay in the brick-and-mortar world

You can accomplish a lot by clicking the same links and reviewing the same pages each time you visit eBay. But once you get used to following the same patterns, you tend to overlook all the nooks and crannies of eBay's web site. I have been exploring eBay for nearly seven years, and I am continually discovering parts of the site that have been newly created, as well as resources for buyers and sellers that I didn't know about before.

You can't be an effective user of any software program or any online service until you are aware of all you can do with it. Once you've registered with eBay and begun to shop and buy, it's important to take some time and explore the resources available to you. You'll uncover some special sales, promotions, sellers, and merchandise you wouldn't have known about otherwise—things you never knew you could do on eBay.

Getting to Know *All* of eBay

Suppose you've stopped at an estate sale—a sale in which all of the items in a household are being cleared out—and you are looking for treasures. Perhaps you want to sell them on eBay; perhaps you want to add them to your collection. Do you only look in the living room and kitchen and then leave? Of course not. You move happily from room to room, looking through boxes, drawers, and closets, hoping to find the ideal object.

In the same way, whether you are shopping or hoping to sell items on eBay, you need to explore the whole site, not just your favorite categories or discussion boards. The following sections describe some parts of eBay's home page and site map that you should visit at least once to know what they're there for and what they contain.

Secret Places on eBay's Home Page

eBay's home page is one of the most popular locations on the Internet. eBay itself reportedly gets 1.5 billion page views each month, so it's safe to estimate that the home page gets millions of page views every day. It's not surprising, then, that eBay stuffs lots of links on its page. Have *you* explored each one of those links?

My guess is that, like many users, after logging on you simply enter some search terms in the search box near the top of the home page, or click a link in the eBay navigation bar. Doing it that way, you miss an incredible amount. Just on the home page alone there is a variety of links that take you to places where you can bid on items or locate sellers you might not know about otherwise. Figure 3-1 displays a few of these unusual links, just begging to be explored.

NOTE   *This section assumes you are looking at the version of eBay's home page that appears after you have signed in with your User ID and password—not the one entitled "Welcome to eBay" that appears before you sign in. See Chapter 1 for more about the two versions of the eBay home page.*

The following describe just a few things you can learn by exploring the links depicted in Figure 3-1:

- **Powered by IBM**   Why care about the IBM link? One trend you should know about, particularly if you are looking for computer and electronic components, is the movement of big businesses to eBay. IBM, Dell, Sun, Sony, and many other big manufacturers all have their own eBay Stores. Shop there for discontinued or refurbished hardware that can be had for cut-rate prices.

- **PayClick**   If you have won an auction or bought something and you're wondering what to do next, click here. You'll get information about PayPal, eBay's payment system, and about your shipping options.

- **Live HelpClick**   Click here and a separate "chat" window will open (see Figure 3-2) where you can submit a message to a support staff person (unless there are so many questions already in the queue that a message appears asking you to wait for an unspecified period before submitting yours).

- **eBay Gift Certificates**   eBay isn't a store, exactly, but you can give that special someone a gift certificate that can be used toward payment of something sold on the site (as long as that something is purchased using PayPal).

Click here to find out
how to pay for auctions
you've won

Type messages to eBay
in a "chat" window

Get a gift certificate
for someone

Shop for vehicles

Buy books and music
cheaply

Click a category name
to go to a category
opening page

Shop for items whose
sellers have paid extra
to feature them

Find items being sold
to benefit charities

Participate in
real-time auctions

Shop for regional
specialties in other
countries

Click here to buy or
sell professional
services on eLance

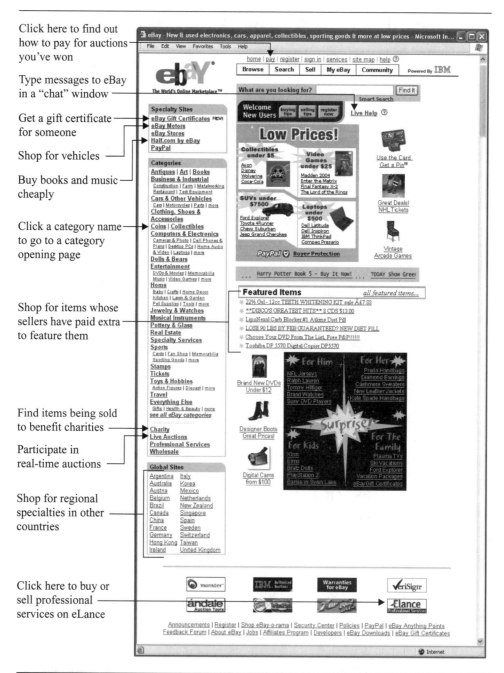

FIGURE 3-1   Don't overlook these unusual links on eBay's home page.

■ **Featured Auctions**   Some of the sales are laughable, while others are intriguing; the only thing that ties them together is the fact that the sellers for eBay must include links to those sales on its prime home-page real estate.

■ **Charity**   This link takes you to the eBay Giving Works page (http://pages.ebay.com/givingworks/index.htm), where you can search eBay for auctions held to benefit special causes.

■ **Global Sites**   eBay's site in the U.S. is considered its "headquarters," but eBay also operates separate sites designed for users in other parts of the world. Contents are presented in different languages as well as different currencies. It's worth your while to shop other sites for local specialty foods and souvenirs of other cities and countries—especially if you are able to read and write in another language. You can find things on the global sites that don't appear on the U.S. site, such as overseas hotel accommodations, discounts on cruises, and other travel bargains.

The parts of the eBay empire that are also mentioned in Figure 3-1 and that allow you to buy and sell specialty items, or sell in different ways than the standard eBay auction format—eBay Motors, Live Auctions, and eLance—are described later in this chapter.

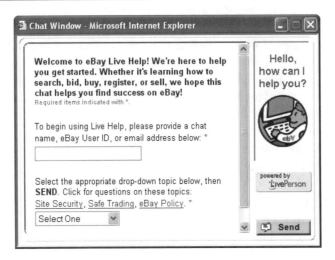

FIGURE 3-2   Have a live "chat" with support staff if you have questions or need help with eBay.

Hidden Areas of the eBay Site Map

Whenever you are looking for a category or other area on eBay and don't know where to find it, the Site Map is the place to turn. You find the link to the Site Map in the set of links at the very top of the eBay navigation bar. (The direct URL is http://pages.ebay.com/sitemap.html.)

Like any site map, this one has links to all of the main areas of eBay. But over the years, as eBay has grown more complex, the Site Map has become crowded. The page holds some links that you might overlook and that can bring you some surprise benefits.

> **TIP** *If you are ever looking for a specific page on the Site Map and you're tired of scrolling through the long lists of links trying to locate it, press* CTRL-F *to open the Find dialog box (or, as Netscape Navigator calls it, "Find on this Page"). Enter the name of the page you're looking for, and then click Find. Your browser will jump to text that matches the search terms you entered.*

Category Opening Pages

The category links on eBay's home page and the Site Map are special: They take you to pages that have been set up as home pages for categories within eBay's site. Each of these pages has its own URL, with links to subcategories within that category. But if you always navigate eBay by searching for terms, or if you click category links that you see on a page of search results, you won't reach the category opening pages.

If you have an area of special interest, either as a collector or because you want to sell, visit that category's opening page. These pages often contain special promotions you won't find elsewhere that eBay conducts with well-known companies. You can also find links that are of interest to sellers. For instance, when I visited the Dolls & Bears category page, Disney was offering holiday toys at special reduced rates. The Antiques category page (http://antiques.ebay.com) contained links to the Rose Bowl Flea Market and the Antiques area of eBay Live Auctions, as well as the following useful links for those who want to sell antiques on eBay:

- **Antiques Newsletter** eBay's category-specific newsletters are a gold mine of tips for sellers. In addition, they profile sellers who offer particular types of merchandise.

- **Popular Searches** This brief list of five words, shown in Figure 3-3, is important for sellers: it indicates the most frequent keyword search terms in a category. You should make it a habit to incorporate these keywords into your own descriptions to increase the frequency with which your sales turn up in search results. For instance, if a category tells you that the most popular terms include "oriental" and "primitive," you should try to work them into your descriptions if possible.

- ■ **Top 10 List**   This list identifies the most popular items in the category in question.

- ■ **Category Community Links**   Visit one of these links to view comments, ask questions, and just gab with other buyers and sellers who are interested in this category.

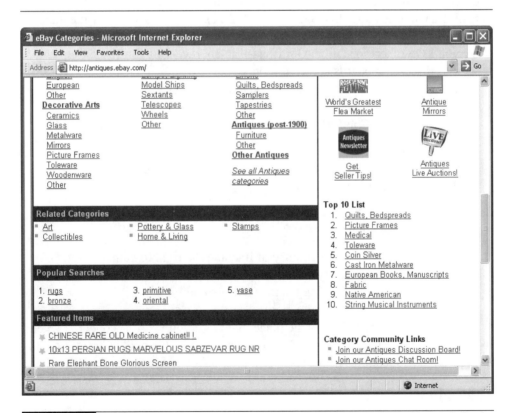

FIGURE 3-3   Links to popular items and search terms can help sellers who specialize in a particular category.

When you incorporate keywords into your descriptions, make sure those terms actually apply to the item you have up for sale. Working them into a title like "Susie doll for sale not Barbie" constitutes keyword spamming, which violates eBay's rules. See Chapter 11 for a description of how to use keywords in a way that won't potentially get you in trouble with eBay or attract negative feedback from other users.

Big Ticket Items

If you have some time to kill or a few thousand dollars to spend on an unusual toy, click the Big Ticket Items link in the Site Map and prepare to be entertained. You never quite know what you'll find in this category: it's eBay's collection of current auctions for which the current high bid (not a starting bid assigned by the seller, but an actual bid) is more than $5000. You'll find some items you only dreamed you'd see for sale, others that leave you shaking your head, and still others that make you LOL (short for Laugh Out Loud—an abbreviation you'll see frequently on eBay's discussion boards and chat rooms).

Here are a few examples I turned up on a random visit:

- A 1906 Louis Comfort Tiffany Jack-in-the-Pulpit vase, with a current high bid of $9505.

- The rights to breed your horse to a stallion named High Brow Cat, with a current high bid of $11,300.

- An upper deck "Legendary Cuts" signature of baseball legend Babe Ruth, with a current high bid $9500.

- Governing rights to the country of Iraq and the right to name yourself emperor of that country—obviously not a serious sale, and not a serious high bid either since it logged in at $99,999,999.

Big Ticket Items is definitely the place to go to if you've ever wondered where to find weird and zany auctions of the sort mentioned in this book's insert, as well as high-priced collectibles of the sort often seen on TV's "Antiques Roadshow."

The Gallery

A picture is worth a thousand words of advertising copy. That's why the sales catalogs you get in the mail are filled with glossy images of their merchandise. Some shoppers prefer to shop by looking at images first and descriptions later. The

Gallery (http://pages.ebay.com/buy/gallery.html) is a set of eBay sales (some of them competitive auctions, some of them fixed-price sales) whose owners have paid an extra 25 cents to have them listed in the Gallery.

Each Gallery item is advertised with a single photo and an auction title, as shown in Figure 3-4. Shoppers can click the title to read the full listing. While it's true that eBay's usual search results contain Gallery photos, too, those photos are smaller, and not all auction listings have them.

Featured Items

When you're browsing or casually shopping, not looking for anything in particular, your eye is often caught by merchandise that is prominently displayed or that is described as especially "hot" or desirable. The equivalent of the table at the entrance to the bookstore or the table full of specials in the department store is eBay's Featured Items category.

FIGURE 3-4   The Gallery includes items that have only Gallery photos available.

If you've never checked out the Featured Items category before, your impulse is to think that they are exceptionally rare or noteworthy in some way. This assumption is not always accurate. Items only get into this category when their owners pay a listing fee. You might get a chuckle out of the listings for products that are supposed to enhance various parts of your body.

In between diet pills and other medicinal items, you do find interesting listings such as antique furniture, collectible rock concert posters, and even, on the day I looked, a family of nine from Atlanta, Georgia, offering to enter into an advertising contract with a company for a year (they will wear the company logo on their clothing).

Charity Items

It's nice to give something to one person while benefiting another person or cause. Even if the person who receives the object doesn't fall in love with it, the cause that actually receives monetary benefits from your gift will surely be pleased. You'll find charitable auctions held by television and movie stars in this category, as well as sales that benefit a wide variety of causes.

Search Secrets

One of the reasons why millions of people around the world have come to love eBay is the ease with which they can find just about anything. Whether it's a coveted long-lost childhood toy, a rare object needed to fill out a collection, or a bargain price for a computer, DVD player, or other mass-produced consumer item, you can find it in a matter of seconds by doing a search.

As described in Chapter 1, you can use one of eBay's many search boxes to find what you want, as well as the Basic or Advanced Search pages. But that's only part of the story when it comes to finding what you want on eBay. Some suggestions for more sophisticated searches are presented in the sections that follow.

Searching Descriptions

Most of the searches you are likely to conduct on eBay, especially when you are first starting out, are searches for keywords that are included in auction description titles. You might want to search for items manufactured by a certain company, or in a certain location. Perhaps you collect sterling silver and want to search for every auction that contains those particular words.

If you check the box next to Search Title and Description, you'll turn up many more listings than you would if you only search titles. You'll also locate auctions that have your desired keywords in the subtitles as well as in the descriptions. If terms like *19th-century, silver, pearl, refurbished,* or *unopened* are included in the descriptions rather than the titles and these terms are important to you, be sure to search auction descriptions. I've used titles and descriptions when I want to find private auctions, or auctions where bidders have to be pre-approved—those explanations are often found in the descriptions, but not the titles.

Searching for People

As you'll learn in Chapter 4, it's not difficult to find people on eBay. It's a remarkably social place. But if you want to find people who have a particular User ID or e-mail address, you can use one of the following special features in Basic Search or Advanced Search.

Search by Seller

After you have been shopping on eBay for a while, you'll notice that certain individuals have objects you avidly collect or that are particularly reputable. When you know that someone has a specialty, and you have a smooth transaction with that person, you naturally want to keep returning to him or her on a regular basis. Some service-minded sellers specialize in encouraging return business by combining shipping costs if buyers purchase two or more items at the same time.

To save time and trouble, you can return to a seller you like by clicking the By Seller tab in either Basic Search or Advanced Search. As shown in Figure 3-5, you can specify that you want to search only sales that the seller is currently offering (by leaving No selected in the Included Completed Items set of options), or sales that have been completed (by checking Last Day or other options next to Included Completed Items).

Researching sellers is an essential part of being a smart eBay shopper. By looking up a seller's current or past auctions, you determine how busy they are, how much interest their sales generally attract, and whether they frequently sell items similar to the one you are considering buying. The more experienced and active a seller is, the more likely you are to have a smooth transaction.

Search by Bidder

If you want to be an eBay "power shopper," learn to research other bidders—those who outbid you as well as those who compete with you for similar items. Suppose you're a numismatist (a coin collector, that is). Certain collectors as well as sellers frequent eBay's coin auctions. Getting to know the bidders who tend to spend a lot

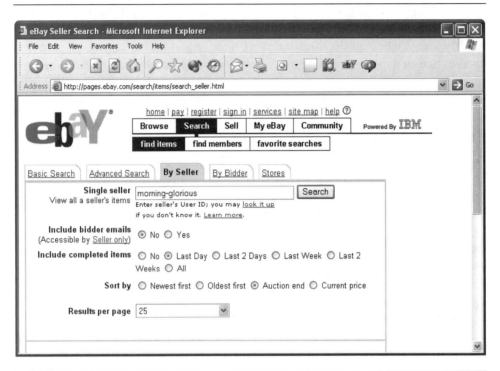

Researching a seller's past sales can help you decide whether or not to place a bid.

on rare items can help when you're deciding whether or not to get in a "bidding war" over something you really want.

To research someone's bidding, click the By Bidder tab in the Basic or Advanced Search form. Enter the member's user ID, then select whether you want to research auctions that have been completed or only those that are still ongoing. If the member has done any bidding, you'll see a report that displays the item number, the current or final price, the name of the high bidder, and the seller of the item.

Finding eBay Members

Suppose you want to research a seller but you can't remember his or her exact user ID. You have to enter the person's user ID exactly in the By Seller tab. If you get one character wrong or forget a single underline (_) or asterisk (*) character, eBay's search utility won't find the sales or the bids for that person. Perhaps you meet someone at one of the eBay venues mentioned in "eBay in the Real World" later in this chapter. If that's the case, you can use the Find Members form.

You connect to Find Members by clicking the link in either the By Seller or By Bidder tab, by clicking Find Members in the eBay navigation bar (this option only appears when Search has been selected), or by going directly to the page at http:// cgi3.ebay.com/aw-cgi/eBayISAPI.dll?MemberSearchShow. You then fill out the Request User ID part of the Find Members form (see Figure 3-6).

As you read in the form, after you click Search in the Request User ID part of the form, you are only presented with the person's actual User ID if you are currently involved in a transaction with the member—say, if you bid on one of the member's sales, or if you are selling something to a bidder. But if that's the case, you'll have access to the person's exact User ID anyway. Most likely, you'll get back the person's Feedback Profile and feedback comments. You'll probably have to e-mail the individual, however, if you really want his or her User ID.

Searching Around the World

Most of the time, the default search options on eBay are pretty straightforward. If you don't choose more specific search options, your search will be confined to your own country. In the U.S., when you enter a term in eBay's search boxes, either on

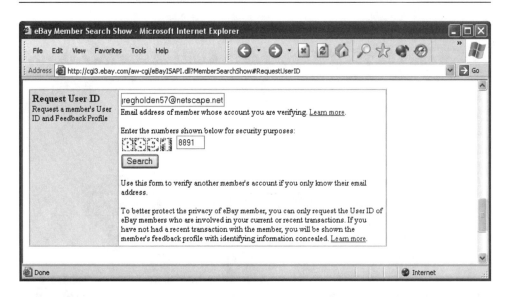

FIGURE 3-6   You can look up someone's User ID or read their feedback by filling out this part of the Find Members form.

the home page or on a search results page, you search for items only in the United States.

In the UK, Canada, Brazil, or another eBay location around the world, the default option is to search only your own country or region. In areas outside the United States, the search box on the home page allows users to search either the home country or Items Worldwide. The UK version of eBay, shown in Figure 3-7, shows the two options.

When you click Search in the eBay navigation bar and then click Advanced (or when you go directly to http://pages.ebay.co.uk/search/items/search_adv.html), your browser connects to the Advanced Search form. By using Advanced Search, you can specify exactly what part of eBay you want to search, either in your own region or around the world. This enables you to take advantage of favorable exchange rates or uncover local treasures you can't find anywhere else.

Searching Locations in Your Own Country

After you enter your search keywords and choose other options, you can optionally narrow the search to different geographic locations by making choices from the Location/International drop-down lists in Advanced Search. If you leave the Items from eBay.com (or eBay.co.uk, or your own country's home address) option selected

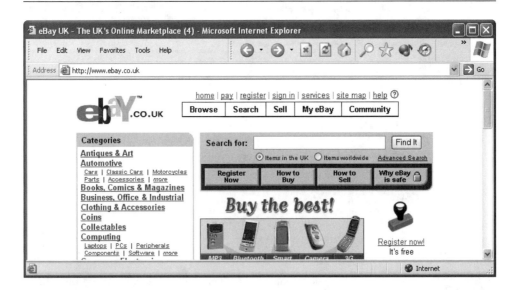

FIGURE 3-7   In locations outside the U.S., the home page search box gives visitors two search options.

and then choose an option from the first drop-down list, you can choose a region within your own country. In the U.S. location (eBay.com), you can choose one of the fifty states. In other eBay locations, you choose one of the major cities.

Items Available To...

The second drop-down list in the Location/International section of Advanced Search, Items Available To..., enables you to search for items that are available only to buyers from a particular country. Select the country from the Items Available To drop-down list. Though some sellers exclude overseas bidders from their auctions, this option lets you find international sales that include your country as well as other parts of the world.

Items Located In...

The Items Located In... drop-down list gives you more specific and focused results than Items Available To... It enables you to choose a specific country in which a seller is located. If you are looking for gourmet cheese from Holland or exotic art from New Zealand, this is the list to use. Whatever country you select, though, make sure their sellers will ship to your part of the world.

> **TIP** *Choose an option from the Currency drop-down list if you want to search for items sold in a particular currency. Even if the item is not being sold in the currency you use at home, you can convert it using eBay's Universal Currency Converter. Afterward, you can have your bank or Western Union convert it to the currency the seller desires.*

Sorting Search Results

When you get a list of search results from eBay, you don't need to accept the default presentation. It's tempting to scroll through page after page of results without making any changes, but you can save yourself some time by sorting the results. At the top of any page of search results, you see the following options: Ending First; Newly Listed; Lowest Priced; and Highest Priced. By default, the items that end first are listed on the first page of search results. But clicking Newly Listed can tell you about items that you didn't see on your present search through the category: you might turn up a Buy It Now item that you can buy before anyone else discovers it.

You can also sort search results by clicking the column headings. Clickable links enable you to sort the results. For example, in Figure 3-8, the headings Price and Time Left are clickable. The results shown have been sorted by price. As you can see, sorting by price tends to turn up items that have had a large starting bid

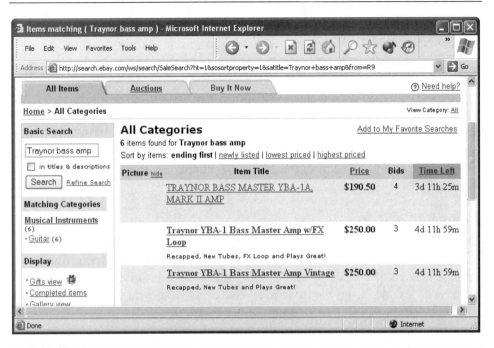

FIGURE 3-8 Sorting by price turns up the items that buyers (and sellers) consider most valuable.

placed on them by their sellers (and not necessarily any real bids). But you also find items that are rare and valuable and that have already attracted attention from other bidders.

Sorting Searches

Suppose you have a favorite item you search for every week on eBay. You construct the exact terms you want, you set up combined search terms (as described in Chapter 2), and you get a good set of results. Do you really want to be retyping, or pasting, the search terms into a search box every time you conduct subsequent searches? You don't have to: you can save as many as 100 favorite searches in your My eBay page. Just follow these steps:

1. Click Search in the eBay navigation toolbar.

2. When the Basic Search page appears, fill in your search criteria—or click options on Advanced Search, By Bidder, By Seller, or Stores and fill out the search terms you use frequently.

3. Click Search.

4. When the search results appear, click Add to My Favorite Searches.

5. When the Add to My Favorite Searches page appears (Figure 3-9), click one of the two buttons that either create a new search or replace a previous search.

6. Check the box next to Email Preferences if you want eBay to e-mail you whenever an item appears that matches your search criteria. (Be aware that you are likely to get lots of e-mail if you check this option, unless your search criteria are very specific.)

7. Click Submit.

When you want to conduct one of your saved searches, click My eBay in the navigation bar. When your My eBay page appears, click the Favorites tab, and scroll down to the Favorite Searches section. When you want to do a search, click its name in the Search Name column (see Figure 3-10). All of the search criteria you stored will be used.

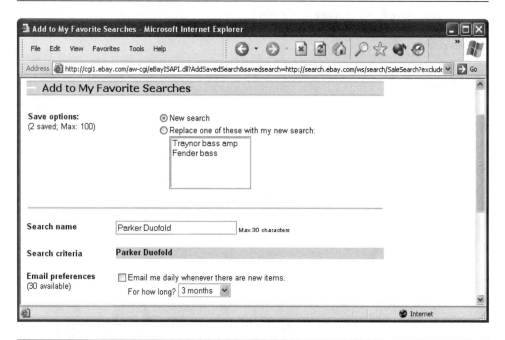

FIGURE 3-9 On the Add to My Favorite Searches page, you can have eBay e-mail you when one of your search items is offered for sale.

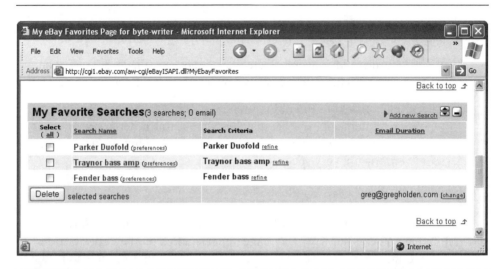

FIGURE 3-10   Whenever you want to conduct a saved search, click its name in this part of My eBay.

What Kinds of Amazing Things Can You Find on eBay?

Once you have learned how to search through eBay's site, what kinds of things can you find? In many cases, you can locate surprising types of merchandise you never thought you would find otherwise. Some examples are described in the sections that follow.

Restaurant Deals

eBay auctions don't always last five, seven, or ten days. Not only that, but you don't always have to wait for what you buy to be shipped to you. The one-day auction option is perfect for restaurant discount coupons, which can usually be redeemed with a special code.

In fact, restaurants around the country offer gift certificates through Restaurant.com, which is one of eBay's biggest sellers (it had a feedback rating of nearly 100,000 when this was written). This company has an About Me page at http://members.ebay.com/aboutme/restaurant.com/ where you can search for gift certificates at restaurants in locations around the U.S. Do a search for restaurants in your own city: you might be able to pay only a dollar or two for a half-price coupon or a gift certificate for a restaurant just a few blocks from your house.

When you win, you receive an e-mail from Restaurant.com. The message contains a link to a secure checkout area, where you pay for your gift certificate with a credit card. You then get a link to a web page that contains the actual gift certificate, which you print out on your home printer.

Vacation and Travel Bargains

More and more, the Internet is becoming the place to arrange travel. Train and air tickets are now routinely purchased online. People who are used to traveling through cyberspace are increasingly reluctant to turn their travel arrangements over to a travel agent. Click the Travel category (http://pages.ebay.com/travel/) to start shopping. You'll immediately see a search box where you can get prices on airfares, hotel rooms, cars, and vacation packages. You can also find links for luggage, cruise deals, and many other travel-related categories (see Figure 3-11).

Web Design and Other Services

If you're going to have a certain type of surgery, common sense would lead you to a doctor who performs the type of operation on a regular basis. So, buying a service through a vendor familiar with eBay makes sense if prospective buyers and sellers on eBay will make up a large percentage of the audience for your site. A person offering to design and maintain your site is likely to already be familiar with your needs and, chances are, will make helpful suggestions that you hadn't yet considered.

eLance is eBay's marketplace for professional business services. It brings together professionals who offer services such as accounting, consulting, and design with businesses who need contractors to provide those services. Freelancers who are looking for work use eLance to find employment; they post descriptions of their business and their experience. Employers, for their part, use eLance to post descriptions of the projects for which they need help.

Freelancers post bids that offer how much they will charge to do the work. It sometimes takes less than a day for several bids to be received (a far cry from the traditional process of soliciting bids, which can take companies days or even weeks). Once the bids are in, the company manager is in the driver's seat: he or she can ask the freelancers for more information about their qualifications or the type of work they plan to do. When the work is done, the company pays the freelancer, and pays a transaction fee of 8.75 percent of either the invoiced cost of the job or the original bid amount (whichever is greater).

FIGURE 3-11   The Travel category opening page contains links to air, cruise, and
hotel deals.

Employers can draw on a large pool of potential service providers and get
competitive bids quickly. Freelancers check eLance periodically and are able to
regularly review new projects on which they might bid.

Business & Industry Supplies

eBay isn't just for people buying and selling in their pajamas at home. In a time of
economic uncertainty and belt-tightening, eBay has become a venue for business
managers who need to procure goods and services for their companies while
maximizing cost savings. It's also a place where commercial operations can sell
off excess inventory and offer professional services in an effort to find customers
for what they have to offer.

Through the Business & Industry category, companies both small and large are
able to conduct business-to-business (B2B) transactions. One company that has
ordered 100 desks too many can probably find an eager buyer for those desks in

this area. Construction companies can find lumber, steel, and other building supplies. This part of eBay has its own newsletter, which is a good source of information for managers who are thinking of buying or selling through eBay (see Figure 3-12).

Planes, Rockets, and Other High-Tech Gadgets

As the years have gone by and eBay has matured, the things that are sold online have continued to grow in size. If you're in the market for a high-end purchase, you probably have the wherewithal to hopscotch all over the world to comparison shop. But why not let your finger do the flying (or rather the clicking of your mouse)? It's not unusual for shoppers to look to eBay for big-ticket (and big-weight) items such as planes, rockets, and high-tech gadgets of all sorts.

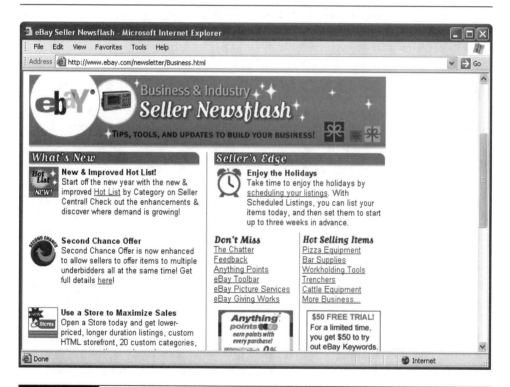

FIGURE 3-12   Read the Business & Industry newsletter if you are thinking of eBay for B2B transactions.

Browsing through eBay can give you a good idea of what's available as well as the item's going rate. After all, even if you save only a small percentage, with a purchase of this magnitude it's likely to add up to hundreds or even thousands of dollars.

Packing Material, Postal Scales, and Other Necessities

What better place to find materials for packing and shipping merchandise sold on eBay than on eBay itself? Pretty much any item that you sell on eBay will require you to somehow get it safely to the buyer, so why waste time reinventing the wheel when you can acquire what you need conveniently and at a reasonable price on eBay? Even better, many of the materials available are designed for your specific purpose.

Do a search on eBay for the single word "packing," and you turn up hundreds of results for packing peanuts, packing tape, foam packing sheets, packing carton boxes, packing labels, plastic bag sealers, and many similar items. A little time spent in research will save you a lot of time in the long run.

Homes, Castles, and Other Real Estate

Every day, thousands of real estate properties are up for sale on eBay. Why turn to eBay rather than your local real estate company if you are looking for someplace to hang your hat? eBay is perfect if you are looking to relocate because of its global reach. It's also great if you are looking to splurge on some luxury vacation property, or if you just want to rent a beautiful condo or apartment for a week. And, if there is more than one of you making the decision on where to move or what property to buy, looking over the possibilities before having an actual onsite visit is the way to go.

There's one very big difference between sales in eBay's Real Estate section and other parts of eBay: many sales are "nonbinding." In other words, even if you turn out to be the high bidder, the owner is not always obliged to sell to you. As eBay obtains real estate licenses for each state, however, it is able to conduct binding real estate sales. Check the real estate section to see what's current in your own area.

If at all possible, arrange to view the property yourself before you bid on it. If you can't take a trip right away, hire a realtor in the area to evaluate the property for you. You'll find realtors and answers to questions about buying and selling real estate in the Helpful Resources section on the right-hand side of the Real Estate category opening page (http://pages.ebay.com/realestate/index.html).

Amazing Sales: How $weet the $ound

The "Spotlight" section at the end of this book presents some of the amazing items that have been put up for sale on eBay. But many of those offerings didn't actually sell. Here are some items that did sell either for surprisingly high amounts or to surprising bidders.

- **The $31,857 fishing lure**   A simple listing with the title "Old Wooden Bronze/Orange Fishing Lure" and a starting price of $9.99 grew into a great fish story, as collectors drove the price up and up for the rare Heddon fishing lure.

- **The $19,000 beer can**   A female seller found a vintage can of 1941 Clipper Pale beer in the crawl space of a home she was remodeling. She thought it might bring a few hundred dollars. The sale was viewed 50,000 times, and the high bidder was happy to find the last item needed to complete his collection.

- **The $12,000 radio**   A radio collector with the User ID of tiptie sold a rare Sony TR55 Radio for $12,000 to a bidder from Japan, where the radio was originally manufactured.

- **The long-lost family photo**   A man with the user ID faraday2 was taking a break from work one night and casually surfed eBay. He found a postcard with a photo of a family taken in the early 1900s. He discovered that the card depicted his own grandfather-in-law, along with that boy's brother, sister, and mother. It was the only record of those family members together. He gave the photo to his father-in-law (the son of the boy on the card) as a Father's Day gift.

Of course, in terms of sheer dollar value, these auctions pale in comparison to things like the sale of one of those ultra-rare Honus Wagner T206 baseball cards, which went on eBay for $1.3 million, making it the highest price ever paid for a baseball trading card. Even this was bested by the sale of the town of Bridgeville, California, which went to a buyer for $1,777,877 in late 2002, as described in this book's insert.

eBay Stores

An eBay Store is a web site on which a seller is allowed to post merchandise for sale at a fixed price rather than having to deal with competitive auction bids. Those who operate eBay Stores tend to be knowledgeable and reputable sellers who know a lot about what they sell. For sellers, eBay Stores have the advantage of enabling you to put up more items for sale than you would otherwise. For buyers, eBay Stores give you a way to buy merchandise instantly, without having to get into "bidding wars."

They also enable you to make purchases from sellers with whom you have already transacted business. If you have a seller from whom you have purchased frequently, go to their eBay Store if they have one; you'll find more of the same kinds of offerings, and you only have to click the Buy It Now button to make them yours, without having to wait for a sale to end.

You have several options for finding and shopping eBay Stores. If you aren't sure what you want and don't have a particular seller in mind, go to the eBay Stores home page (www.ebaystores.com). Browse through the categories of merchandise offered through the stores, or enter a search term in the search box near the top of the page (see Figure 3-13) if you aren't looking for something special.

When you click a category, a page of results appears. But rather than showing individual items for sale, the page displays eBay Stores that contain categories of merchandise for sale that match the category you were looking for. For instance, if you click Sports, a page appears that has lots of stores containing sports-related material.

A set of subcategories also appears on the left side of the page, under the Sports category, in case you want to get more specific with store merchandise (see Figure 3-14). Eventually, if you keep drilling down through subcategories, you'll find an individual store you want to explore that specializes in the type of item you want.

> TIP   *Once you find a specific subcategory that you want to explore, you can enter search terms in the Search Stores box on that subcategory's page. Be sure to specify whether you want to search for specific Buy It Now items or store names/descriptions.*

The other way to find a store is to click the eBay Stores icon next to a seller's User ID. If you see such an icon, it means the seller has his or her own store. An eBay Store owner has the store advertised in the Seller Information box at the top

FIGURE 3-13   You can browse or search eBay Stores the same as eBay auctions.

of his or her auction descriptions. The store icon and link for Lori Baboulis's store, NYC Designs for Less, is shown in Figure 3-15.

Once you locate a set of specific items either through browsing or searching through stores, you can do some quick comparison shopping. Scroll down to the bottom of a page of search results. You'll see the link Find Related Auction Items in All eBay. Click this link if you want to find eBay auction items that resemble or match your search terms.

It's a good idea to compare what you find in a store with the rest of eBay— you might be able to find a sale in the auction categories that can save you money. You might not always get the best price in an eBay Store, but you can often find things there that aren't up for auction at all.

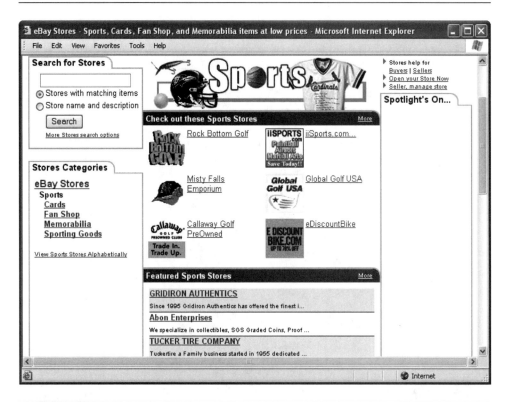

FIGURE 3-14   Drilling through categories leads you to stores, not individual items.

Half.com

At this writing, Half.com is changing. It originally existed as a thriving e-commerce web site that was known for offering books, music, and video entertainment at half price, and separate from eBay. (It also existed as a town that received money from Half.com for officially changing its name to Half.com, Oregon.) eBay eventually purchased Half.com and made its web operation part of eBay's own (its URL became http://half.ebay.com). Now, in early 2004, there are plans to dissolve Half.com as a separate area within eBay, and make its sales part of the main eBay web site.

Even when Half.com's name goes away, its sales are likely to retain their bargain nature. Anyone who is a registered seller on eBay can put books, computer equipment, music, games, trading cards, and much more up for sale and name their price. Sellers don't pay a listing fee to put things up for sale—only a percentage when the sale

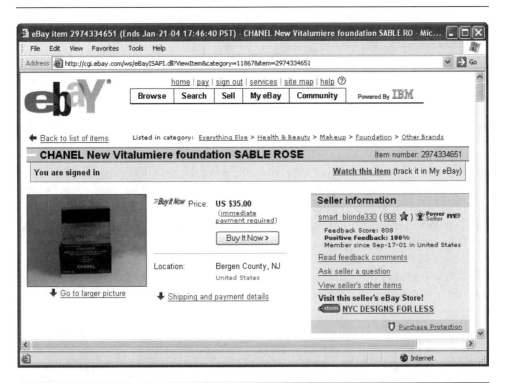

FIGURE 3-15   A seller who has an eBay Store has a clickable icon and a link at the top of each auction description.

actually goes through. It's a great place to find cut-rate items and buy them with a minimum of trouble.

eBay-o-Rama

You don't hear much about this part of eBay's marketplace, either on eBay itself or in books like this one. I'm not sure why. Maybe eBay is too busy promoting sales at auctions and through stores to promote its own store. If you are just crazy about eBay and want to tell the world about your love affair with the world's most popular auction site, click the eBay-o-Rama link at the bottom of the home page and go to a page where you can purchase clothing, coffee cups, and other items with the eBay logo on them.

 *PowerSellers and Trading Assistants can get their own posters, logos, and advertising goodies through other parts of eBay. PowerSeller paraphernalia is described at http://pages.ebay.com/services/buyandsell/powerseller/benefits.html, while benefits to Trading Assistants are described in general terms at http://pages.ebay.com/tradingassistants/marketingyourself.html.*

eBay Motors

eBay is fast becoming one of the biggest and most active dealers around for devices that run with a motor. That includes cars, of course. But it also encompasses other motorized vehicles, such as planes, boats, motorcycles, and sidewalk scooters. eBay Motors is also the place to find accessories for those vehicles, including tools to fix them, parts to make them run better, and manuals so you can learn more about them.

The process of bidding on and winning items in eBay Motors is pretty much the same as on other parts of eBay. But there are a few considerations to keep in mind. Some sellers will require you to put down an "earnest money" deposit at the end of the bidding. Not all sellers do this, however—make sure you read the terms of sale carefully before placing a bid.

Then there is the question of how the auto or other vehicle actually gets to you. Many buyers only shop for items offered in their geographic location, so they have a chance to inspect the vehicle (if it is a vehicle) beforehand, and then pick it up in person. Otherwise, you'll need to have the item shipped.

 *You use eBay's Basic Search or Advanced Search forms to shop for items available to a particular location, as described earlier in this chapter.*

Inspecting the Vehicle Beforehand

If you are looking to purchase a motorcycle, mobile home, truck, or auto that you intend to drive around for years at a time and that costs thousands of dollars, it only makes sense to "kick the tires" beforehand. You can't get your mouse or trackball to interact with a photo of a vehicle in this way, of course. "Virtual inspections" are available and highly recommended, however. Many sellers hire one of two inspection services that are available through eBay. (The one conducted by Pep Boys costs only $24.99.) They get the vehicle checked out beforehand through a comprehensive inspection that covers the appearance as well as the operating condition. The resulting inspection report is then made available to bidders like you.

You can find vehicles that have been inspected when you browse the eBay Motors category; they have an inspection item next to the title. The first three cars shown in Figure 3-16 include the inspection item. The car below has the dollar sign ($) icon, which means buyers can use a secure escrow service to handle payment.

If an inspection has not yet been conducted and you really want the vehicle in question, you can also pay an inspection service to check it out. Most sellers will agree to this (if they don't, it makes them look untrustworthy).

You can also do a "Lemon Check" through the eBay Motors link to Carfax. Just copy and paste the Vehicle Identification Number (VIN) listed in the auction description and submit it to Carfax. Such a check can tell you if the vehicle has been in a major accident and undergone significant repairs, among other things.

Shipping, Insurance, and Warranties

eBay has entered into an arrangement with a shipping company that specializes in autos, DAS Auto Shippers, to get vehicles from seller to buyer. You can and

FIGURE 3-16   Vehicles that have undergone an inspection are marked with inspection icons.

should visit the company's Web site (http://pages.ebay.com/ebaymotors/services/
das-shipping.html), before you bid in order to calculate how much the shipping
will actually cost, unless the sales description includes an interactive shipping cost
calculator that streamlines the process for you. (Not all sales include this, because
it requires the seller to set up the function during the process of creating the item
description.)

Shipping can add a significant amount to a vehicle that otherwise seems like a
bargain. Table 3-1 gives you some examples of how much it costs to ship a 2001
Volkswagen Passat from Chicago to various points around the country.

After you buy a car, you should have insurance to help recover repair costs if
the vehicle is damaged, or to cover your liability in case of an accident. eBay Motors
provides links to two insurance companies that have agreed to provide quotes to
eBay auction buyers. If the car you are considering is more than 20 years old, you
can get low-cost insurance through eBay Motors' arrangements with Insurance.com
and Allstate. Find out more at http://pages.ebay.com/ebaymotors/services/
insurancecenter.html.

 *If you see a license plate for sale on eBay Motors that claims to resemble
license plates currently in use somewhere in the country, don't bid. Their
sale is prohibited on eBay, and it's likely the sale will be taken down
before long.*

eBay Live Auctions

The Live Auctions area of eBay is where you get a taste of how the traditional
auction world conducts sales. On eBay Live Auctions, sales are conducted in real
time. You browse the catalog of items for sale and, if you see something you want
to bid on, you register to participate in the sale. You then either place a proxy bid
in advance or return when the sale is being held. If you're present at sales time,
you watch as groups or auction items called lots are put up for sale. It's fascinating
to connect to the site and watch auction lots being put up for auction, one by one.

From	To	Cost
Chicago	New York	$405
Chicago	Los Angeles	$590
Chicago	Miami	$540

TABLE 3-1 Vehicle Shipping Cost Examples

3

Often, sales end without any bids. Occasionally, someone who placed a proxy bid in advance turns out to be the winner. On other occasions, bidders in a real-world auction house (such as Sotheby's) compete against cyber-bidders, like you, for items. Even if you don't compete, it's exciting to watch the action, especially when bids climb high. Of course, it's even better when you see something you want and there are no bids, or the current bids are within your price range.

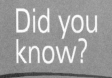

eBay in the "Real World"

You find eBay in many places online. Some online retailers advertise their eBay sales on their web sites along with their other catalog merchandise. One of the most surprising places you are likely to find eBay is at a storefront near you.

One of the newest trends n the online auction business in 2003 was the emergence of eBay drop-off stores: real brick-and-mortar storefronts where anyone could drop off items so they could be photographed and put up for auction on eBay. See Chapter 8 for more about this new combination of traditional and cyber-commerce.

You can also find eBay itself, as well as thousands of its members, at eBay Live. "Live," as it is sometimes called, is a user convention held over several days somewhere in the country. Events include panel discussions held by eBay staff as well as longtime sellers, vendor booths, and panel discussions. Attendees can take classes, meet other users, and get tips on using special features on the site.

Books like this one allow you to learn about eBay at your own pace. But they don't give you face time with real eBay buyers and sellers. For personal interactions, you need to enroll in eBay University, a series of classes held around the country where you can learn about eBay and meet other users. An eBay University seminar consists of either half-day or full-day workshops held in a single city somewhere in the country. Seminars take place during a period of two weeks throughout the year. If you find a University workshop in your area, consider signing up: you'll be able to join as many as 500 to 1000 eBay buyers and sellers of varying levels of experience. It's a terrific way to meet eBay staff people, get the latest news about developments on the site, and socialize with other people who live in your own area and who share your enthusiasm for eBay.

Find out more about eBay University and the eBay Workshops by checking the eBay Calendar of Events. To find the calendar, click Community in the eBay toolbar, and then click Calendar on the Community Overview page. An upcoming calendar page is shown here.

Where to Find It

Web Site	Address	What's There
eBay Giving Works	http://pages.ebay.com/givingworks/index.htm	A search box that lets you find auctions that benefit charitable causes
eBay Site Map	http://pages.ebay.com/sitemap.html	An extensive page full of links to all areas of eBay's web site
Find Members	http://cgi3.ebay.com/aw-cgi/eBayISAPI.dll?MemberSearchShow	Enables you to find a member based on their User ID or e-mail address, and to search for a member's feedback

Web Site	Address	What's There
Advanced Search page	http://pages.ebay.co.uk/search/items/ search_adv.html	Options for searching by geographic location, currency, and completed auctions
Community Events: Calendar	http://pages.ebay.com/community/ events/	A monthly list of workshops, eBay University classes, and events such as street fairs

3

Chapter 4

Participating in the eBay Community

How to…

- Get questions answered on eBay's Help boards
- Find friends in eBay's chat rooms
- Participate in eBay discussion forums
- Solve problems in the Answer Center
- Revise, update, or otherwise manage feedback
- Join a user-created eBay Group—or start your own

When you become a member of eBay, it isn't like signing up for a diet program or becoming a customer of a commercial operation that has a sales catalog on the Web. You become a member of a community—a group of like-minded individuals whose interactions really influence the effectiveness of the marketplace.

Consider the group of female PowerSellers called PowerChicks. In summer 2003, when eBay first let members form their own eBay Groups, a group was started by a seller named Chez, whose User ID is chezgems. Less than six months later, with 90 active members, PowerChicks had become a supportive mini-community. "It is wonderful to be able to network with other women doing the same thing, running businesses on eBay, and it seems someone is *always* online in the group, night or day," says PowerSeller Jennifer Karpin-Hobbs, who is profiled later in this chapter.

In recent years, big corporations have become more of a presence on eBay. But without a dedicated core of regular folks who want (even need) to generate some income and who love to shop for bargains, there wouldn't be an eBay. The community is still where you find the real, personal side of eBay, and this chapter describes how to participate in that community and take advantage of the tips, warnings, answers, and friends you can find there.

Turning to eBay's Discussion Boards

It's hard to work alone, in a vacuum. But whether you are a buyer or a seller (or both), that doesn't need to be the case on eBay. You can always turn to the site's wide selection of discussion boards when you need to complain, get motivated, receive free advice, or find the answer to a question. For many members, eBay's community venues are the most personal, freewheeling, and enjoyable parts of the entire web site—surpassed only by finding a bargain or making a big sale, of course.

eBay has lots of ways you can meet and talk things over with other members. Most of the groups are run by eBay itself, but a new category, eBay Groups, enables individual members to establish and moderate their own discussion boards. Within the groups run by eBay, you have discussion boards, chat boards, and the Answer Center—a list that can be difficult to keep straight, when you're trying to figure out where to go. Table 4-1 provides some suggestions.

Getting Started

All of eBay's discussion areas work the same general way. If you are familiar with the newsgroups that populate the part of the Internet known as Usenet, or with online discussion areas known as message boards, you'll have no trouble getting used to participating in eBay's community boards. The general idea is the same: people connect to the forum and type messages to one another. The resulting back and forth exchange of messages is called an online discussion. You might get involved in discussions by following these general steps:

1. You connect to the forum you want. The quickest way to find eBay's community groups is to click the Community button in the eBay toolbar.

If You...	Turn to this Community Option	How to Get There
Want to make friends and have fun	General chat rooms (like eBay Café) or discussion boards such as the Town Square, the Front Porch, the Homestead, and so on	Go to the Discussion Boards page (http://pages.ebay.com/community/boards/index.html) or the Chat Index page (http://pages.ebay.com/community/chat/index.html).
Have a specific question about eBay	Turn to the Answer Center	Click community, and then click Answer Center.
Have a specific question about buying or selling something	Turn to the category-specific discussion boards	Click Community, click Discussion Boards, and then click the name of the board you want.
Are having a problem with eBay or need general advice	Turn to the Community Help boards	Click Community, click Discussion Boards, and then click the name of the board you want.
Want to meet people with similar interests	Turn to the category-specific chat rooms	Click Community, click Chat, and then click the name of the chat room you want.
Need to learn how to use eBay software or complete a procedure on eBay	Attend a workshop or review the transcript of an archived workshop	Click Community, click Workshops, and then click the name of the workshop you want.

TABLE 4-1   eBay Community Options

This takes you to the Community Hub Overview page (http://pages.ebay .com/community/index.html) where you can find the group you want under the general heading Talk. This page, shown in Figure 4-1, enables you to connect with eBay members in different ways.

- **Talk**   This section contains links to the primary discussion areas: the discussion boards, chat boards, and the Answer Center. Start here if you want to connect with other members.

- **News**   This area contains the announcement boards where eBay publicizes new features or makes note of service outages. It also includes the community newsletter.

- **Events**   The most useful thing here, to my mind, is the Workshops link. Online workshops are often held by experienced eBay members, and typically provide a wealth of information about a particular aspect of eBay's operation.

- **People**   eBay Groups are the most exciting area here—you can start your own group or join one that other members have formed and which they moderate on an ongoing basis.

2. Suppose you have a question about paying for something you purchased on eBay. You click Discussion Boards, and then scan the list of topics. Each group has a set of discussion topics posted on its site, along with the number of comments in that particular discussion. The number of topics gives you an idea of whether or not a topic is particularly "hot."

3. Click a topic to view the comments.

4. You either read, or you can post your own message. To post, click Board Log-In at the top of the discussion board. Sign in with your username and password. You return to the discussion board, where you scroll to the bottom of the page and click the Post Message button to post your own message.

Reading without posting is an activity known in traditional newsgroups as "lurking." There's nothing wrong with lurking. It gives you an idea of the flavor of discussion in a particular community area. Some groups, like the Town Square, are quite informal. Participants meet there on a regular basis, become friends, and chit-chat like housewives talking over the backyard fence. People speak in a sort of shorthand that can be mystifying for newcomers, using abbreviations like:

- **BBL**   Be Back Later

- **FVF**   Final Value Fee

- **FWIW**   For What It's Worth

- **LOL**   Laughing Out Loud

- **NARU**   Not a Registered User

- **NPB**   Non-Paying Bidder

- **POOF!**   "I'm Leaving," or "I'm Outta Here"

It's entertaining to scan the messages in these groups and observe how members add a personal note to their communications. Some format their words in color using HTML; others add extra blank spaces or insert special icons that become a sort of informal "trademark."

FIGURE 4-1   The Community Hub includes four areas where you can find out about other eBay members.

You'll find a set of eBay-related acronyms on the About Me page for eBay member blue*eyes at http://members.ebay.com/aboutme/blue*eyes.

Other groups are more formal. Someone suggests a topic of discussion, such as "Anyone having problems using Checkout?" Someone responds with a comment. Someone else reads the original comment or the response and responds to either one (or both). Others join in and a lively discussion develops. Oftentimes, the discussion isn't lively. Sometimes topics are suggested but they get no responses; other times, only one or two responses are posted. The response depends on how many members share the same concerns and have something to say about them.

It's important to shop around the discussion areas to find the one that is best suited to your concern. If you just want to say hi to other people who collect antiques like you do, go to the Antiques chat board. If you have a problem with eBay Stores, go to the eBay Stores Answer Center. If you want to discuss ways to accept payment from buyers who live overseas, try the International discussion board. Some specific boards that are well suited to beginners are listed in the following section.

As the preceding steps demonstrate, you need to be a registered member of eBay in order to post messages or respond to questions in any of the discussion boards. That's one of the advantages of turning to the boards for help: you're sure to get a response not from just anyone, but from someone who actually uses eBay. Feedback ratings play the same sort of role on the boards as they do in auction categories: members with higher feedback are more likely to have more experience than those with low feedback, and their comments are likely to be more useful and valuable. If someone misbehaves or tries to abuse someone on the boards, you can click the Report button next to the person's name, which enables you to send a message to eBay about it.

General Discussion Boards

You can ask questions of other members in virtually any eBay discussion area. But eBay has set aside several forums especially for those who are new to eBay and who are seeking help from more experienced buyers and sellers. You find them when you go to the Discussion Boards page (http://pages.ebay.com/community/boards/index.html), under the heading General Discussion Boards. The following sections present some suggestions of where to turn.

If You're Just Starting Out and Are Bewildered or Uncertain...

If you're a beginner, go to the New to eBay Board (http://forums.ebay.com/db1/ forum.jsp?forum=120). You'll find discussion topics on when to charge sales tax, how to add HTML formatting to an auction listing, and fake e-mails that purport to be from eBay but that are really from criminals trying to "hijack" legitimate accounts. If you're just starting out as a seller, you can get useful tips on how to attract bidders or buyers to your sales. You'll also get answers to questions such as:

- Should I let someone pick up sales merchandise in person and pay in cash? (Opinions vary widely; use your judgment, but be careful. Consider meeting in a public place rather than your home.)

- What do you do when you pay for something but the seller does not ship it? (Within a month, you can file complaints with eBay and with the payment service PayPal, if you used it; you can also file an insurance claim with eBay, and leave negative feedback for the seller.)

Occasionally, tips are posted by eBay staff members (look for the topic "Best Tips for New Members" on the site). But usually, answers are given by dedicated members who take pride in helping others buy and sell successfully—exactly the kind of dedication that makes eBay work.

If you're just starting out with eBay and need some questions answered, click Chat and visit the eBay Q & A Board or the Images and HTML Board.

If You Want to Relax and Visit with Other eBay Members...

Most of the other boards under the General Discussion Boards heading are social rather than instructional in nature. You'll find comments about dieting and stopping the smoking habit, as well as jokes, games, and topics that go on and on with thousands of contributions piling up over time. These boards include the following:

- **The Front Porch**   Arranged by topic. Some questions about eBay operations mixed in with social chit-chat.

- **The Homestead**   What herbs do you use? What do you do about stress? What are your New Year's resolutions? Find out more on this board.

- **The Park**   You'll find lots of word association games here, as well as many other types.

- **The Town Square**   For some reason, there tend to be more comments about politics and news stories on this board.

- **Soapbox**   Contains virtually identical subject matter to the Town Square board.

- **Night Owl's Nest**   The idea is that eBay buyers and sellers who are up late at night tracking sales can go here to contribute to poems, jokes, and ongoing topics that have thousands of individual message postings.

The other two groups—eBay Live and Do It eBay—are intended to promote events that bring community members together. Do It eBay is a party in which members can give advice and help and have fun at the same time.

Some of the most useful topics on the New to eBay Board discuss fraudulent e-mail messages that seem to be from eBay. Typically, the messages have warning signs that point to them as being fraudulent: the English grammar is poor; the e-mail refers to the recipient as "Dear Customer" and not by name or User ID; the message claims that the recipient is being suspended, or needs to verify his or her identity; the recipient is asked to click a link in the e-mail message body or respond to the message and provide identification such as name, address, and financial information. Don't respond to such messages; rather, report them to eBay's address for fraudulent e-mail: spoof@eBay.com.

Getting Help on the Community Help Boards

From its earliest days, eBay has provided online forums where users could help one another. Experienced users provide answers to those who are just starting out and wondering about how to pay for something, how long to wait before it is delivered, how to use the feedback system, and many other basic questions. One place to go to get general help with eBay is the set of Community Help Boards.

You get to the Community Help Boards by clicking Community, then Discussion Boards, and then scrolling down the list of boards on the left-hand side of the page. You might well ask what, exactly, is the difference between the Community Help Boards and the Answer Center. In terms of content, there isn't a lot of difference. Both venues provide you with a place to ask questions and get advice from other eBay members.

The way questions and answers are presented is different. The Answer Center groups discussions by question: you view a list of questions, and see a link indicating how many people, if any, have responded. Click the link and you view the answers.

In the discussion boards, you see a list of topics, which aren't always presented in the form of questions (see Figure 4-2).

Category-Specific Discussion Boards

While the Community Help boards give members a place to discuss aspects of eBay itself, category-specific boards are focused on the types of merchandise commonly sold on eBay. If you want more specific advice about how to improve sales in an area, or if you have a question about how much something is worth, you are likely to find members who are experienced in a particular sales category and who are willing to help.

You may well ask (again) what the difference is between the category-specific discussion boards and the category-specific chat rooms. The names of the forums are virtually the same: antiques, comics, collectibles, dolls, photography, and vintage clothing. The difference is in the way the discussions are presented. Chat room discussions tend to be short, while discussion boards promote longer, in-depth exchanges on topics related to the subject at hand.

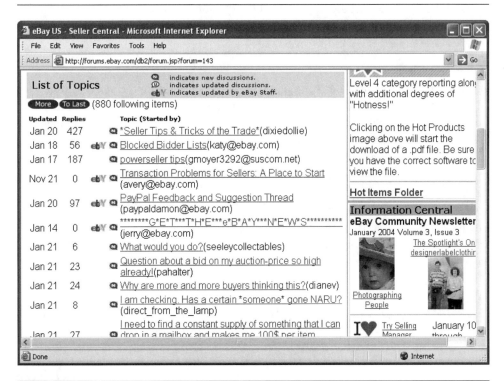

FIGURE 4-2   Discussion boards present lists of topics that others have raised.

 *Don't try to advertise your sales or your eBay Store on the discussion boards. Such marketing is prohibited; the boards are only for discussions, not for doing business.*

Getting Solutions in the Answer Center

If your child gets sick and has a temperature and it's the middle of the night, do you know what to do? Chances are you feel the need to ask a doctor or nurse for advice. Web sites are now available for these and other medical problems. Similarly, eBay's Answer Center functions like a round-the-clock database of questions and answers that have been posted in the recent past, as well as a place to turn to describe your current situation and get answers from eBay members who are willing to help.

As stated in the preceding sections on discussion boards, the Answer Center is specially designed for members who want to ask a question—or, just as often, present a problem they're having with a feature on eBay that's not working right or that they don't know how to use. When you connect to part of the Answer Center, such as the Photos / HTML forum shown in Figure 4-3, you see a list of questions or topics that users have submitted. The number of replies to the question is given in parentheses. You then are able to read the question or learn about the problem. If you click the name of the question/problem, you can read the responses.

Workshops

It's always best to learn from someone who has gone through the same kinds of problems you are encountering. If you and your instructor are in the same community and speak the same language, you are likely to learn more and have a more rewarding educational experience. That's the idea behind eBay's Workshops, which are among the best features in the community. They are places where new or less-experienced users can learn from veteran buyers and sellers who are willing to share their knowledge.

Workshops are often led by individual eBay members, but they are also frequently conducted by eBay staff members. In any case, eBay employees are usually on hand to offer advice and answer questions that arise. The workshop is conducted like this: at a preannounced time, all interested parties connect to the same workshop web page.

Wait until introductory remarks have been made until you post a question. It's easy to think that the discussion phase of the workshop has started before it really has. As a result, you post a question immediately and it is overlooked because the instructors and eBay staff are still presenting introductory material.

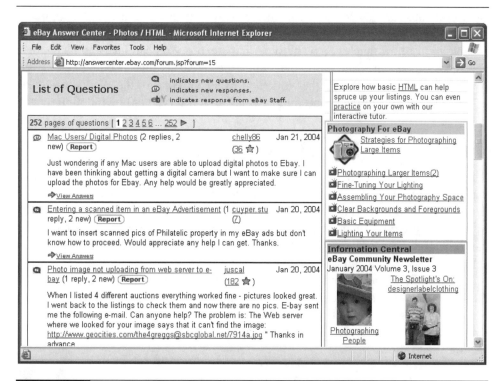

FIGURE 4-3   The Answer Center lets you read a full question or problem without having to click a topic name.

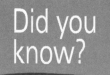

About AuctionBytes

eBay isn't the only place where you can exchange news and views on auction sales. AuctionBytes, a web site which reports on eBay and other online auction venues, has its own set of discussion boards. This is the place to go if you have a problem with fraud or a question about marketing and you want to see if others have had the same experience. It's also a good place to find out about other auction venues, and to meet online collectors, too. Find out more at www.auctionbytes.com/forum/phpBB/index.php.

Workshops are also good because they give you freedom. For one thing, you can attend class in your pajamas from the comfort of your own home. You are flexible in just how much you want to participate, too. You can lurk and listen, or you can post messages and participate while the actual seminar is being held. Even if you can't be present during the workshop, you can return to the Workshops area and read transcripts of the proceedings, which are preserved online indefinitely.

Expanding Your Social Life on eBay

Why is eBay so successful? Is it because you can find, and then buy, that particular variety of stuffed animal you had when you were six years old and haven't seen for decades? Is it because you can supplement your income or even start a new career by selling those old trinkets that have been cluttering your basement? That's a big part of it. But why do so many of those buyers and sellers keep coming back, and actually make eBay a part of their lives?

In my opinion, people are initially attracted to eBay because of the money—the chance to either save money, or to make money—and they keep returning because of the social life. eBay's chat rooms enable people to make friends, or simply make connections by interacting with one another, as described in the sections that follow.

NOTE   *eBay's chat rooms are different than the sorts of chat rooms your teenage sons and daughters (or your friends' sons and daughters) frequent. On eBay, "chat rooms" are more like message boards. Participants simply post messages on web pages. Responses and resulting "conversations" don't take place in real time—there's a delay in between. Teenagers are more familiar with chat rooms in which messages and conversations scroll along a computer screen as fast as participants can type.*

General Chat Rooms

Time was when neighbors talked to one another over the backyard fence. Vendors in street markets shared their thoughts as well as their wares. If you feel connected to eBay members, you have more fun participating—you sell more, you bid more wisely, and your whole experience improves.

Most of eBay's General Chat Rooms are primarily intended for fun. The eBay Q & A Board and Images/HTML Board are exceptions—they emphasize instructions and tips. But this part of the eBay community is best known for the eBay Café, the original eBay community discussion board, a place where longtime members go every day and greet one another like the old friends they are. The Holiday Board, Giving Board, Discuss Newest eBay Features Board, and the International Boards are designed with specific interests in mind.

One board in this section, Emergency Contact, deserves special mention. If you are attempting to contact a buyer or seller with whom you have conducted a transaction and that person has not responded to your inquiries, it can naturally be upsetting. The Emergency Contact Board is intended for people who aren't getting responses from buyers or sellers. Scanning through the messages on this board can be upsetting, because almost all of them consist of problems of one sort or another.

Keep in mind that the problems you see listed here are the exception rather than the rule on eBay. It's good to be aware of what can happen, however, by reading the messages posted to the Emergency Contact Board, and posting your own message if someone proves to be nonresponsive.

Category-Specific Chat Rooms

When you go to a party, to whom do you naturally gravitate? Someone who shares your interests or who has the same background as you, right? The same is true on eBay. If you want to share stories and dreams with like-minded individuals, the category-specific chat rooms give you a place to do it. Chat boards have been set up for people who love Elvis and memorabilia associated with him, as well as those who are enamored with Barbie dolls, Beanie Babies, and other objects.

Scrolling through messages in the Diecast chat room, the Glass chat room, or any number of other chat rooms can be a bewildering experience. You don't necessarily see lots of comments focusing on diecast collectibles, or glassware, or whatever the ostensible subject of the board happens to be. You usually see a lot of greetings, jokes, experiments with HTML formatting, and humorous icons.

The thing that ties people together in the chat rooms is their shared interest, and the fact that they are eBay sellers. You can ask questions about manufacturers, models, or makers' marks in the chat rooms, but if you want an in-depth discussion, you might be better off visiting the category-specific discussion boards.

Share-Your-Wares Events and Street Faires

eBay's discussion boards and chat rooms are the scene of two kinds of periodic events that bring sellers together to have some fun and possibly do a little business as well. They're called Share-Your-Wares events and Street Faires, and they are an attempt to offer merchandise for sale using a theme. In both cases, sellers post messages on the discussion boards that describe what they have for sale. Interested buyers can follow links included in the messages in order to view the descriptions and either place a bid or click the Buy It Now button.

Street Faires bring together buyers and sellers from many parts of the eBay community. As this chapter was being written, a Street Faire was being planned for February 2 in honor of the upcoming leap-year day, February 29. The twist was that participants could offer items for sale that had anything to do with "leaping" (see Figure 4-4).

FIGURE 4-4   A Street Faire enables sellers to offer merchandise connected to a playful theme.

Share-Your-Wares events, in contrast to Street Faires, are held on only one of eBay's community venues—The Park, which is one of the General Discussion Boards. A Share-Your-Wares event usually has a theme, too. If it occurs in May or June, the theme might have to do with Memorial Day or the upcoming Fourth of July holiday. But a Share-Your-Wares event only consists of a single set of discussion messages posted on The Park when the event starts. Along the way, sellers often tell funny stories about their merchandise. They also post messages or photos offering virtual food to the group, such as the ever-present "choklit."

 *You can find out about upcoming Share-Your-Wares events and Street Faires at the following About Me page: http://members.ebay.com/ aboutme/sywstreetfaire.*

Managing Feedback

In Chapter 2, you learned what feedback is and how to look it up. But after you start buying and selling, how you actually use the feedback system affects your experience on eBay. What constitutes good feedback? How can you respond to feedback or manage it? That's what this section discusses.

Making the Most of the Feedback You Leave

Feedback comments are among the most important types of communications between buyers and sellers on eBay, yet most members toss off feedback comments quickly without giving it a lot of thought. The comments you leave for other people are easily accessed as part of your member profile, along with the comments others leave for you.

In order to build a good reputation and develop trust, try to make your feedback comments courteous yet specific. Often, members simply reuse standard feedback phrases, such as "smooth transaction" or "fast response." They use lots of quotation marks and make comments like the following:

- "AAAA+++++!!!!! Smooth transaction!"

- "Fast shipping, good item. Thanks!"

- "Speedy delivery, good customer service. Highly recommended!"

There's nothing wrong with such phrases. But consider describing, simply and briefly, the exact experience you had with someone during a transaction. To me, the most valuable feedback comments are those that get more precise about how long it took to receive something, or how an item was shipped. For example:

- ■ "Shipped in less than 5 days; video was good quality."
- ■ "Received CD-ROM within three days of payment."
- ■ "E-mail responses came in less than six hours; shipment received 3 days after payment."
- ■ "I appreciated double-boxing and Priority Mail option."

Also be aware of the option to leave neutral feedback. A negative comment should be left if you feel someone didn't behave in a satisfactory way—if an item arrived damaged and you weren't offered a refund or discount, if the high bidder didn't pay up, or if the seller didn't ship. Neutral feedback is appropriate if something went wrong with the transaction but it wasn't necessarily the buyer or seller's fault—for instance, payment was slow because the buyer was out of town, or the package got lost by the shipping company, and so on.

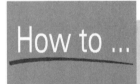

Be careful when deciding between positive or neutral feedback. Neutral feedback is perceived by most eBay members as having a negative connotation, so only leave such comments if you were really unhappy with how a transaction turned out.

How to ... Responding to Feedback Someone Has Left about You

You need to protect and manage the feedback you receive, either as a buyer or a seller. After all, a few negative feedback comments can damage your reputation in a marketplace populated by more and more PowerSellers with 98 or 99 percent positive feedback ratings.

One way to ensure the accuracy of the feedback left about you is to provide a response when you feel one is needed. You don't need to start an argument, necessarily. By adding a response to someone else's comment you can make it more professional. Just fellow these steps:

1. Click the My eBay button in the eBay navigation bar that appears at the top of virtually every eBay page.

2. Click Feedback to bring this tab of My eBay to the front.

3. In the box labeled Leave Feedback Links, click Review and respond to feedback left about you.

4. Look over the comments that have been left for you, and click the Response link just to the right of a comment you want to respond to.

5. Type a response of up to 80 characters in the Your Response box on the eBay Feedback Response page (see the following illustration).

6. Click leave response to post your response along with the original comment.

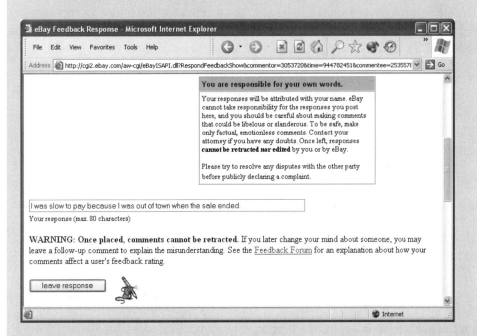

TIP *BayCheck Pro, a software program created by HammerTap and designed to help eBay power users quickly investigate and analyze feedback received by their fellow members, also includes the ability to sort feedback—a feature not available on eBay's site. By sorting feedback, you are able to group all of a user's positive, negative, or neutral comments in one place, even if those comments were left months or even years apart. Find out more at www.hammertap.com/BayCheckPro.html.*

Adjusting Feedback

Most feedback comments are straightforward. Someone posts a phrase or some descriptive comments about you, it goes online, and it sits there for months or years, being reviewed by both you and those who are thinking about doing business with you. But what happens if you disagree with the comments, or if something happens that requires a comment to be clarified? If that's the case, eBay gives members the chance to adjust their feedback in various ways in order to keep them accurate—and giving other members the complete and truthful picture about someone is part of being a good member of the community.

Clarifying Feedback

The feedback response steps detailed in the preceding section needn't apply only to feedback that others have left about you. You might also want to post a response to feedback comments that you left about someone else. It's always a good idea for buyers and sellers to wait as long as possible before deciding to leave feedback.

For buyers, that means not leaving feedback the moment the seller says a package is out the door, but to wait until it actually arrives, and even to try the item out (if it is a toy or object that can be used) to make sure there aren't any problems. For sellers, it means waiting until the check is cleared, or until the buyer leaves feedback, before you leave feedback about the other person.

In either case, if comments are left too soon, they might need to be "revised" as the situation changes. You can't erase your original comments, but you can add new information—a statement of regret, for instance, if you said something unfair earlier.

Erasing Feedback

eBay itself won't erase feedback comments on its own. The process is involved, but those buyers or sellers who dispute comments left by someone else or who want to "clean up" their feedback comments in order to improve their overall rating can pay a fee to have them reviewed by a third-party company called SquareTrade.

SquareTrade (www.squaretrade.com) is in the business of giving a seal of approval to companies that want to do business online. It has entered into a partnership with eBay to provide arbitration services in case of a feedback dispute.

The process works like this: You go to SquareTrade's web site home page, and click the eBay icon under the heading Dispute Resolution. On the next page, click Find Out How to Get Feedback Removed. You read an overview of the process, then file a case and pay a $20 fee to SquareTrade. At this point, two things can happen:

■ If the other party responds, SquareTrade mediates between the two parties and hopefully you can reach an agreement to have the feedback removed. The feedback isn't automatically removed, however. The request is forwarded to eBay, which has the final say on whether to remove it or not.

■ If the other party does not respond, SquareTrade forwards your request to eBay. If eBay approves the request, the feedback is removed.

Some sellers with deep financial resources regularly use the SquareTrade feedback removal process, and they improve their feedback because the other party often does not respond at all.

Keeping Up with the eBay News

Like any commercial operation, eBay is constantly changing the way it does business in order to respond to trends and economic conditions. eBay's policies have a bearing on the way you do business, so it pays to stay on top of events and changes as they occur. The primary source of news is described in the sections that follow.

Announcement Boards

When you click Community in the eBay navigation bar and then click News, you connect to two announcement boards that eBay uses to report on new policies, new features, or explanations of service outages. If you encounter a problem yourself or if you want to learn about new features, go to the announcement boards.

The System Announcements Board

Any web site functions only as long as its web servers can handle requests from visitors. If the servers cease to function, either part or all of the site goes offline. eBay calls such unfortunate episodes "system outages." Over the years, eBay has gone offline occasionally because it received more requests than its computers could handle.

Periodically, all or part of eBay goes offline in the early morning hours for scheduled maintenance. Because eBay auctions end at a precise time, system outages can affect sales. Such events, whether they are scheduled or not, are noted on eBay's System Announcements Board (www2.ebay.com/aw/announce.shtml).

If eBay or one of its categories is not functioning at the moment a sale ends, bidders cannot place last-second bids. In such cases, eBay sometimes issues refunds to affected sellers, but not always. If eBay makes an announcement that it will be offline at a predetermined time, you need to be aware of it and make sure none of your sales ends at that time.

If you find you cannot view auctions or place listings in your chosen category for a period of time, check the System Announcements board after the fact to find out what happened. Auctions slated to end during a scheduled downtime, or that end during unexpected downtime, are automatically extended to compensate.

The General Announcements Board

eBay frequently comes out with new features designed to improve your buying or selling experience. There may be a new and improved version of the software eBay makes available to sellers, such as Seller's Assistant or Selling Manager, or there may be new sales categories that more closely fit your area of interest than previous categories did. You'll almost certainly want to know about special sales, free listing days, or other promotions being held on eBay. Whatever the development, you can find it and other new tools and marketplace features listed on the eBay General Announcements Board.

You'll find the General Announcements board at www2.ebay.com/aw/ marketing.shtml. You can also find it by clicking Community in the eBay navigation bar, and then clicking News. You can switch to the System Announcements board by clicking the System tab.

The Community Chatter

To keep up with the public face of the eBay community—at least, the part of the community that eBay chooses to make public—get in the habit of visiting the Community Chatter once a month. People learn in different ways and, if you are more at ease reading a newsletter than typing messages on discussion boards, the Chatter (shown in Figure 4-5) can help you learn how to be a better buyer or seller.

You'll find articles by eBay members talking about how they use selling tools such as Seller's Assistant. You'll also find profiles of eBay staff members, and how-to pieces explaining ways to take photos, handle returns, and the like. Perhaps the best thing about the Chatter is the fact that all back issues have been archived, so you can browse through past issues for subjects you want to explore. Find out more at http://pages.ebay.com/community/chatter/index.html.

FIGURE 4-5   Another way to keep in touch with eBay's community is through the monthly Chatter newsletter.

Joining eBay's Do-It-Yourself Community Center

The most exciting part of the eBay community (at the time this was written, anyway) was the area where anyone could create his or her own user group. It's called eBay Groups, and it enables you to create or join a forum where you can share news and views with similar-minded members. eBay Groups have less supervision than other parts of the eBay community, but on the other hand, they place more of a burden on members to keep a close eye on the goings-on there and manage them so the discussions are useful. Groups can be created in keeping with a wide variety of criteria:

- **Geographic location**   Some groups bring together buyers and sellers who live in the same U.S. state or country, for instance.

- **Type of merchandise**   There are collectors' groups for those who love coins, glass, stamps, porcelain, and toys, among other things.

- **Type of activity**   There are groups for people who do scrapbooking, who are interested in genealogy, who work from home, and who use Macintosh computers on eBay.

Groups aren't all the same. Some are public: they are open to everyone who is already a member of eBay. Public groups want lots of members to join up. Others, like the popular PowerChicks group, are private: they are only open to members who have asked to join and have had their requests approved, or who have been invited. Private groups want to keep the membership low.

> **TIP**   *If you are looking to make a name for yourself as an authority in the category where you do business, consider starting your own eBay Group. You'll have to put in a lot of time in terms of advertising your group, suggesting topics for discussion, and the like. But you gain a lot of credibility as well, which can boost your eBay business if you decide to run one.*

Becoming a Group Member

Have you been asking yourself questions like these: "I wonder how many eBay users there are in my city (or state)? I wonder how many people on eBay have the same religious beliefs, or political beliefs, that I do?" Or perhaps you've been asking more unusual questions such as: "I wonder if anyone else on eBay suffers from Dulcimer Acquisition Disease (DAD)—the desire to buy those American folk music instruments called dulcimers?"

Normally, these kinds of personal affiliations aren't accounted for in eBay's own discussion boards or chat rooms. But you might be able to find such like-minded individuals by joining an eBay Group. You only need to find the group you want by connecting to the Groups home page (http://groups .ebay.com/index.jspa). Click through the available categories of groups, as shown in Figure 4-6, or enter a ZIP code or keyword in the search box to locate the one you want.

> **NOTE**   *You may need to join more than one group in order to find the one that's right for you, since you can't actually read group discussions unless you are a member.*

4

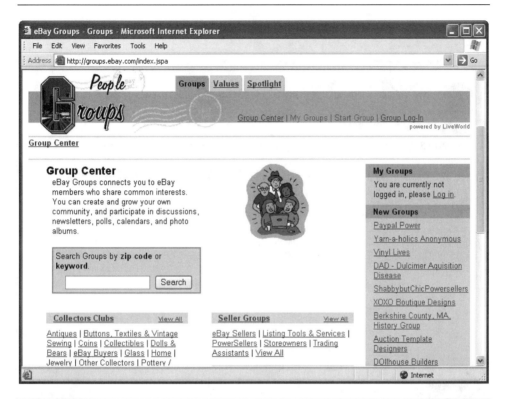

FIGURE 4-6   Go to the eBay Groups page to find a home-grown group you want to join.

When you first click a group's link on the eBay Groups home page, you access the group's Welcome page. Click the big Join Group button, and then log in with your User ID and password. Click Sign In, and the group's Home page will appear.

Unlike the Welcome page, the links on the left side of the page under Choose an Activity and Group Controls (see Figure 4-7) are now clickable links. They enable you to view photos that members have posted, learn about upcoming events, and join discussions.

CAUTION   *Even though boards are created by users, that doesn't mean you can do anything you want on them. You can't post someone else's contact information, and you can't make profane comments. See the list of Restricted Group Activities at http://pages.ebay.com/help/welcome/ group-restricted-activities.html.*

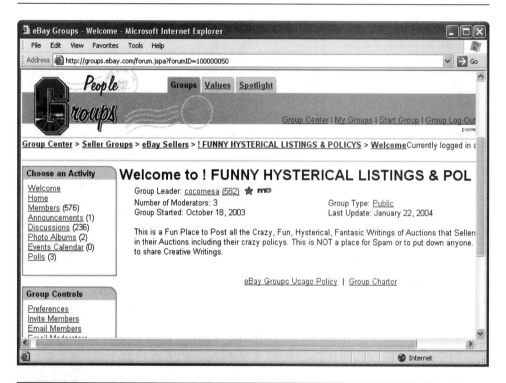

FIGURE 4-7   A group's Welcome page contains the links you need to begin
participating.

Stories and Experiences Make eBay a Way of Life

"eBay is a very important part of my life," says Jennifer Karpin-Hobbs.
"I use eBay to promote two different businesses, as well as to shop and bid."
Hobbs, whose User ID is morning-glorious, and who is shown here, has two
businesses: Morning Glorious Collectibles, an antiques business, and The
Grafton Homestead, a Bed & Breakfast she and her husband run together in
their Vermont home. She is one of four moderators of the popular eBay group
for female PowerSellers called "eBay PowerChicks."

"It's definitely a social bonding experience," Hobbs says of the group. "It also helps me as an eBay seller in concrete ways. The PowerChicks display a logo in their auctions that buyers have started to search for, especially in the wake of recent media publicity for our group. Many of us have noticed an increase in our sales from displaying the 'PC' logo. We have events like the 'Fugly Contests,' where we auction off the 'funniest, ugliest' items we can find. Prizes are awarded for the tackiest item, the one that sold for the highest final bid price, and so forth. It's a great motivator. I also use the discussion boards at times, to get answers to questions, or help others if I know the answer to their concerns. The boards are so diverse, from Vintage Textiles to Travel to Jewelry, that there seems to be one for every need or interest. I would highly recommend that anyone start an eBay Group or join an existing one that meets their needs and interests."

Jennifer Karpin-Hobbes

Running a business (or, in her case, two businesses) on eBay is different than selling part-time, she says. "For me, the difference is in the care with which I treat each transaction. It is my reputation at stake and this is how I make my living. I want every customer to be thrilled with their purchase and with every aspect of the auction experience. I communicate with my customers every step of the way: they get an e-mail from me when the auction ends, when their payment is received, and when the item has shipped."

Karpin-Hobbs says the eBay community extends to her promotion on eBay of a getaway suite at The Grafton Homestead. "I find that advertising on eBay, in the Travel category, is a great way to fill our empty B&B rooms, especially midweek days or off-season when people aren't traveling as much. Plus, we get to meet these winning bidders in person! Our guests really love the spaciousness and privacy of their accommodations here. We've made many eBay friends from our Grafton Homestead auctions."

In fact, keeping up with customers is one of the best things about selling on the auction site, she says. "My favorite thing about selling on eBay is hearing from bidders who share with me why the item they won is special to them. In one case, a man saw an article in a 1930s magazine I was selling that profiled his own grandfather! Another time, a lady bought an 1890s cabinet card photograph from me that actually was a picture of her own great-aunt. I had the privilege of selling an original 19th-century Currier & Ives print of the Brooklyn Bridge to a man who ran across that bridge on September 11th, 2001— running to safety on that terrible day of tragedy. The stories and experiences shared with me by my buyers, regarding their special purchases, are what makes 'doin' it eBay' a really great way of life for me!"

Forming Your Own eBay Group

Once you have participated in some eBay Groups and have a feel for how they work, you can consider starting your own group. As long as you have the required feedback rating, you click the link Start Group near the top of the eBay Groups home page to get the process started. But before that, you should join a group called the eBay Groups Information Center. This group contains all the instructions you need on how to operate a group after you have formed it.

In order to be successful, a group needs care and tending, just like a web site. You need to develop a schedule of events, and you need to be available to moderate discussions. You might be called to handle complaints and disputes between members, should they occur. In order for your group to get off the ground, you might want to invite friends and other members with whom you've done business to join your groups.

Don't Overlook eBay's "Suggestion Box"

As eBay has grown, it has become more complicated to get in touch with eBay staff members. It's not impossible by any means; it's just more complicated than in the "old days" when people like founder Pierre Omidyar could be found on the discussion boards and you could simply e-mail him a question. Today, if you send an e-mail message regarding a problem you are encountering, someone at eBay will get back to you. But, in my experience, it takes a couple of days to get a response.

You'll probably only take the trouble to find and then fill out the Contact Us page (http://pages.ebay.com/help/contact_inline/index.html) or connect to the Live Help system (click Live Help on the eBay home page) if you actually have a pressing problem. What if you just want to be a good member of the community and make a suggestion?

eBay does provide a place for this, but it's not easy to find. Go to http://pages.ebay.com/help/welcome/suggest.html, and click one of the two Send Us Your Suggestion links. One enables you to suggest a new category for buying and selling, while the other lets you make a general suggestion about how to improve eBay's web site.

4

You need to maintain interest in your group: if there has been no activity for 90 days, eBay will delete it.

NOTE
To start a group, you need to have a minimum feedback of 50 and have been registered on the site for at least 90 days.

Where to Find It

Web Site	Address	What's There
Community Hub Overview page	http://pages.ebay.com/community/index.html	Links to discussion groups, workshops, announcement boards, and other community forums
Share-Your-Wares and Street Faires pages	http://members.ebay.com/aboutme/sywstreetfaire	Announcements of events where sellers offer merchandise for sale that's in keeping with a particular theme
Contact eBay page	http://pages.ebay.com/help/contact_inline/index.html	A form you fill out in order to submit questions or comments to eBay
eBay Groups home page	http://groups.ebay.com/index.jspa	Links to eBay Groups created by members, and links to help you set up your own group
General Announcement boards	http://www2.ebay.com/aw/marketing.shtml	Announcements of new features and system problems on eBay

Chapter 5

Cool Tips for Beginning Buyers

How to…

- Become an eBay "Power Shopper"

- Automate your bidding with a bidding service

- Communicate with sellers to ensure smooth transactions

- Keep in touch with eBay no matter where you are

Some of the people who get the most attention on eBay are known as PowerSellers—members who have displayed high competence in selling and customer service. I don't think there is any scientific study of this, but I have a theory that many of those PowerSellers are also Power Buyers—people who are able to win auctions, get bargains, and gain high feedback for the way they deal with sellers.

This chapter provides some tips on a subject that's often overlooked when discussing eBay: how to bid effectively. Bidding seems all too easy. You see what you want, you click the Place Bid or Buy It Now button, and you're done. One danger is that you end up making "impulse purchases" that bust your available budget. Another, commoner problem occurs when you reach the exciting moments near the end of an auction when you are trying to get in the last bid, and you are either outbid or you fail to meet the seller's reserve.

How can you ensure that you come out as the high bidder or buyer when the sale ends, without spending more than you want to? These and other strategies for Power Buyers are described later in this chapter.

Becoming a Power Buyer

If you are a smart shopper, you will be a smart bidder on eBay—someone who gets what they want and gets bargains, so they can save money, and resell what they buy in the hope of making a profit. Many of the same practices that make sellers successful apply to buyers, too: building up good feedback, searching regularly for what you want, and bidding with your head rather than your heart.

Building Up Your Positive Feedback

Sellers react to feedback numbers the same as buyers. When they notice that their high bidder has a feedback rating of 0 or 1 (or worse, a –1 or –2), they tend to get worried. Some sellers who have encountered Non-Paying Bidders (NPBs) actually specify in their Terms of Sale that they will not sell to anyone who has a certain amount of feedback. The amount of feedback varies depending on the seller.

Some pick a feedback rating of 1 or 0. For some especially expensive sale items, sellers specify that they won't sell to anyone with a rating of less than 10. One of the eBay Groups described in Chapter 4, the PowerSellers Discount Forum, will only sell to Power Buyers who have feedback ratings of 200 or more (see Figure 5-1).

The point is that you need to build up positive feedback numbers by being a good citizen and either paying for what you buy quickly or shipping quickly. Positive feedback will build trust. It also gives you access to special features like starting up an eBay Store (you need a feedback rating of 10 or more, or

5

FIGURE 5-1   Buyers who maintain high positive feedback can take advantage of special offers like this.

pay $5 to have your identity verified) or starting an eBay Group, as described in Chapter 4 (you need a feedback rating of 50 and need to be a member of eBay for at least 90 days to start your own group).

How do you get started, if you only have a feedback rating of 0 or 1 to begin with? Consider buying something at an eBay Store at a fixed price. Don't just buy anything at random. Buy things you really want and that you'll be happy with. When you receive the items, be sure to leave positive feedback for the seller, and wait to see if the seller leaves positive feedback in turn. If you don't receive feedback for a week or two, send a gentle reminder to the seller, if necessary. Soon, you'll have a feedback rating in the double digits, which will help instill more confidence in prospective customers once you decide to sell.

Bid with Your Head, Not Your Heart

The people who end up with many varieties of eBay junk sitting on their shelves that they never use and no money to pay their bills are the impulse buyers—the ones who don't think before they buy. Some ways to avoid this situation are described in the sections that follow.

Know What the Item Is Worth

Before you place a bid or buy something, make sure you know its value. Experienced collectors and dealers in antiques and collectibles nearly always have a set of collectibles price guides—books that describe various things and provide estimates of what they are worth. eBay, in fact, is making such guides obsolete. You get real-world, up-to-date information on the value of items from eBay's database of Completed Items. You access this database by following these steps:

1. Go to the Advanced Search page (click Search, and then click the Advanced Search tab, or go directly to http://pages.ebay.com/search/items/search_adv.html).

2. Enter the search term in the Search keywords or item number box.

3. Check the Completed Items Only box.

4. Click Search.

5. Log in with your User ID and password, and then click Log In.

When the search results appear, you can scan about two weeks' worth of past auctions on eBay. You can see which sales ended without any bids, and which ended with a huge number of bids. A book might say that a Beatles *Yellow Submarine* toy is worth $50, but if it fetches $100 in bidding on eBay, that's a more accurate estimate of its value. Nevertheless, price guides are still good because they provide easy-to-scan lists of model numbers and product names. You can learn about all the different variations of an item.

Even if you are unable to get more up-to-date, real-world prices on eBay, you can find sales data that indicate the relative values of a model compared to similar ones. You might find that a first edition of an Ernest Hemingway novel with a letter *A* next to the publication date is worth $100, but a first edition without the *A* is worth $50. Armed with the right model numbers, you won't place a high bid on an item that isn't a valuable one. See Chapter 2 for some more suggestions on knowing the value of an item and doing comparison shopping.

5

> TIP
> *Price guides are going online, and some provide you with databases you can search. The Kovels Online Antiques and Collectibles Price Guide (www.kovels.com) lets you search its database if you sign up for a free account. Many of the prices are several years old and may be out-of-date, but they can give you a good starting point.*

Patience Is a Virtue

You have more control than you think when bidding on eBay auctions. You know when the sale ends; you know what the high bid is; you can even see who the other bidders are (unless you are participating in a private auction, which doesn't happen most of the time). You can also shop around eBay to see if any similar items are being offered, and search through eBay's database of recently completed auctions to see what similar items have fetched in the past. In other words, keep your cool; don't get caught up in bidding wars.

Like the participants in traditional auctions, you need to set a limit for your maximum bid. If someone goes beyond your maximum, take a deep breath and stop bidding. It's likely that the same item will turn up eventually on eBay, and you might find it for a lower price.

> TIP
> *You can configure My eBay to send you an e-mail message when an item comes in that matches the description of one that you bid on unsuccessfully. You can use this feature to track the high and low prices for such items. See Chapter 2 for this and other features of your My eBay page.*

Reading those Descriptions Closely

Because many PowerSellers are also Power Buyers, they know about the kinds of subtle tricks that can be inserted into auction descriptions. They read descriptions closely for phrases such as:

- **"Like new" or "Almost new"**   This can mean virtually anything other than brand-new. Ask for more specifics to find out exactly how far removed the item is from the designation brand-new.

- **"Minor bumps and bruises"**   Again, this is vague. It says nothing about exactly how many flaws the object has or where those objects are located.

- **"Reconditioned" or "factory serviced"**   This, too, is *not* new! Ask why the object was reconditioned—was it used slightly and then returned for a cosmetic flaw, or did it have to be extensively rebuilt?

In any case, such items should sell for perhaps 20 to 40 percent less than new. If you have *any* doubts or suspicions about something mentioned in the auction description, e-mail the vendor and get more information before you bid on the item.

> TIP   *If shipping and handling aren't listed in the description, they should be. Power Buyers know that this is a way where they can get an unwelcome surprise in the final cost of an item. Make sure you know exactly how much the shipping and handling costs will be before you bid.*

Keeping Track of What You've Purchased

When you are a Power Buyer, you might make a dozen purchases or more each week. It's easy to lose track of some of these sales. Don't keep sellers waiting for payment because you forget to pay them in your haste to pay for other auctions (it can happen). Get in the habit of checking My eBay's Bidding/Watching tab in the Items I've Won section and pay up promptly so you don't risk being labeled a Non-Paying Bidder (NPB).

Watching for Misspellings

As time goes on, it gets harder to find genuine bargains on eBay—things that sellers have undervalued and that other bidders have not hit upon. Sellers are getting smarter, and more and more buyers are joining eBay all the time, bringing their accumulated knowledge to the process of searching for, and finding, auction items.

One of the few ways you can find something that's a true overlooked gem, these days, is to search for misspellings in auction titles. A misspelled item won't show up in search results. You might find it by laboriously scrolling through each of the listings in a category, one page at a time. You also might find it by entering spelling variations in the Basic Search or Advanced Search form. For instance, if you're looking for CD-ROMs of symphonic works by the Russian composer Tchaikovsky (a name that is easily misspelled), you should enter a search like the following:

```
Swan Lake (Tchaikovsky, Tchaikovski, Chaikovski, Chaikovsky)
```

In fact, when I conducted a search for any of these terms, I turned up the following items:

- Chaikovski Symphony #2

- Tchaikovski Symphonie en Mi Mineur CD Album

- Tchaikovsky CD Swan Lake

The first two listings, obviously, would never have turned up in a search for the correct spelling. Because of this, relatively few bidders are likely to find the sale and participate. You might well be the only bidder and, if there's no reserve, you might walk away with a true bargain.

Knowing When to Buy It Now

I was looking for a desirable fountain pen for a long time—a Waterman #7 red ripple with the extra-flexible pink nib. Over the years, I found one or two of these models on eBay, but I was outbid at the last minute both times. I kept scanning the pens for sale on eBay, and saw one that had just been listed—it had no bids as yet, and a Buy It Now price of $195. It was a little more than I had hoped to buy for this pen, but I clicked the Buy It Now button and purchased it anyway. Why? I didn't want to risk being outbid for this desirable model once again. I was willing to pay a little more in order to avoiding bidding wars and get the pen shipped to me right away.

If you see something you really want advertised with a Buy It Now price that you know is reasonable, strongly consider bypassing the bidding process and simply making the purchase immediately. If the Buy It Now price is really good, you'd better move quickly—someone might just purchase the item out from under you while you are thinking about it. (This has happened more than once to me.)

5

Sellers like Buy It Now because it ensures that they will get paid right away. It doesn't necessarily mean that the item is not rare or exceptional. In fact, many items are offered with both a Buy It Now and a reserve price. You can search for Buy It Now items by checking the appropriate box in the Advanced Search form. If you are concerned about paying too much for something through Buy It Now, you can even specify a price range (see Figure 5-2).

 *Keep in mind that, if the item is being offered with no reserve, the Buy It Now price is no longer applicable after the first bid. If the item is being offered with a reserve, then the Buy It Now price is no longer applicable after the reserve is met.*

The Joy of No Reserve

The items that have the promise of being real bargains are the ones being offered with no reserve price. (Such no reserve auctions are frequently designated with the abbreviation NR.) The seller simply puts the item up for sale on eBay

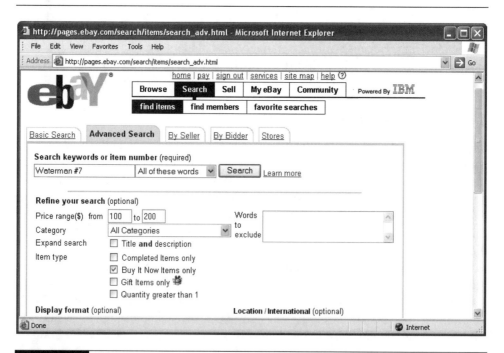

FIGURE 5-2 You can search for Buy It Now items and limit your search to a desired price range.

No Reserve Attracts Competition

Jennifer Karpin-Hobbs, an eBay PowerSeller, knows what happens when items are offered with no reserve price. "I used to use reserves more than I do now," she says. "I now think reserves can really turn off bidders who assume the reserve must be higher than they want to pay—it stops them from bidding in the first place.

"These days, I only set a reserve if the item I am selling is on consignment, and it belongs to someone else who just will not sell it without getting a certain price. I actually do not like to take on consignments with reserves. I find items sell the best when they start well below their retail value. In many cases, I open my auctions at $9.99—or even $1.00—regardless of what I have paid for the inventory I'm auctioning. This is definitely a risk, and sometimes I lose the gamble. Other times I win; I just start low and if the item has value, the bids will come."

with the certainty that it will go to the highest bidder. The "joy" of NR auctions is the prospect of actually getting an item at far below its market value.

But, as described in the sidebar, savvy sellers know (and therefore, savvy buyers should also know) that NR auctions tend to attract more attention from bargain-conscious shoppers, so they can easily lead to bidding wars.

Such sales can be a gamble for sellers as well as buyers. For buyers, the danger is that they can become caught up in the fever of wanting to win and maybe even bid more than the item is actually worth.

Going Dutch (Auctions, That Is)

Maybe they are called "Dutch" auctions because the concept can throw a monkey wrench into the windmill of your mind. Just hang in there, however, because if you want to buy multiple instances of the same item, this is the kind of sale to look for. In a Dutch auction (actually, eBay usually refers to them as multiple-item auctions), a seller offers at the same time two or more identical items. Winners obtain the amount of items they want if they have the lowest bid that is above the minimum price.

Dutch auctions are often overlooked in the rush to find bargains at standard or reserve auctions. But savvy buyers know that Dutch auctions can provide bargains for just that reason. Let's say you're a buyer who finds five identical Precious Moments figurines for sale in a Dutch auction. You really only need one figurine to add to your own collection. Why would you consider bidding on two or three? You can resell the others on eBay to help recoup your cost.

The seller has specified a minimum bid of $10 for each of the five figurines. You see that the current bidders have bid $15, $13, $12, $11, and $10. You don't want to be close to the low bid; that means you would be "on the bubble" and in danger of being outbid. You bid $14 for two items. If you win both, you can keep one and wait a few weeks to sell the other one. If you are able to sell the item for $20 or so, you can recoup much of the cost.

Wholesale Lots

Suppose you are hoping to purchase a large quantity of items (more than you typically find at a Dutch auction) at a discount to sell on eBay or at the local flea market. Or, suppose you need some prizes for the school carnival. In either case, the place to turn is eBay's Wholesale Lots area.

Wholesale Lots (http://pages.ebay.com/catindex/catwholesale.html) is a category where sellers try to unload groups of items at once, often at cut-rate prices. It's a perfect place for manufacturers to clear out unused inventory and supplies. Their priority is to sell, not to get the highest price. You're probably already familiar with warehouse and wholesale stores, which sell items in greater quantities than retailers, but at lower overall prices.

Wholesale Lots works in the same way: hopefully, you'll save overall by buying lots of things at once. It's up to you to figure out what to do with two dozen refurbished computers, 48-plus teddy bears, or "lots" of items such as the ones shown in Figure 5-3.

Creating Two User IDs

Some PowerSellers, or sellers who don't have that designation but have a high profile on eBay, make use of two separate accounts. They use one for selling: this one has their high feedback number, their star icon, perhaps their PowerSeller icon if they have one. The second has lower feedback and no PowerSeller icon: it's one they use only for bidding.

The idea is that, if they bid with their high feedback and other icons, people will be attracted to compete with them for items—the moment they see that a PowerSeller is the high bidder, they realize that there must be something desirable about the item, and they decide to bid, too. Keeping a lower profile by using the buyer's User ID helps reduce competition.

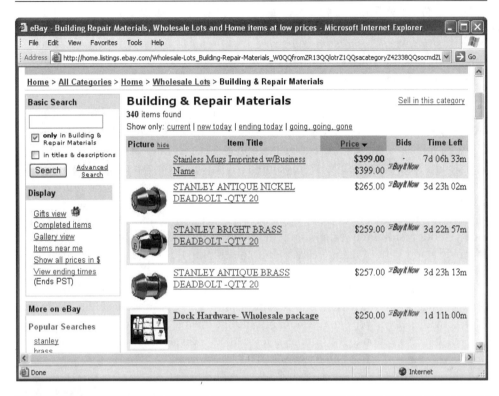

FIGURE 5-3   If you need large quantities of identical items, shop eBay's Wholesale Lots category.

Automating Your Bidding

Chapter 2 described the common practice of *sniping:* the practice of placing bids at the last possible moment in the hope of avoiding counterbids and winning an auction. That chapter described one way to snipe: setting up two or more browser windows (or two or more computer monitors) and being present at your computer at the end of the sale.

When you are tracking multiple sales, many of which end on weekends, you can't always be physically present. If you want to snipe, you need to install special software or subscribe to an online service that lets you configure to place bids at a time interval you specify (a minute or 30 seconds or 15 seconds before the auction ends). You also tell the software or service how big your bid should be. Many applications and services enable you to place snipe bids automatically. This section of the chapter focuses on one online service, but you should shop around to find the best one for your needs.

 *Sniping is not foolproof. Nor is it the only way to win an auction. If someone places a snipe bid that's larger than your snipe bid, you can still lose out. And snipe bids can be beaten by bigger proxy bids placed well before the sale ends. See Chapter 2 for tips on these alternate ways of winning auctions.*

HammerSnipe is a sniping service provided by HammerTap, a company that specializes in creating software applications for bidding and managing sales on eBay. In this case, the software does not come in the form of an application that you download and install on your computer. Instead, you use the software by connecting to a web site on which the software runs. You're using an online service rather than an installed application. There are lots of advantages to subscribing to software services—you save on disk space, and you don't have to worry about maintaining or updating the software. Perhaps the biggest advantage, from the standpoint of using eBay, is that the sniping doesn't have to be limited by your computer or your Internet connection.

If your computer crashes or runs slowly or your Internet connection is slow or breaks down at the critical moment, sniping won't work. Because the sniping software is on someone else's web site (presumably, the site operated by a company with a fast and reliable connection to the Internet), you can be reasonably certain that your last-second bid will arrive before the sale ends.

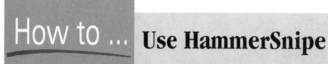

How to ... Use HammerSnipe

In general, using HammerSnipe is easy: you enter the eBay item number of the auction you want to bid on, your maximum bid, and the "buffer time" (the number of seconds before the end of the auction when you want to place your bid). To get started, follow these steps:

1. Go to the HammerSnipe New Account Sign Up page (http://hammertap .auctionstealer.com/secure/signup.cfm) and fill out the form to apply for an account.

2. Click Sign Up.

3. When the HammerSnipe Confirmation page appears, follow the instructions to activate your copy of HammerSnipe.

4. Scroll down to the Add a New Item section. Choose the eBay area where the sale is located from the Auction Site drop-down list. (The service supports sales located in many foreign countries as well as eBay Motors.) Paste the item number in the Auction Number box.

5. Click Verify Item. Scan the Auction Information section. Then enter your maximum snipe bid and the quantity you want to bid on in the Snipe Information section (see the illustration).

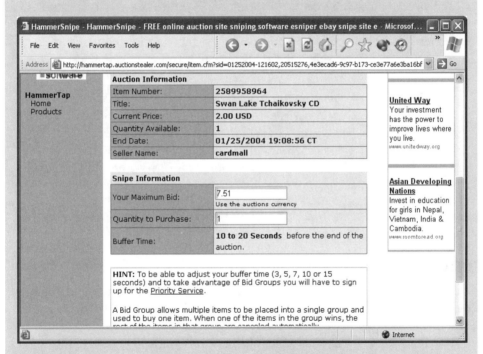

TIP   *Don't enter an even dollar amount for your snipe bid. In the event someone bids the same amount you do, add one or two cents to your bid in an attempt to beat out the competition.*

6. Click Save Item to save your item in HammerSnipe's database. You can review your item by returning to the Current Auctions page while the sale is going on.

It's worth noting that the free version of HammerSnipe only gives you an allotment of 15 "points" per month while the Priority Service gives you an unlimited allotment. You use up a point each time you place a snipe bid using the service. You can upgrade to the Priority Service version at any time. Priority Service carries a monthly subscription fee. If you pay with PayPal, a one-month subscription is $8.99, and a three-month subscription is $19.99. Many other payment options are available; check http://hammertap.auctionstealer.com/pricing.cfm for more information.

HammerSnipe is hardly the only type of service that enables shoppers to place snipe bids on eBay. eSnipe (www.esnipe.com) doesn't charge a monthly fee. Instead, you are charged points each time you win an auction using the eSnipe service. When you accumulate 500 points, you pay the service $5. Another sniping service, AuctionSniper (www.auctionsniper.com), charges you one percent of the final sale price of each auction you win using the service.

> **NOTE** *HammerSnipe comes in two versions: a Free Service and a Priority Service. One of the biggest differences between the two programs is the minimum time when the last-second bid can be placed: the Free Version lets you bid up to ten seconds before the auction ends; the Priority Service extends the time to only three seconds before the end. The Priority Service carries fees of up to $1 per auction, however. Find out more at http://hammertap .auctionstealer.com/info.cfm.*

Communicating Effectively

One quality shared by Power Buyers is the ability to communicate clearly and courteously with sellers. You don't have to make friends with all the sellers you encounter, of course.

The more you know about a seller, the better off you will be as a bidder. Check a seller's bidding history to see if he or she has switched User IDs frequently. Also check the feedback profile to see if there is any neutral or negative feedback. The law of averages dictates that everyone will hit a few bumps in the road on a long trip. But use the resources available to you to get acquainted, at least in a virtual way, with the person you're trusting to keep up their end of the bargain.

Using the Auction Number in All Your E-Mails

One piece of specific information is worth a thousand guesses. Don't keep your sellers guessing when they read your e-mail. Sellers who run through dozens of eBay sales a week can easily lose track of what you, specifically, have just purchased from them. Don't make them look up your User ID. Be specific and include your item number and perhaps even the auction title in all of your e-mail exchanges with the seller. A typical end-of-sale e-mail might look like this:

```
I am pleased to be the winning bidder on item #1122334455, the
Fender Coronado bass guitar. I will do my part to make this a
smooth transaction for both of us.

I see you accept PayPal, personal checks, cashier's checks, and
money orders. My first choice is cashier's checks. Will this add to
the time required to ship? Please send me a total of what I need to
send you and where to send it and I'll get a check out to you in
the next day or two.
```

5

Your goal is to make the sale go as smoothly as possible, and anything you can do to reduce the possibility for a mix-up is well worth the extra effort. Suppose, however, that you are the high bidder on an item but your bid did not meet the reserve. In that case, a different kind of communication is needed. The seller is not obligated to complete a sale if his or her reserve amount is not met. However, many sellers will follow through if you offer to meet the reserve, or at least a higher amount than your high bid. You can do one of two things:

- Make an offer that is higher than your maximum amount.

- Ask the seller what the reserve was to see if you want to pay it.

The first option at least gives you a slight chance of getting close to your high bid. The seller might say, "My reserve was higher than your offer, but I'll sell anyway." Of course, its far more likely the seller will say, "My reserve was $X amount, so if you want to buy it at that price, it's up to you." At that point, you have to decide if you want to accept the reserve or not. This is where any research you have done on the market value of the item comes into play (see Chapter 2).

If you have an idea what the item is worth, you can evaluate whether you want to pay the seller's price or not. If you do, keep in mind that you won't be able to take advantage of eBay's fraud protection for buyers and sellers—you either pay the seller directly or use a payment service such as PayPal or Western Union BidPay to give yourself some measure of protection.

Chasing Down Nonresponsive Sellers

If a seller doesn't respond immediately to your inquiries, don't immediately assume that there's a problem with the transaction. Wait a couple of days, and then send a polite reminder e-mail:

```
Dear Seller,
I'm the winning bidder for your item #11223344, the Extra-Large
Widget Shredder. I'm still waiting for the shipping information and
will be happy to send you payment as soon as I hear from you.
Sincerely,
[Your Name]
```

Any number of things can keep sellers from responding to a buyer on the day an item is sold, or the day after. They may be sick or out of town; they may be busy working at their "day job." eBay's rules state that a seller has 30 days to ship an item to you. If the seller responds and says the item has been shipped on a specified date, give the package about two weeks to get to you. Even then, you should do your best to be professional and courteous: just tell the seller that two weeks have elapsed and the package hasn't arrived. It may have been lost in transit, after all.

> **TIP** *You can ask eBay to send you the Seller's contact information. Fill out the Contact Info part of the Find Members form (http://cgi3.ebay.com/aw-cgi/ eBayISAPI.dll?MemberSearchShow) and you'll get the seller's address and phone number. You can only get the phone number of a buyer or seller with whom you are involved in a transaction, however.*

Many problems can be resolved with a phone call. If you have not yet received what you purchased, you should give the seller a call about two weeks after the sale ends. If you still haven't received the item after 30 days, you should file a fraud alert with eBay; click the fraud alert link at http://pages.ebay.com/help/confidence/isgw-fraud-protection.html.

After that, you should file a claim with your credit card company, if you paid with a credit card. You can then file a claim with eBay's Fraud Protection

Program, which gives you a reimbursement of up to $200 in losses, minus a $25 processing cost. If you paid with PayPal, you may also be eligible for its own Buyer Protection Program, which provides up to $500 of coverage. See Chapter 6 for more information.

Keeping in Contact with eBay

These days, everyone needs to be mobile. You probably need to keep in touch with home, office, or friends using your cell phone. You might also be able to use a wireless laptop or Personal Desk Assistant (PDA) to check your e-mail.

To be an effective eBay Power Buyer, you need to keep on top of sales. Specifically, you need to know when you have been outbid, so you can place a counterbid. You also need to know when a sale is about to end in case you want to place a last-minute bid. The following sections explain how to keep in touch with eBay when you are away from your home or office computer, or even when you're surfing sites other than eBay.

Setting Your Notification Preferences

eBay can send you e-mail messages or even text messages to your pager or cell phone when certain events occur. If you want to receive such messages from eBay (and, if you really consider yourself a Power Buyer, you might want them), you begin by setting your notification preferences and telling eBay how to get in touch with you. The following How To section outlines the setup.

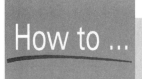 **Tell eBay How and When to Contact You**

If you want to receive messages from eBay when you're "on the road," you must give eBay a number or e-mail address where you want to be reached. Then you tell eBay what sorts of messages you want to receive. Follow these steps:

1. Click My eBay.

2. Click Preferences.

3. Under the heading UserID/Email address, click Change My Wireless Email address. The Add/Change Wireless Email Address page appears.

NOTE   *Many cell providers give subscribers who choose to send and receive e-mail on their phones special e-mail addresses that take the form myusername@cellprovider.net. You can choose to receive such messages at such an address if you have one.*

4. Enter your e-mail address in the box provided, and then click Save Wireless Email Address.

5. Sign in with your User ID and password if you are prompted to do so. The Change Your Notification Preferences page appears (see the following illustration).

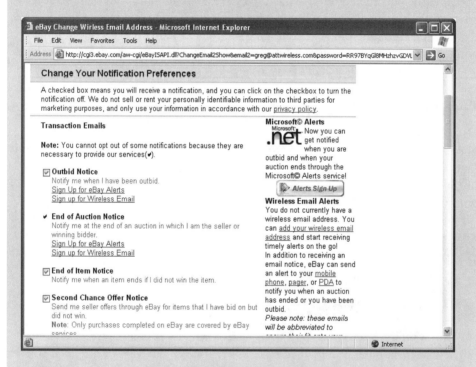

6. Check the box next to the type of notification you want to receive. For wireless e-mail purposes, you'll probably want to check Outbid Notice, so you can receive a message if someone has outbid you.

7. Under the heading Transaction Emails, choose one of two alternatives for receiving alerts: Click the Receive Wireless Email box if you want to receive alert messages from eBay, or click the Sign Up for eBay Alerts button if you want to use the Microsoft Alerts system to receive

alert messages. If you choose the Microsoft Alerts option, you are prompted to use a Microsoft Passport account or sign up for one (see the following illustration).

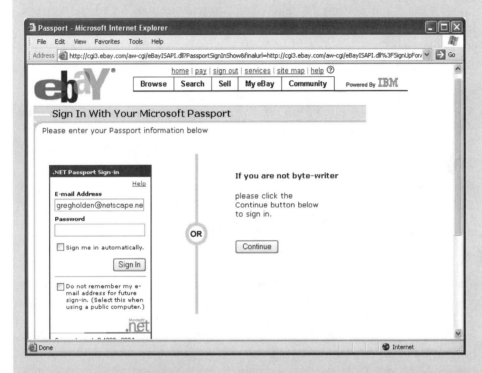

8. Type your Microsoft Passport username and password, and then click Sign In. (Click the small link, Get a Passport, just beneath the sign-in form if you don't have an account yet.)

9. Sign in with your eBay User ID and password, and click Sign In.

10. Click Finish Signing Up for eBay Alerts. When a license page appears, click Accept. A page with the heading "Where do you want your eBay alerts delivered?" appears. Follow the instructions shown on this page to select an e-mail address where you want the alerts to be sent.

You may need to do some configuration of your wireless device to notify you when an e-mail message is received (if such a feature is available). More likely, you won't have to do any configuration; the text message from eBay will be sent to your cell phone, and you'll automatically receive an alert. Check with your cell phone or PDA manufacturer for detailed instructions.

Adding eBay to Your Browser's Toolbar

A free utility called eBay Toolbar lets you search eBay while you are surfing other web sites. It also gives you a set of toolbar buttons that are added to your web browser's usual toolbars and that take you to various locations on eBay's web site. The toolbar gives you a way to search eBay from wherever you are on the Web and receive alert messages in your browser window if you are outbid in an auction where you were the previous high bidder.

NOTE *eBay Toolbar only works with Windows operating systems; Macintosh and Linux users can't install it. The toolbar works with Microsoft Internet Explorer 5.01 or later, or Netscape Navigator 4.51 through 4.79. You can find out more about eBay Toolbar at http://pages.ebay.com/ebay_toolbar.*

How to ... Install the Toolbar

eBay's toolbar gives you a connection to eBay from your web browser. You can search eBay whenever you want and reach favorite categories with just one or two mouse clicks. You install the toolbar by following these steps:

1. Go to the eBay Toolbar page (http://pages.ebay.com/ebay_toolbar). Make sure you have turned off any firewall programs you have running, at least during the download process.

2. Read about the toolbar, make sure you have the required software to run the toolbar, and then click Download.

3. When the license agreement page appears, read the license terms, and then click Accept.

4. When a security warning page appears, click OK (if you use Internet Explorer) or Grant (if you are using Netscape Navigator).

5. Your browser window refreshes, and eBay Toolbar is instantly added to the toolbars just above the main display area. The sign-in page then prompts you to enter your User ID and password (see the illustration).

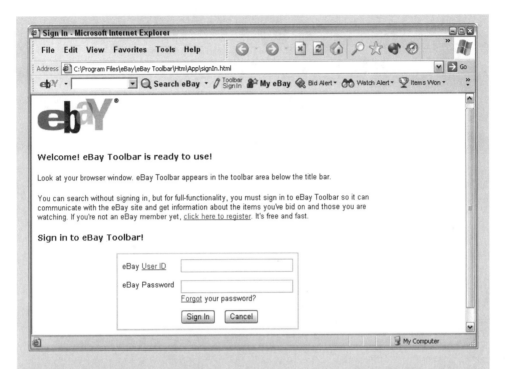

> **NOTE** *eBay Toolbar only works with Windows computers. Macintosh users can use Apple Computer's tool called Sherlock to receive special content from web sites. Find out more at www .apple.com/macosx/features/sherlock.*

Searching with the Toolbar

The toolbar's primary function is to let you search eBay. The search box keeps a record of the most recent searches you have done (as many as 25 previous searches). Click the drop-down arrow next to the search box to access one of the previous searches. This search history list can be a convenient way to save and reuse searches you conduct frequently.

If you click Search eBay, a long list of search options appears. The options at the top of the submenu let you choose how you want to search eBay. The others provide you with categories and subcategories for searching. You choose an option, and then enter a word or phrase in the toolbar's search box to actually conduct the search. You can also search within eBay Stores, by seller, and for Buy It Now items (see the illustration).

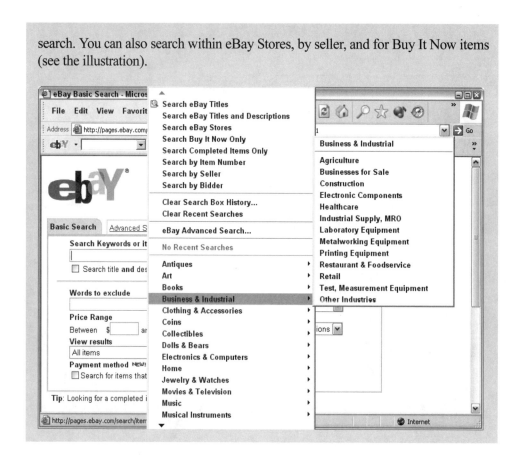

eBay Toolbar contains a set of buttons that take you to different parts of the eBay web site, no matter what web site your browser window is displaying at the time. On the left of the toolbar is a search text box, which functions like the search boxes on eBay's site. The buttons to the right of the search box include:

- **Toolbar Sign In**   This takes you to eBay's Sign In page, where you can enter your username and password. You need to sign in so you can receive Bid Alerts and Watch Alerts.

- **My eBay**   This takes you to your My eBay page.

- **Bid Alert**   If you have bid on an auction and adjusted your My eBay preferences so that you receive Bid Alerts, you'll receive notifications 10, 15, 30, 60, or 75 minutes before the end of the auction. Such alerts give

The Weirdest, Wildest eBay Auctions Ever

Looking Back...

- Historic sales that influenced eBay's development
- Body parts and people for sale online
- Celebrity sales that dished the dirt
- Childhood homes of the rich and famous
- Gastronomic delicacies, or did you say disasters?

Over the years lots of wacky and weird things have been put up for sale on eBay. You've probably heard of some of them because whenever one of these incidents occurs, it's picked up by the news media, leaving you to wonder "Whatever happened to those sales?"

eBay is approaching its first decade of business, and a look back at some of its most famous sales can give you some perspective on what you might sell yourself, or how you might decide to sell it. Many of eBay's activities, and the business decisions that have shaped its history, have revolved about certain items that were sold at critical periods of time.

Legendary eBay Sales

O ver the years, eBay has evolved in response to how people have used it—and, occasionally, how they've abused it. Its site operations and the organization itself have been influenced by some noteworthy sales.

Sometimes, sales have proven so popular that they have exposed technical limitations associated with conducting online transactions. In some cases, eBay has been flooded with requests and been forced to improve its ability to handle simultaneous connections.

On other occasions, the fact that eBay sellers can put virtually anything online for sale has forced the company to examine its user policies. Everyone has heard of instances in which people have tried to put materials up for auction that were obviously illegal or offensive. At the same time, as eBay has extended its reach to include other countries, where language barriers and other regional differences have resulted in sales that have violated trade laws. eBay often reacts by hurriedly taking the sale down, contacting law enforcement authorities, and devising new rules to prevent repeat occurrences.

The Earliest Items Sold on eBay

There is, apparently, no accurate record of the very *first* items ever sold on eBay. In a book about eBay entitled *The Perfect Store,* Adam Cohen describes the contents of a September 12, 1995 newsgroup posting that Pierre Omidyar made to provide examples of what was up for sale on AuctionWeb, which was then less than two weeks old. Table S-1 provides a few examples of the early bidding, along with comparisons of what 2003 bids were offered for the same items. In some cases, demand has gone up; in others (for example, Michael Jackson paraphernalia), demand has fallen over time.

The Beanie Baby Craze

One of the first marketing sensations to fuel AuctionWeb's transformation into eBay was the humble Beanie Baby line of toys. These days, Beanie Babies are only one of a raft of plush bean-filled toys, and are greatly outnumbered by the volume of promotional items occasionally given out for free by fast-food restaurants. Beanie Baby products were small, lightweight and, in 1996, somewhat hard to find.

That's when Ty Inc., the company that manufactures the creatures, began to "retire" individual models in order to make them scarce and drive up demand. Each time a Beanie Baby was retired, auction sales on AuctionWeb became more and more frenzied. The harder-to-find models were in the possession of collectors who were scattered around the United States and overseas. The online auction site was the perfect place to trade them. By spring 1997, Beanie Babies that

Item	Asking Price on Sept. 12, 1995	What It Sold for in 2003
Superman metal lunchbox, 1967	$22	$87.02
Autographed poster of Michael Jackson	$400	$152.50
Hubley #520 Cast Iron Hook and Ladder Truck	$300	$255.00

Table SL-1　Earliest Recorded eBay Sales

had an original purchase price of only $5 were selling for an average of $33 on eBay. In May 1997 alone, the site was responsible for the sale of $500,000 worth of Beanie Babies.

eBay Gets Flooded

Many of the restrictions imposed on users who are found to have broken one or another rules were originally devised during a period in which the site was overwhelmed by its own success. In early 1997, nearly 200,000 sales began to be held every month. During this period, eBay held its first promotion, the sale of a football autographed by a Green Bay Packers football team of the 1960s. The heavy load placed on servers forced them to take the first measures against deadbeat sellers—people who would put merchandise up for sale and then take bidders' money without ever delivering what had been purchased.

Another flood took place during the 1997 holiday season. That was the year of the Tickle Me Elmo craze. During the 1998 holiday season, the hottest toy was the Furby—a lovable ball of fur that spoke a strange language called Furbish. The demand for such creatures caused eBay's servers to crash over and over. The technical setup was revamped. Today, outages still occur, but not with the frequency or duration of those in the late 1990s.

Firearms Get Banned

Some strange and possibly dangerous people probably look back with nostalgia on the days when you could buy or sell firearms on eBay. Before 1999, you might see auction listings in an eBay firearms category. The sales would bear titles such as "pre-ban Hungarian AK 47" or "pre-ban Uzi."

Since it was too difficult for eBay staff people to monitor which sales were peddling antique firearms that were nonfunctioning and those that were truly dangerous, the auction site decided to ban firearms sales altogether in February 1999, a policy that remains in place today.

Part I: Animals and People

Shortly after Saddam Hussein, the former president of Iraq, was captured and shaven by U.S. doctors, a television host I saw remarked, "How long will it be before those whiskers are put up for sale on eBay?" Sales of objects that are physically connected to the rich and famous (or infamous) are so well known that we now look to eBay the moment something notable happens to those celebrities. But you don't need to be famous to gain attention on eBay. Some of the most remarkable sales involved just plain folks who found their 15 minutes of fame on the world's most popular auction site.

They Tried to Sell Their Family on eBay

Life's not always easy for freelance writers, as this book's author can tell you. I have a certain amount of sympathy for a freelance television writer named Steve Young. He had just written an article about the town in California that sold for $1.78 million (a sale described later in this insert), and was tired of the financial ups and downs of the life of a freelance writer. "If a town could be sold online, then how much could you get for a family?" Young later explained to the *Los Angeles Times*. "As I was writing, I turned to my wife and said, 'We can do this.'"

Young eventually convinced his wife and two children to auction themselves off on eBay for $5 million in January 2003. The winner would receive a life's worth of platonic companionship from the family. The parents would even agree to change their surnames. After appearing on a television talk show, Young claimed he actually got the $5 million minimum bid he had asked for. He was sure the offer was legitimate; the bid, like all those over $15,000, was secured with a credit card number. But eBay eventually pulled the sale, saying it violated the company policy to sell human beings.

In another sale, 24 small children were put up for sale by a seller in Osaka, Japan. The kids were supposedly two to five years old and came with "warranty papers." Supposedly, the children spoke Japanese and had training in factories owned by the Disney company "making Donald Duck velcro wallets." Bidding reached $51 before the sale was stopped. But that's not all. The feedback left for this sale turned out to be equally repulsive:

> "Child at the back, third from right, smells
> a bit off. A replacement please ! How
> much for the mothers? How much for
> your wife?"

What's in a Name?

The moment a baby is born these days, most parents start to wonder how they're going to pay for his or her education. Heather and Steve Johnson of Lacey, Washington (shown in Figure 1) had a creative idea. Why not follow the example of baseball parks and other sports arenas and sell naming rights to their baby to the highest bidder on eBay?

Steve and Heather said they would name their son anything the bidder wanted, including brand names such as OshKosh, Baby Gap, or Pepsi Cola. They figured the money would be more than enough to pay for a college education for the youngster. The only restriction was against names that were "inherently evil," such as Hitler or Osama bin Laden. Unfortunately, no one bid on the naming rights.

The Kidney that Caused a Furor

The single most notorious auction ever held on eBay was probably the offer entitled "Fully functional kidney for donation," which went online in September 1999. According to the Online auction Museum of Weird and Zany Sales (http://auctionknowhow.com/museum),

Figure SL-1. For at least $250,000 you could name their baby whatever you wanted.

which preserves the auction headline shown in Figure 2, the description read, in part:

> "Will donate perfectly healthy kidney for a reciprocal donation of 2.5 million dollars to a charity of my choice. Absolutely serious inquiries please. Kidney recipient to pay all medical expenses for both parties."

With the sale nearly over and a top bid of $5,750,100 on the table, eBay finally pulled the sale offline. Trafficking in human body organs is a felony in the United States and carries a minimum of five years in prison and fines of up to $250,000.

The Serial Killer's Fingernails

Some people are just fascinated with serial killers. The Web abounds with pages devoted to their misadventures, their tortured childhoods, or their whereabouts in prison or in the graveyard. Souvenirs associated with killers are desired by those who have a morbid fascination with them. One of the oddest "souvenirs" was a set of fingernails alleged to have belonged to a serial killer named Roy Norris. A note from Norris—and his thumbprint—covered part of the card. Only one bid was recorded, for $9.99, before bidding was halted (see Figure 3).

NOTE

At this writing, a search for the terms "serial killer" turns up a variety of books, DVDs, videotapes, and posters related to famous mass murderers such as Jeffrey Dahmer, John Wayne Gacy, and the like. But eBay's ban on selling parts of the human body prevents auctions like the preceding from appearing online.

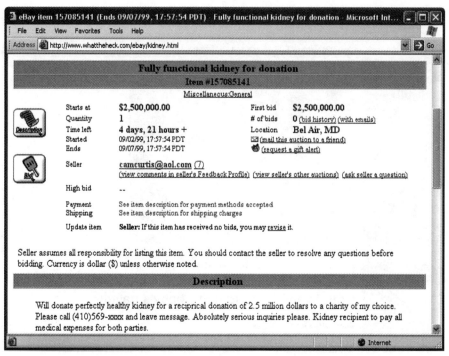

Figure SL-2. Bidding reached $5.75 million for a "fully functional kidney" before eBay removed the sale.

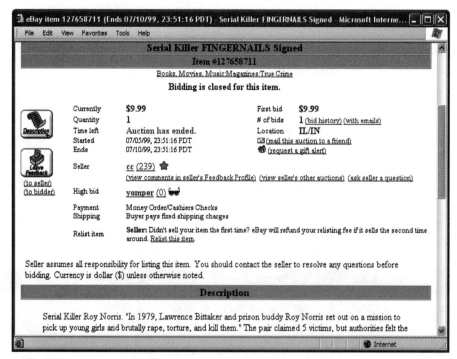

Figure SL-3. A serial killer's fingernails, accompanied by his thumbprint, were up for sale briefly on eBay.

Norris is hardly the only mass murderer to have his personal effects put up for auction on eBay. Consider Arthur Shawcross. He was released from prison in New York after serving a 15-year term for killing two children in the 1970s. He proceeded to kill 11 prostitutes in Rochester, New York in the early 1990s, and was sentenced to 250 years' worth of jail time for those murders. Before he was banned from creating "art" and mementoes, he, too, sent parts of himself to others who would put them up for sale. In May 2000, a hunk of his hair sold on eBay for $20.

Take My Grandma, Please

Auctions on eBay don't always bring out the best in people. In fact, they occasionally bring out the worst—especially when people attempt to sell off family members. One auction seller was particularly mean-spirited: in it, the person offered his or her own grandmother. Accessories included with grandma included two pairs of dentures, one quilt, three bottles of foot ointment, and one rocking chair.

Bidding went over more than a million dollars before the sale was stopped. Only when potential bidders read down toward the bottom of the description did they discover that grandma would come delivered in "jumbo bubble wrap, in a crate that doubles as a wooden coffin when she dies."

Take His Virginity, Please

It was bound to happen. Think about all the young people who have nothing valuable to sell on eBay—except their virtue, that is. In August 1999, a 17-year-old member of the National Honor Society decided to sacrifice his honor—more accurately, his virginity—to the highest bidder. Interestingly, the auction description, which is preserved in part in the Online Auction Museum of Weird and Zany Sales (see Figure S-4), did not specify whether the winner need be male or female ("I'm willing to experiment," the seller claimed). Perhaps it didn't matter, since bidding reached $10,000,000 before eBay took the sale down.

Justin Timberlake's French Toast

Justin Timberlake, a singer who was once a member of the boy group *NSYNC, and later became known as the boyfriend of teen heartthrob Britney Spears, was never associated with French toast. Not, that is, until he and his *NSYNC band mates paid a visit to radio station WHTZ-FM, otherwise known as The Zoo, back in the year 2000. It was breakfast time, so the Zoo decided to feed their guests some French toast. Ever conscious about his weight, Justin only took a bite or two out of his breakfast. When they had gone, an alert employee realized that here was an artifact that would be perfect for eBay.

So it was that Justin Timberlake's partially eaten French toast was put up for auction, with the proceeds designated for charity. It started out as a joke. The surprise was that bids for the toast kept piling up like flapjacks. According to the image of the auction shown in Figure S-5, bids soared over $3000.

The eventual price paid for the toast is unclear. News reports state that the winner, an *NSYNC fanatic and student at the University of Wisconsin named Kathy Summers, placed the winning bid of $1025. Was the bid actually $1025 or more than $3000? Whatever the price paid, it was an astonishing amount for a piece of half-eaten food. Summers eventually had the toast freeze-dried and preserved in her dorm room.

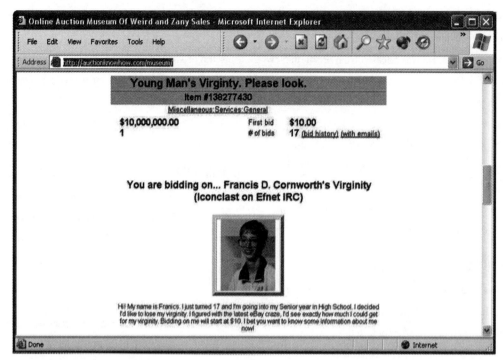

Figure SL-4. This young man's virginity fetched a bid of $10,000,000 before eBay ended the sale.

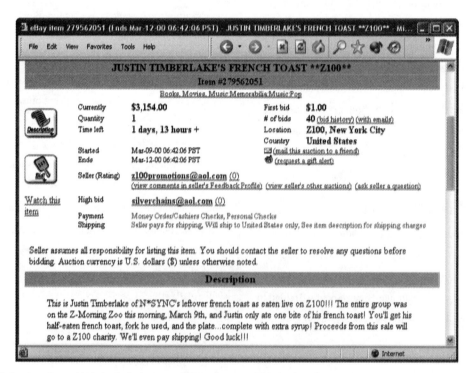

Figure SL-5. A student paid big bucks for a pop star's French toast, which she then freeze-dried.

Ozzy Osbourne's "Holy Water"

Timing is everything. Sometimes, it pays to hold on to relics associated with celebrities until those celebrities hit the big time. Back in 1999, Ozzy Osbourne was only known as a heavy-metal rock star. His main claim to fame was supposedly biting the head off a live bat during a concert. He did some other odd things, too. Apparently, he "personally blessed" 100 containers of water, which someone in North Carolina put up for auction on eBay. At the time, no bids were received. If the same water was sold today, now that Osbourne and his family are famous around the world for their reality TV show and other exploits, bidding wars would be more likely to erupt.

A variation on the theme of water somehow associated with someone famous surfaced on eBay in August 1999: someone attempted to sell 50 vials of water taken from Cape Cod. The only significance was the fact that John F. Kennedy, Jr. and his fiancée had perished in the same body of water in a plane crash. No bids were believed to have been placed. The same seller had better luck with water taken from the pool used in the 1990s television show Melrose Place. Two bidders won vials of the water in which the show's stars allegedly cavorted. They paid $7.99 each.

eBay Auctions Made for Dr. Frankenstein

If Dr. Frankenstein, the mad scientist who created the monster of the same name, were really alive today, he wouldn't bother lurking around cemeteries and digging up corpses. He'd be able to save time and trouble by surfing eBay. The following auctions come close to violating eBay's prohibition on selling real body parts. But in both cases, the items being sold aren't really "real."

Seller Offers to Lend a Hand—and Rest of Arm

In my book *How to Do Everything With Your eBay Business,* I profiled a seller who put an artificial leg up for sale on eBay almost as a joke, to see if anyone would bid on it at all. To his surprise, he ended up selling the leg for $430. Artificial body parts are occasionally sold on eBay. Real body parts are prohibited from sale on the site. But the sale shown in Figure 6 was allowed, apparently because the seller was only renting out one of his arms. The seller specified in the ad that the winning bidder was required to pay airfare to transport the arm and its owner to and from the winner's location. Another important caveat: nothing illegal could be conducted "in the presence of my arm." The item was listed as a gift item: the seller would gift wrap the arm for presentation to the bidder.

Uncle Bob's Glass Eye

The eBay seller mojo-man tells a colorful story about the real glass eye he put up for sale with no reserve in late 2003. He said it belonged to his Uncle Bob who, it seems, lost an eye in World War II. The replacement eye (blue in color, shown in Figure 7) was given to him by the U.S. government. The seller went into amazing detail when he recalled:

> "It matched Uncle Bob's real eye perfectly. I used to tell him, 'Uncle Bob, you can't tell that it's not real.' Of course, you could tell it wasn't real because it never moved. Remember how Sammy Davis Jr.'s eye never moved and Columbo's eye never moved? Well, Uncle Bob's was the same way. I think it made Uncle Bob feel better when I would say that you couldn't tell it from his real eye."

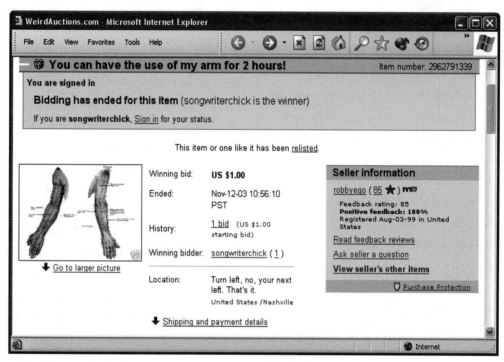

Figure SL-6. Why lend a hand when you can rent out your own arm? That's what this eBay seller apparently thought.

When Uncle Bob died, the story goes, his body was cremated. His will was read, and the seller was surprised to find that Uncle Bob had left his glass eye to him. Now, he says, his girlfriend was frightened by discovering the eye in a drawer and he was forced to sell it. "Well, what do you do with a damned used glass eye?" he concludes. "eBay, of course!"

Figure SL-7. What do you do with a used glass eye? Sell it on eBay, of course!

Basketball Signed by Murder Victim, Alleged Killer

eBay sales are often strange, but they don't often have a connection to a real-life murder mystery. The basketball shown in Figure 8 certainly does. In summer 2003, Patrick Dennehy, a star basketball player for the Baylor University team, was found murdered, shot twice in the head. His teammate Carlton Dotson was eventually charged with the murder. He pleaded not guilty and, at this writing, is still awaiting trial.

The story doesn't end there, however. The coach of the Baylor men's basketball team, Dave Bliss, resigned his job after inquiries into Dennehy's death revealed NCAA rules violations as well as an attempt to mislead investigators. An assistant coach at Baylor made a secret recording in which Bliss encouraged his players to say that Dennehy was a drug dealer. He also admitted he had been involved in tuition payments to two players that violated the NCAA's rules. Bliss's signature was also on the basketball being sold on eBay.

The seller of the basketball, who said in an addendum to his description that he only expected to sell the ball for $50, expressed interest in donating the money to charity. The ball eventually sold for $1,026 after receiving 59 bids.

Life After Death—Frozen in Place

Occasionally, eBay auctions feature something that has to do with one's death. You find such things as embalming fluid, coffins, cemetery plots, and cremation urns. But one auction posted in summer 2003 promised to have you frozen after death. It also gained some negative publicity by liberally throwing around the name of the most famous person ever to be cryogenically preserved (in other words, have his body frozen) after his death.

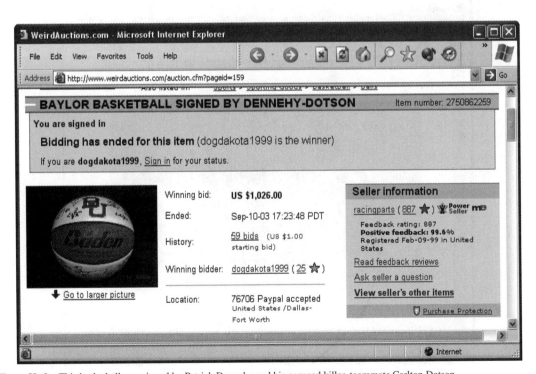

Figure SL-8. This basketball was signed by Patrick Dennehy and his accused killer, teammate Carlton Dotson.

This is Ted Williams, one of the greatest baseball players of all time. Williams was known as The Splendid Splinter during his playing days, but he might now be called The Incredible Iceman. Williams' photo was included in the auction description shown in Figure 9.

There were several odd aspects to the sale besides the use of Williams' name: anyone who bid and won received all arrangements to be frozen after "death" and maintained in a state of "cryonic suspension." However, in order to have the procedure done, the winner would have to take out *life insurance*. An estimated annual fee of $1000 would be required. The starting bid for the auction was $5000, which turned out to be dead as a doornail, as no one actually bid. But of course, the auction is now preserved after "death" within the pages of this book.

Figure SL-9. This auction gained negative responses from baseball fans who said it tarnished the name of Ted Williams.

Auctions that Tried to Make Political Hay

Most people put things up for sale on eBay in order to clean out their storage areas, or to make some extra money. A few, however, try to mix politics with commerce. The administration of President George W. Bush and Vice-President Dick Cheney has frequently been the subject (or the target) of sales items on eBay, if only because eBay grew so quickly in popularity after he was elected in 2000. But President Bill Clinton and Vice-President Al Gore showed up in eBay auctions, too. Some examples of auctions that stirred up political controversy are listed below.

"Axis of Weasels" Sale Stirs Up Trouble

In July 2003, a Canadian named John Steins decided to do a parody of the famous playing cards issued by the U.S. government during the war in Iraq. The cards depicted 50 members of the Iraqi regime of Saddam Hussein, including Hussein and his sons Uday and Qusay. The original deck of cards was frequently offered for sale on eBay; at this writing, you could still find them for sale on eBay for as much as a Buy It Now price of $14.99.

Steins decided to create his own deck of 50 cards, but with a difference. These cards (shown in Figure I-10) depicted members of the Bush administration, and was called the Axis of Weasels (a play on Bush's famous phrase "Axis of Evil").

eBay took the sale offline, and Steins received howls of protest from eBay members who objected to his political jibe at the government. Steins protested

to eBay, and eventually, was invited to put his deck of cards up for sale again. He apparently didn't take up eBay on its offer, but sells his deck of cards at http://www.thebushadministration.com/bush.

Mrs. Cheney's Potboiler Attracts Big Bucks

Lynne Cheney, the wife of vice-president Dick Cheney, wrote a novel called *Sisters* back in 1981. The original hardcover edition of the book sold for only $2.50. When the book's publisher planned to reprint the novel in the election year of 2004, Mrs. Cheney stepped in and did a surprising thing for a writer: she prevailed upon the publisher to *not* reprint the book. Why? According to *USA Today*, the novel features "brothels, attempted rapes, and a lesbian love affair." Cheney reportedly said the article did not represent "her best work." A savvy eBay seller put a copy on eBay in April 2004, around the time news reports surfaced about the publishing flap. As I write this, the book has attracted 21 bids and the high bid is $100–quite a profit for a book signed not by the author but by the book's previous owners.

Figure 1-10.   eBay took the sale of these cards offline, then relented and invited the creator to put them up for sale again.

Clinton's Boyhood Home Brings Hope to eBay Buyer

Just to show that Democrats can get on eBay as well as Republicans, it should be noted that the boyhood home of President Bill Clinton went up for sale on eBay in March 2004. The small (950 square foot) home in Hope, Arkansas was Clinton's home for about three years, starting when he was about age 5. The seller, Gary Johnson, wanted to sell when he was married. The starting bid was $200,000, but the house attracted no bidders who wanted to match that price.

> **NOTE**
>
> Also on the Democratic side, a rare album by a musical group called The Electras, a band made up of students attending St. Paul's School in Concord, NH in the early 1960s, made several appearances on eBay around 2003-2004. That's when the group's bass player, one John Kerry, was running for U.S. President. The album has reportedly sold for $2,500 on eBay; when it was up for sale in April 2004, bidding was at $450, and the reserve had not yet been met. Only 500 copies of the album were reportedly pressed.

Part II: Places and Objects

Need ideas for a gift to delight that special someone who has everything? Look no further than the world's most popular auction site. eBay is known as a place where you can buy hard-to-find and one-of-a-kind objects such as collectibles and antiques. If you're in the market for something a little more substantial, you might even shop for a car online. The Brooklyn Bridge is not yet available online, but you can buy a piece of the planet that was significant in the life of someone famous. This chapter examines some of the places, objects of interest, and downright strange things that have sold on eBay.

We Call It Home...

Everyone needs a place they can call home. Of course, what one person might call "Home Sweet Home" might be seen as a dump by someone else. If you're looking to make a deal with someone who'll pay what you think your piece of property is worth and you want to cast the widest possible net, turn to eBay. People have bid on an island off the coast of Maine, amazing luxury homes, and entire towns online. Then there are foodstuffs that kids would find disgusting and items that are so personal you can't believe someone would admit to owning them. If you build your description on eBay, people will come to bid on it—to paraphrase the theme of the movie, *Field of Dreams.*

The homes of the rich and famous (or just famous) have occasionally come up for sale on eBay. But the deal doesn't always go through, however. As reported in an article on Forbes.com (www.forbes.com/home/2003/01/24/cx_bs_0124home.html), many of the bids are fraudulent,

---

NOTE

Speaking of *Field of Dreams,* the film featured the legendary baseball star Shoeless Joe Jackson. Yes, he too has a tie to the Internet. The famous "Black Betsy" bat used by Jackson throughout his major league career sold for a record $577,610 on eBay in 2001.

---

put forth by fans who are only interested in committing pranks—for example, the home in a downscale neighborhood in Detroit in which rap singer Eminem was raised was put up for auction in eBay's Real Estate section. The bids soared above $13 million, but it was discovered that most of the high bids were from pranksters, and the reserve price was unmet. The childhood homes of Madonna and President George W. Bush, respectively, were also both listed on eBay at one time or another. The homes listed in the following section were actually sold on eBay.

Indeed, purchasing such a home can give you an insider's perspective: If becoming rich and famous happened to them, maybe it could happen to you. But you'll be surprised to learn that the individuals who actually purchased the homes weren't always looking for some form of stardom to rub off on them, as you'll read in the sections that follow.

A Buyer Who Has Some 'Splaining to Do

TV's "I Love Lucy," ran from 1951 to 1957 and is considered to be one of the greatest comedies of all time. Lucille Ball wasn't much of a homemaker, though, and many of the show's episodes followed Lucy as she coped with various domestic disasters.

Lucy's fans have naturally wondered whether many of the hilarious scenes depicted on the small screen were based on events that occurred in her own life. As many of those devoted fans know, the little house in which Lucy spent much of her childhood is in the town of Celoron, New York. The house is located on a street that has been renamed 59 Lucy Lane, in fact. It was Lucy's home from the time she was eight years old until she was midway through high school.

Lucy's daughter Lucie Arnaz and her brother, Desi Arnaz, Jr., had been trying to buy the house and incorporate it into the Lucy-Desi Museum in nearby Jamestown, New York. The museum had been under the control of the Chautauqua County Arts Council under a

ten-year contract with the Arnaz family that recently expired. When no deal was made, the home (shown in Figure 11) was put up for sale—on eBay.

The listing prompted more than 30,000 visits, and after six weeks was finally sold—not to a fan or museum, but reportedly to a lady from Florida who was merely looking for a summer home near her native Buffalo, New York.

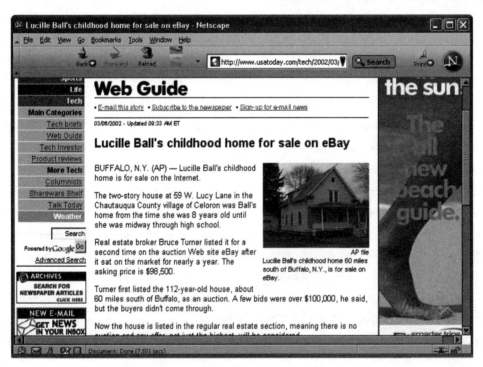

Figure SL-11. "Lucy, I'm home!" Lucille Ball grew up in this home in Celeron, N.Y.

The Times They Are A-Changin' for Bob Dylan's Home

Folksinger Bob Dylan's home in Duluth, Minnesota (where he grew up with the name Robert Zimmerman) was actually sold on eBay for $94,600, after receiving 25,000 visitors during the 30 days it was up for sale. The house supposedly featured, according to the description "original woodwork still shows the innitials [sic] young Dylan scratched in his bedroom." (The seller later backpedaled on this claim, saying that previous owners had noted the alleged initials but she had not seen them herself.)

Jimi Hendrix's Home Undergoes Rocky Experience

Jimi Hendrix's boyhood home in Seattle, Washington came with a big catch: the property on which the house stood had been sold; only the house at 26th Avenue East and South Washington Street was for sale. Anyone wishing to purchase it would need to move it or it would be torn down. The house's cabinets and walls had been painted purple, lavender, and other wild colors by previous tenants who wanted to commemorate the singer and guitarist, an icon of the psychedelic 1960s.

The house did sell in August 2001 to a Michigan-based buyer for $43,500. But the buyer backed out after the terrorist attacks of September 11, 2001. The owners made a pitch to Microsoft co-founder Paul Allen, who created the Experience Music Project, which has a permanent Hendrix exhibit, but Allen showed no interest. Only two weeks before the home was scheduled to be demolished, a developer said he had a plan to raise the money and move the house to a new location, where it would be turned into a museum.

Bidding Your Way to Luxury and Privacy

You can buy some really cool expensive places if you have a cool million or more to spend. For sellers, eBay is often the only place where they can get the price they want for their special piece of property. Here are examples of high-priced places that have sold online.

Your Own Special Place Will Call You

In the dead of winter 2003, eBay bidders were tempted with a piece of paradise. Thatch Cay, which was described as the last uninhabited island in the U.S. Virgin Islands (see Figure 12), was put up for sale on eBay. Three lots were priced at $2 million each, but the owner, Scott McIntyre, was hoping to fetch a whopping $25 million for the entire island.

As McIntyre discovered, eBay bidders are looking for bargains, even when they're bidding in six or seven figures. Although bids came in totaling more than $4 million, McIntyre said such amounts were insufficient to part with the island. He said his development company would embark on plans to create a "luxury estate community" and private retreat on Thatch Cay.

> **NOTE**
>
> Coincidentally, the United States purchased all of the Virgin Islands from Denmark in 1917 for the same price McIntyre was asking for his one island—$25 million.

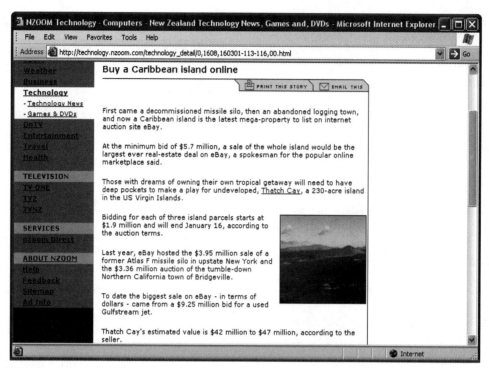

Figure SL-12. You, too, could buy your own piece of the Virgin Islands.

A Tale of One City

Joe and Elizabeth Lapple had been trying to sell the 82-acre town of Bridgeville, California, for some time, but no one had ever come close to the asking price of $775,000—not until the town went up for sale on eBay, that is.

Bidding started at $5000. When the bidding ended in late December 2002, the town went to the buyer who put in a bid for $1,777,877 just seconds before the Internet auction closed.

Bridgeville was the first town to be sold on eBay. Almost 250 bids were cast during the town's month on the electronic auction block. The town, which was described as a "fixer-upper," came complete with a post office, a mile and a half of river bank, a cemetery, and more than a dozen cabins and houses. "Your own zip code will now be 95526," the eBay description read.

But this is a neighborhood full of catches: Final bids for real estate posted on eBay aren't binding. The buyer and seller have to close the deal offline. Most of the "residents" of the town don't actually live onsite. The sale did not include the local school or the state roads, and Humboldt County, California, had previously declared some of the homes "uninhabitable." The Los Angeles businessman who reportedly purchased the run-down town has—perhaps wisely—managed to stay anonymous since the gavel closed the sale.

It's a Bird, It's a Plane——No, It's a House

Most people get in a plane to take a trip when they want to get away from their house. But what would they do if their house was a real Boeing 727 jet airplane?

A total of 31 bidders decided they could live in the airplane, which was offered on eBay by a company called Max Power Aerospace, Inc., and working through a consignment seller. The plane would be suspended on a column and allowed to rotate in the wind like a weathervane. To enter the home, you climb up a set of stairs wrapped around the center column. The wings could be outfitted with handrails so you and your guests could sit on them like sun porches. The multiple photos included with the auction description showed how a fully functional kitchen, furnishings, and even a hot tub could be added (see Figure 13).

Airplane homes are described as being perfect for people who live in a flood plain area because they can be suspended as high as 40 feet in the air. The sale attracted a high bid of $49,544, which did not meet the seller's reserve. As a result, the plane was later relisted.

The Door to Elvis's Home—— After Death, that Is

As all of rock star Elvis Presley's fans know (except the ones who believe he is still alive and wandering the countryside, that is), The King's final resting place is at his home in Memphis, Tennessee. However, before his body was moved to Graceland, it was at Forest Hill Cemetery, where fans made pilgrimages and often left their signatures on the door. The door, covered with writing (see Figure 14), was recovered by a devoted fan, and it reportedly included two of the seller's own signatures left on earlier visits.

The seller even offered to personally deliver the 8-foot by 3-foot, 3-inch door to the lucky winner's home. But no one was willing to match the $35,000 starting bid, and the door went unsold.

The Secret of Life, eBay Style

Some eBay sales can be described (by those who think too much) as existential or even philosophical in nature. Most web surfers, though, would describe the following sales as just plain silly:

- **"The Meaning of Life"** The description read: "I have discovered the reason for our existence and will be happy to share this information with the highest bidder." The high bidder paid $3.26.

- **"The Secret of Life"** Similar to the preceding sale, but with some tantalizing detail: "I was eating a Der Wienerschnitzel Polish Sandwich while parked under the shade of a tree and gave this some thought. My conclusions are yours for the highest bid. Shipping is 33 cents."

- **"My Dignity"** This sale attracted seven bidders; the winner bid $10.50: "The winner will receive a piece of paper that says 'My Dignity' on it, with my signature. Warning: I may become a sad man after relinquishing my dignity."

- **"My Appreciation"** Surprisingly, no one bid on the following: "Rather than clutter your lovely house or apartment with more useless gewgaws and trinkets, I am offering a very unique item for bidding: my appreciation. Unlike poorly crafted Korean electronics or American watches, this intangible gift will last a lifetime."

Figure SL-13. What do you do with an old jet airplane? Some eBay sellers would like to turn them into homes.

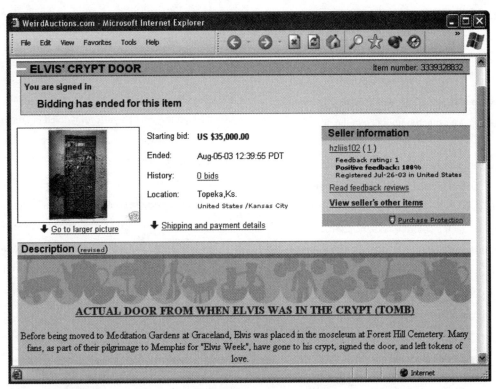

Figure SL-14. The door to Elvis's original grave failed to sell for $35,000.

Many people have put their souls up for sale on eBay; at least one person offered thanks; another, like Wizard of Oz, offered to present a testimonial to the winner.

Real Fairy Dust!

Finally, a way to obtain that magical material used with great effect by Tinkerbell, Peter Pan, and other famous figures in fairy tales and literature. For only $1.75, 12 bidders were able to obtain "Fairy Dust with Love, Hope, Luck & Kindness." The dust was said by the seller to have been mixed by the Good Fairy herself: The Good Fairy gathers a pinch of LOVE, a pinch of HOPE, a pinch of LUCK, and a pinch of KINDNESS. She magically mixes them all together to make Fairy Dust." Visitors were directed to a web site run by the good fairy, but apparently the fairy had disappeared into fairyland—the site was no longer operating.

Elian Gonzalez's Life Raft

These days, he is well on his way to becoming a young man in Cuba. He's also well on his way to becoming the answer to a trivia question back in America, where he lived for a short and turbulent time. His name is Elian Gonzalez and, back in the year 2000, he was the center of one of the year's biggest social controversies. He and his mother, along with others, floated all the way to Florida from Cuba in a bid for freedom. His mother died along the way. The controversy concerned whether he should be allowed to stay in this country or not. His father eventually arrived from Cuba and was allowed to take him home.

eBay is often a barometer of the big social events of the moment, and this was no exception. Plenty of traces of Elian appeared on eBay in the spring of 2000, not the least of which was the supposed raft on which he traveled (see Figure 15). It was described as "the most desirable piece of memorabilia from the new millennium."

At least two sales attempted to auction off Elian himself. One depicted him clinging desperately to the neck of then–Attorney General Janet Reno. Another attempted to sell a coloring book he allegedly had. Perhaps the most humorous attempted to capitalize on the endless publicity about the young man by attaching his name to a piece of computer equipment: "This is Elian Gonzalez favorite networking card that he loved so very much!!" screamed the description for the 3COM 3C509B-TP ISA networking card.

A Used Handkerchief

You can only shake your head over an individual who goes through the time and effort involved in creating an auction listing for his own used handkerchief, with a starting bid of 99 cents.

A related item—a roll of toilet paper that also functioned as a fortune cookie, since it had a series of fortunes printed on it—somehow failed to attract a bid.

Yet another related item—a "barf bag" used in Disneyland on one of its rides and handed out to riders in case they became ill—only attracted a bid of $3, which failed to meet the reserve.

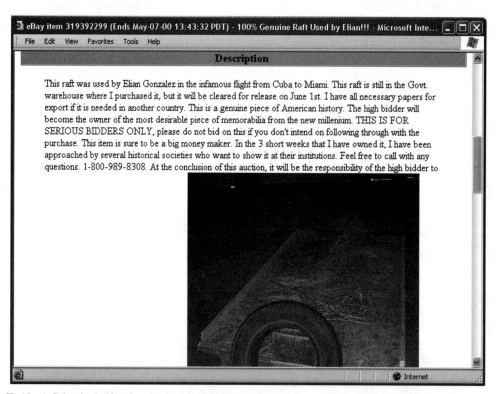

Figure SL-15. A Cuban boy's life raft, a simple slab of wood covered with straw, attracted more than 35 bids on eBay.

Trying to Sell Mother Nature

By now, you probably don't need proof that anything can be put up for sale on eBay. It doesn't matter if the substance you want to offer is as plentiful as air, snow, or dirt. Consider the following examples in which sellers attempted to peddle some of Mother Nature's own property.

Let It Snow, Let It Snow, Let It Sell

When the garage is cleaned out and you don't have anything left to sell—and the weather is so bad you can't go shopping for more inventory to auction on eBay—where else can you look but your own backyard?

In North Carolina, they aren't used to getting more than a foot of snow. One winter when it was really coming down and four-wheel drive vehicles were having trouble negotiating the roads, an ingenious seller

decided to call on eBay buyers to help with snow removal. The sale was entitled "Snow, powder, 12"+, buyer must pick up."

Although the seller could not ship the snow because neither dry ice nor FedEx packing materials were available, an offer was made for something extra: "We'll be happy to throw in a hot meal if you come to pick up the snow. Our selection is getting a little thin, though, so it may come from a can."

Airheads Try to Sell Air on eBay

If you have ever been accused of having nothing between your ears, you can prove your accusers wrong by selling air on eBay. You might just turn out to be pretty smart after all. An example is shown in Figure 16. The British seller is offering an air guitar—but not just any air guitar: it's a bass guitar, and a "supernatural

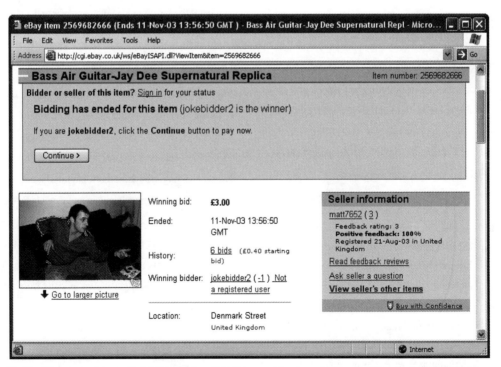

Figure SL-16. It's not surprising to find sales of air on eBay. It *is* surprising to see bidders for this easy-to-find substance.

replica" at that. As you can see, this sale actually attracted a bidder—though considering the negative feedback rating and the Not a Registered User (NARU) designation, payment is not likely to be forthcoming.

Other examples of "air sales" crop up regularly on eBay. Another example was an air gun. As the article about the sale on the Weird Auctions web site (www.weirdauctions.com) points out, the weapon is easily concealed and can even get past the security measures in place in airports around the world.

Then there's the bag of air captured at the height of Hurricane Isabel at Cape Hatteras in September 2003. The bag (see Figure 17) was sold with a certificate of authenticity and the disclaimer that the seller, "'Cane Capturers," was not responsible for any damaged caused by the release of the air inside. The bag received 19 bids and sold for $123.50.

Dirt from...You Name It

People have always wanted to own their own plot of land. Those who live in high-rise apartments or are stuck in submarines patrolling the briny deep probably wish they had some earth to call their own. Thanks to eBay they, too, can point to a box or jar filled with what other people would call mud, or dirt, and say, "This is mine." Here are just a few examples of the "earthy" sales that have been held on eBay over the years:

- A seller located in Memphis, Tennessee (Elvis's home) offered to provide any item located within the city limits, except for anything "illegal."

- Someone posted a winning bid of $2.75 for one pound of Arkansas dirt—dirt that was somehow associated with the Civil War. Shipping, by the way, was said by the intrepid seller to cost $3.20—not exactly dirt cheap.

- Everything is bigger in Texas, but one seller offered just one bucket full of "100% original TEXAS dirt, and is capable of growing assorted plants." The starting bid was placed at a Texas-sized $50,000.

- A lump of coal from the mines of West Virginia was offered for 50 cents (no takers).

- A sample of "Big Apple" dirt from New York City was sold for $3.25. ("Mix it in with your backyard soil to render your home as 'partial' NYC real estate, and watch its value soar through the roof!"

- The entire planet Earth was sold for a mere $10 million; the seller's location was given as "Galaxy Coordinates: +3221353, –9424543, –3243234.

In other auctions, the sun was put up for sale, as well as the entire colony of Palm Beach, Florida, and sand from the beach in Los Angeles where the television show "Baywatch" was produced.

A Famous Phone Number

What's in a name? What's in a number? When the name is "Jenny," and the number is 867-5309, apparently there is a great deal, indeed. In a pop song called "867-5309," released in 1982 by a group called Tommy Tutone, the singer lamented not having the courage to call a girl named Jenny. The Urban Legends Reference Pages report (www.snopes.com/music/songs/8675309.htm) that phone companies all over the country were driven crazy by owners of the number, who complained about getting crank calls from young men supposedly looking for Jenny.

In February 2004, the controversy cropped up again when a New York lawyer who owned the number 212-867-5309 attempted to auction off, on eBay, the

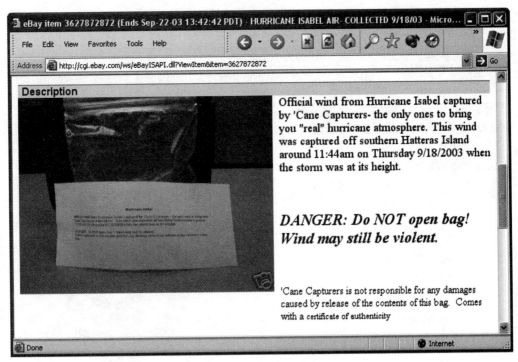

Description

Official wind from Hurricane Isabel captured by 'Cane Capturers- the only ones to bring you "real" hurricane atmosphere. This wind was captured off southern Hatteras Island around 11:44am on Thursday 9/18/2003 when the storm was at its height.

DANGER: Do NOT open bag! Wind may still be violent.

'Cane Capturers is not responsible for any damages caused by release of the contents of this bag. Comes with a certificate of authenticity

Figure SL-17. You, too, can get close to a real hurricane just by opening this bag.

rights to own it. As you can see in Figure 18 that at least 177 bidders were anxious to get their hands on this recognizable phone number, and the price reached $80,000. But the sale was never completed. The telephone company Verizon complained that private phone numbers could not be sold, and eBay agreed to end the sale early. That didn't stop copycats from attempting to cash in on interest over the magic number themselves.

Weeks after the sale ended, eBay was still crowded with listings for the domain name 867-5309.com, lotto tickets bearing the number 867-5309, and even the privilege of having someone sing the song over the phone for the high bidder.

Fantastic Food Finds

It might surprise you to discover that you can find a variety of delectable, rare, and exotic foodstuffs on eBay. From truffles to chocolates to salmon and steaks, the Food & Wine category contains it all. The auction listings in this section are totally different, and only fall into a few people's description of "gourmet delicacy."

Spotted Dick, Canned Possum, and Other Delicacies

Readers in the U.S. will get a giggle out of the term "spotted dick," but it's a real foodstuff in the UK. It's a pudding made of flour, currants, butter, and the like. The clever seller tried to make bidders believe the auction was for something else; in reality, it was a sale of photos of the foodstuff, the recipe "signed by the artist," and all of it saved on CD.

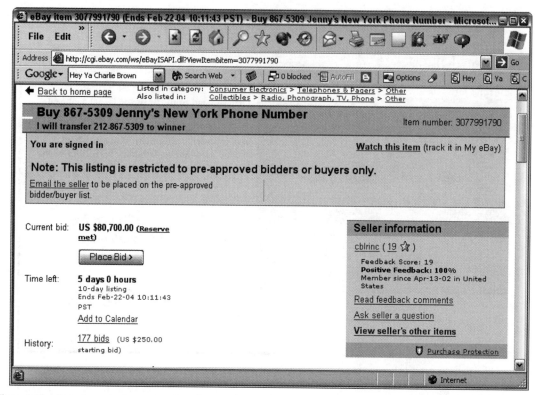

Figure 1-18.   This phone number was music to the ears of some high bidders until the phone company played a sour note.

Cash-strapped American states looking to raise some extra money might take a cue from what one enterprising eBay seller sold for $3.50: canned possum (see Figure 19). The description states that it was canned "on Hwy. 78 between Tupelo, Mississippi and the Tenn-Tom Waterway, or at one of our many roadside canning facilities" and that the canning was done "under the authority of Highway Department Road Crew #21."

World's Longest—and Most Expensive—French Fry

The really successful eBay sellers are always on the lookout for things they can resell online. Even when they take a break for lunch or dinner, their bargain-obsessed minds are always working. One day, when the eBay seller known as reeledit was wolfing down a bag of French fries, he spotted a sure winner:

the six-and-three-quarter-inch-long crinkle-cut spud shown in Figure 20.

The fry, which was reportedly purchased from a Wisconsin fast-food restaurant, gained a lot of attention in the local Wisconsin media. The seller wisely included links to newspaper and TV news stories about the French fry. (It must have been a slow news day in the land of cheese.)

Customized Beanie Baby Meat Grinder

At the time this sale was listed in 1999, the Beanie Baby craze was near its height. eBay was awash in sales for rare and "retired" models. The auction was listed not under the Beanie Baby category, however, but under Collectibles:Kitchenware:Utensils. "This grinder can be set for fine, medium or coarse grind. We want to fill it with Beanie Babies," the seller said.

Figure SL-19. This road-kill delicacy should be served on a cracker with "an RC Cola and a Moon Pie," according to the description.

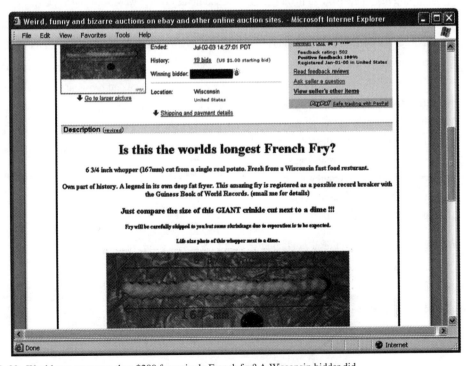

Figure SL-20. Would you pay more than $200 for a single French fry? A Wisconsin bidder did.

Old (Hopefully Not Used) Embalmer's Fluid

The seller who offered a bottle of embalmer's fluid (the label read "EMBALMERS SUPPLY CO–WESTPORT CT") for sale on eBay placed it in the category Collectibles:Bottles:Medicine and Cures. There might as well be a category called Death and Preservation on eBay, because so many things are put on the site that are no longer among the living. Here are some other examples:

- **"Liquid Roadkill...SICK STUFF!"** Forty-one bidders agreed to pay $10 for bottles of this stuff, described as "Incredibly Foul Smelling, Highly Concentrated ... give the gift that keeps on giving."

- **"Rare Mummified Cat"** The poor feline was described as having been "preserved by mother nature and transformed into an unusual work of art." Not something most people would like to hang on their wall, however.

- **"Collectible Old Bottle with dead mouse"** The item was described as "A real conversation starter."

- **"Real Stuffed Frog Playing Bongos Mexico"** Unfortunately, no photo was available for this treasure, described as follows: "From Mexico, a real frog stuffed and on a block of wood, playing the bongos. Pretty weird. In great shape for a dead frog." The high bidder paid $16.66.

Anytime frogs appear on eBay, things are bound to get strange. There's a frog-related item that I can't even describe in the pages of this book; check out the description on the WhatTheHeck.com web site: www.whattheheck.com/ebay/frogpenis.html.

Military Sales on eBay

Some of the items put up for sale on eBay only *seem* dangerous. But eBay has seen some weapons put on its site that are *truly* dangerous. Reportedly, eBay works with law enforcement officials to police sales like the ones described next.

Guns: No Can Sell. Missiles? OK

As you learned in this book, guns and other weapons are banned on eBay. Oddly, some larger and more powerful weapons have been put up for sale on the auction site. In August 1999, a seller who appeared to be reputable (with a feedback rating of 141), offered a Hughes HIM-4D Falcon missile for sale on eBay. The seller explained that the Falcon was the United States Air Force's first air-to-air guided weapon and was once delivered by an F-102 fighter plane. Happily, the missile was unarmed (no warhead). Visa, MasterCard, American Express, and money orders were accepted as payment.

A December 2000 article in *The Industry Standard* reported that eBay works closely with the FBI, the Department of Defense, and other government agencies in an effort to locate and prosecute people who attempt to sell stolen or illegal items. "In one case, eBay found a missile for sale, but kept the item listed so the Defense Department could go undercover to arrest the seller," the article stated. The same article claimed that sellers had placed the following for sale:

- Three grams of plutonium
- AK-47 rifles
- Cuban cigars
- A nuclear submarine that could carry cruise missiles
- A Russian-made rocket launcher

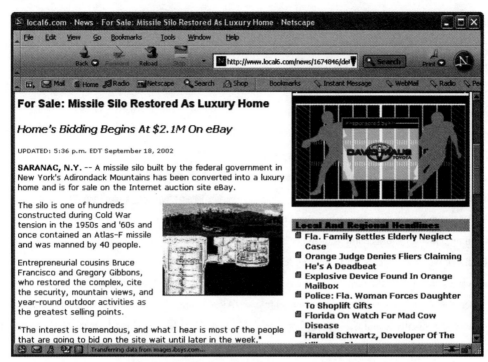

Figure SL-21. This luxury home boasted a 14-story-deep missile silo, airplane hanger, and runway.

You can read the full story at www.findarticles.com/cf_dls/m0HWW/46_3/77033852/p1/article.jhtml.

That same month (August 1999), a new Russian military patrol boat was posted on eBay by a seller located in Baltimore, Maryland. This intriguing note was posted at the end of the description:

"Russian Citizen with PHD in International Law and expert in Russian Military Craft will provide all training and expertise to ensure that you are familiar with all aspects of this superb vessel! If you have a serious inquiry, please do not hesitate to e-mail me. I understand that with a purchase this large that questions will arise. I am happy to speak to anyone about this boat but please send serious inquiries only: Ivan[e-mail address]."

Trying to unload used missiles on eBay is one thing. But what do you do with one of the facilities that used to house missiles? In 2002, a missile silo that was built during the Cold War and later converted to a luxury home was put up for auction on eBay with an asking price of $2.1 million (see Figure 21). The sale closed without a bid; the owners slashed the minimum bid price to $550,000 and enlarged the property. Eventually, the property was sold for the original price of $2.1 million—one of the highest-price sales ever held on the auction site.

Bizarre Clothing

eBay is a great place to buy clothing in the privacy of one's home. Men and women alike can purchase elegant evening gowns at bargain prices. Risqué "adult" outfits are sometimes sold online, too. Parents on a budget can often uncover bargains in clothes especially for babies and small children. But the most memorable clothing sales are of clothes that were used a long time ago, often by people who were notable for one thing or another.

The Weird Gross Bra that Fell from the Ceiling

Sometimes, the sales that get the most attention on eBay are the ones that have the best stories. The items themselves might be repulsive in some way; it almost seems as though the bidders are attracted by the stories about the items.

The eBay seller known as mamasoul reported that she was pulling down some old ceiling tiles in her house that had suffered water damage, when something fell from above and struck her on the head. After frantically batting at her head for a few seconds in an effort to rid herself of what she initially feared was a living creature, she discovered what she later described as the Weird Gross Bra that Fell Out of My Ceiling (see Figure 22).

This sale took on a life of its own. The seller was apparently bombarded by inquiries from curious and highly amused (and amusing) prospective buyers. eBay reportedly removed the sale because the seller played up the "fetish element" involved. She eventually rewrote the description without the offending words, and even added a pair of latex gloves to the sale so no one would actually have to touch the bra.

World's Tallest Man's Shoes Take Final Walk on eBay

If you, like me, have scoured the Guinness Book of World Records, you have probably discovered that the world's tallest man was a fellow named Robert Wadlow, who was born in Alton, Illinois and was known as the "Alton Giant."

Because he was 8 feet 11 inches tall, Wadlow had to have special shoes made for his enormous pedal appendages. A pair of shoes reputed to have belonged

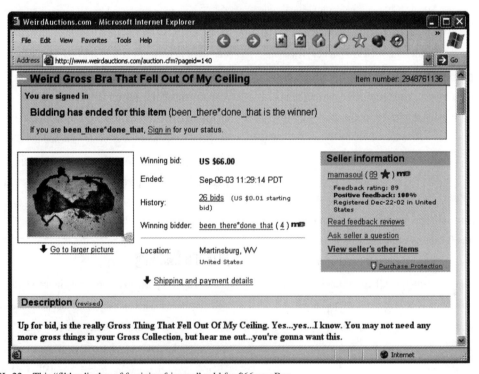

Figure SL-22.   This "filthy display of feminine frippery" sold for $66 on eBay.

to Ludlow (shown in Figure 23) sold on eBay for $355 in late 2003 to a buyer with the User ID of freakmuseum.

The description of the sale included some interesting information about Ludlow and his shoes. The shoes cost a whopping $100 in the 1930s, when Ludlow was alive. Ludlow died in 1940 of an infection reportedly caused by—ready for this?—a foot blister. One hopes the shoes sold on eBay were not the cause.

Levi's Pays $46,532 for 120-Year-Old Jeans

One of the best-known sales of clothing ever to occur on eBay centered on one of the world's oldest pairs of Levi's jeans ever found. The anonymous seller, who reportedly found the jeans in the mud of an old Nevada mining town, brought the jeans to an eBay appraiser. eBay itself promoted the auction in conjunction with the History Channel.

Not surprisingly, the jeans had faded more than a bit over the preceding century. However, despite a rip in the inseam, they were intact and could even be worn. Historians for Levis examined the fabric and rivets in the old pants (see Figure 24) and concluded that they were made between 1880 and 1885.

The jeans were offered over one weekend in 2001 with a starting bid of $25,000. Only two minutes before the sale ended, a flurry of five bids was received, and Levi's came up the winner.

Figure SL-23.   Shoes supposed to have been made for the world's tallest man took their final walk on eBay.

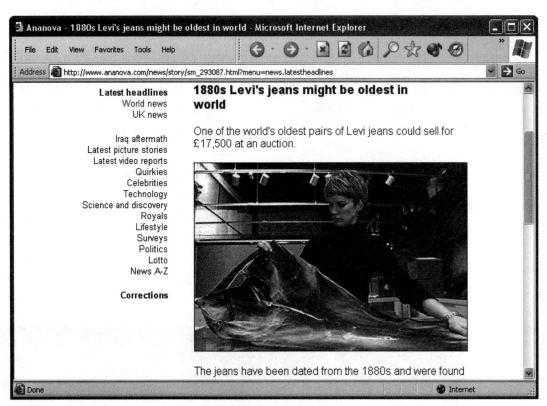

Figure SL-24. Levi's bought back the 1880s jeans so it could use them as a template for a new line of "vintage" pants.

Where to Find It

Web Site	Address	What's There
eBay Real Estate section	http://pages.ebay.com/ realestate/index.html	Links to all of eBay's real estate listings
eBay Other Real Estate section	http://listings.ebay.com/pool2/ plistings/list/all/category1607/ index.html	This is where you'll find island estates, brothel museums, ranches, and all kinds of dream properties up for sale.
eBay Weird Stuff category	http://listings.ebay.com/aw/ plistings/list/category1466/ index.html	List of current auctions being conducted that fall under the description of "Weird Stuff." Subcategories include "Really Weird Stuff" and "Totally Bizarre."

you a chance to return to an auction if you want to place a last-minute bid. The Bid Alerts button opens a Bid Alerts menu, which displays all of the auctions that are still active and on which you have placed bids. Choose Refresh Bid List if the list is not up-to-date.

- ■ **Watch Alert**   This button provides you with a list of items you are "watching" in My eBay (see Chapter 6 for more on how to "watch" auctions).

<table>
<tr><td>NOTE</td><td>Some users (including the author) reported technical difficulties (specifically, JavaScript runtime errors) when attempting to install eBay's toolbar. Problems frequently occur if you once had an early version of the toolbar installed, then uninstalled it, and then tried to install it again. The only solution is to contact eBay support staff directly. I was sent a software utility that erased references to the toolbar from the Windows Registry and that enabled the toolbar to be installed.</td></tr>
</table>

Customizing Your Browser's Links Bar

Some eBay users are suspicious of eBay's toolbar. It takes up space in both your browser window and Windows' system tray, and tracks your searches and movement from page to page through eBay. Plus, for users of Macintosh, Linux, and Unix computers, and those individuals who are still using Windows 95, the toolbar doesn't work at all. As an alternative, you can add custom buttons to your browser's Links bar.

A Links bar is a toolbar included in both Microsoft Internet Explorer and Netscape Communicator that you can customize with quick links to favorite web sites. Internet Explorer calls it the Links toolbar; Netscape calls it the Personal toolbar. The process for customizing the Links bar to include eBay web sites is similar for both browsers. These instructions apply to Internet Explorer:

1. Choose View | Toolbars | Links to display the Links bar.

2. The Links bar comes with some preset link buttons. Delete the buttons you don't want by right-clicking each one and choosing Delete from the shortcut menu.

3. Once you have opened up space on the toolbar, you can add buttons by dragging and dropping web page links directly onto the Links bar, or dragging the icon that appears next to the URL in the browser's Address bar onto the Links bar.

You can duplicate some of the functions of eBay's toolbar by adding links to your About Me page, your My eBay page, eBay's Basic Search page, or links to other pages you often visit into the Links bar.

Taking eBay to the Beach

You never have to be very far from eBay. A special version of eBay's web site, Wireless eBay, enables you to browse categories and search for listings through your web-enabled cell phone or PDA that uses Wireless Application Protocol (WAP) to present web content. You can even use Wireless eBay to send you e-mail notifications or pager messages when someone bids on an item you are watching.

You'll have to work out with your wireless Internet access provider how to get online. Once accomplished, you can then access a version of eBay that's been specially designed for the "small screen." Even with a conventional web browser, you can get an idea of how the simplified version of eBay looks by entering http://mmm.ebay.com in your browser's address bar (see Figure 5-5).

You can't place bids or put items up for sale with eBay Wireless. However, you can search the site, browse auction listings, and check everything on your My eBay page. Most importantly, you can arrange to have eBay send alerts to your wireless device. Such alerts require you to do three things. First, since the alerts

FIGURE 5-4   eBay Wireless is a simplified version of the site formatted for wireless devices.

come via the Microsoft Alert system, you have to obtain a Microsoft Passport account. Passport is a sign-in system that enables you to sign up for services quickly. Second, you need to sign up to receive eBay Alerts. Third, you need to make sure your wireless e-mail address is on file with eBay if you have not done so already.

Where to Find It

Web Site	Address	What's There
Wholesale Lots category	http://pages.ebay.com/catindex/catwholesale.html	Listings by category of large groups of supplies, equipment, and other items
Fraud Protection	http://pages.ebay.com/help/confidence/isgw-fraud-protection.html	Information on eBay's Fraud Protection Program and how to apply for insurance
eBay Toolbar	http://pages.ebay.com/ebay_toolbar	A link that enables you to download and install eBay's toolbar
EBay—Wireless Version	http://mmm.ebay.com	A version of eBay's home page formatted for a wireless device

5

Chapter 6

Avoid Fraud and Resolve Problems

How to…

- Protect your identity and privacy on eBay
- Recognize warning signs of attempted fraud
- Minimize your loss due to fraud
- Handle buyers who don't pay
- Respond when sellers don't ship

Most of the people you meet on eBay are friendly and honest. Unfortunately, the few who are dishonest cause concern for everyone and keep many from participating in online auctions. Fraud is a problem that affects buyers as well as sellers, and it's a problem that has been much in the news of late. You hear, all too often, about members who have their identities "hijacked" by thieves, and who lose thousands of dollars to criminals who manage to induce them to give up their money, but who never ship what they originally advertised.

The good news is that, if you play by eBay's rules and observe some simple commonsense procedures, you won't lose lots of money or your identity. Most of the time, victims of fraud fall prey to time-honored techniques that "con artists" have employed for years. People succumb to the temptation of easy money, or are fooled into thinking that something is wrong with their account and that it needs to be "verified." eBay has protections in place to help keep buyers and sellers from becoming victims of fraud. But the best protection is to simply be aware of what can go wrong and how to avoid it—and that's what you'll learn in this chapter.

Avoiding Identity Theft

Identity theft is the practice of stealing information that is normally used to establish a person's identity (such as his or her name, User ID, password, or social security number) and using that information to make purchases or accept money. eBay claims that identity theft is relatively rare. In a story on CNN.com about identity theft on eBay (www.cnn.com/2002/TECH/internet/02/18/ebay.identity.theft.idg/), a spokesman said that fraud occurs in less than .01 of 1 percent of all transactions.

But stories about fraud and complaints on eBay's discussion boards and chat rooms show just how serious fraud is when it occurs. Since eBay operates in large measure on a network of trust, fraud erodes the system and makes new users wary of trying to buy and sell online. Much of the danger can be avoided simply by being aware of what can go wrong and taking safety precautions, as described in the sections that follow.

Understanding What eBay Knows about You

eBay seems safe. After all, you shop from the comfort of your home, behind closed or locked doors, where no one can get into your wallet or purse and rob you. The truth is that you have already revealed a good deal about yourself to eBay, and unscrupulous individuals can make use of the information you have released for their own profit—and your loss. What exactly does eBay know about you? Here are some examples:

When you first register to become an eBay member, you provide some minimal information:

- Your name

- Your address

- Your phone number

- Your e-mail address

- The password and User ID you will use on eBay

- Your date of birth

That seems harmless enough. But even this simple set of information can threaten your privacy. Marketers would be only too happy to get their hands on your mailing address, phone number, or e-mail address. Thieves, too, can make use of a valid User ID and password: they can use the information to put up items for sale, take the money, and never ship the products, which creates a significant negative impact on your eBay reputation. As part of your registration, you might decide to pay your fees to eBay by charging your credit card. If you do so, you give eBay the following information:

- Your credit card number

- The address associated with the card

- The expiration date

It should be obvious why this information is dangerous if it falls into the hands of a criminal. Suppose, further, that you sign up to pay your eBay fees by making automatic deductions from your checking account, or you decide to have your identity verified through eBay's ID Verify program. You submit the following information:

- Your social security number (for ID Verify)

- Your bank name

- Your checking account number and routing number

eBay stores your information securely, but it doesn't necessarily keep your information to itself. If you check the Appendix to the Privacy Policy page (http://pages.ebay.com/help/community/privacy-appendix.html), you get a complete picture of all the different kinds of information eBay actually collects about you, and how they share it. Some information is shared with advertisers, and some is shared with companies called internal or external service providers (see Figure 6-1).

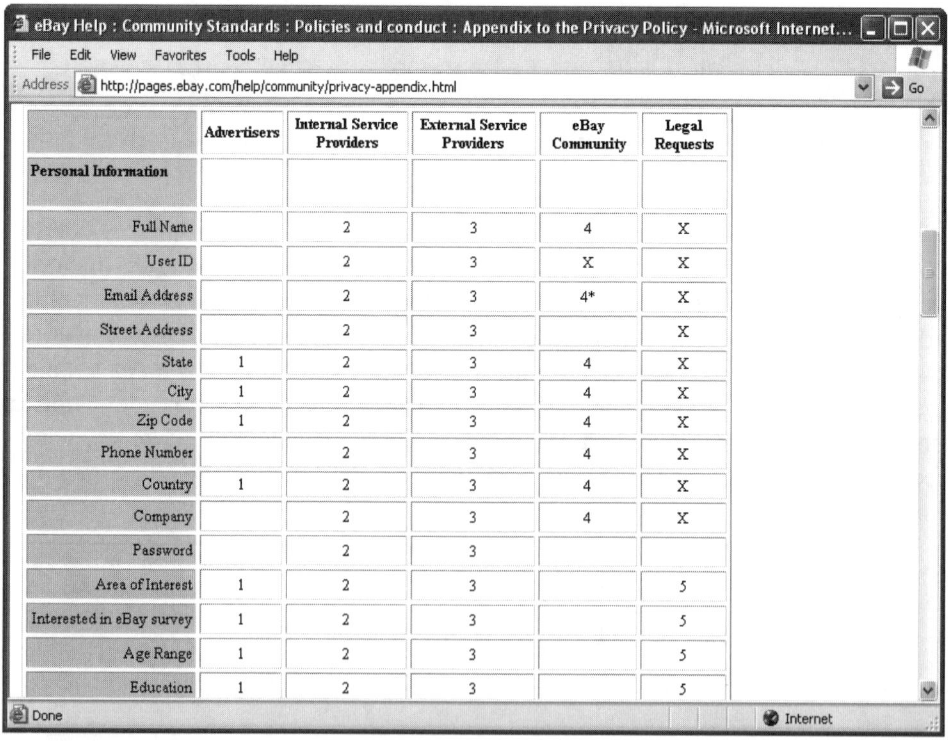

eBay Help : Community Standards : Policies and conduct : Appendix to the Privacy Policy - Microsoft Internet...

File   Edit   View   Favorites   Tools   Help

Address http://pages.ebay.com/help/community/privacy-appendix.html

	Advertisers	Internal Service Providers	External Service Providers	eBay Community	Legal Requests
Personal Information					
Full Name		2	3	4	X
User ID		2	3	X	X
Email Address		2	3	4*	X
Street Address		2	3		X
State	1	2	3	4	X
City	1	2	3	4	X
Zip Code	1	2	3	4	X
Phone Number		2	3	4	X
Country	1	2	3	4	X
Company		2	3	4	X
Password		2	3		
Area of Interest	1	2	3		5
Interested in eBay survey	1	2	3		5
Age Range	1	2	3		5
Education	1	2	3		5

Done   Internet

FIGURE 6-1   eBay already knows a lot about you and how you use its site.

As you learn from the table shown in Figure 6-1, eBay not only gathers personal information from you, but it tracks the time of day when you visit its site, what pages you view, what type of browser you use, and other information. Criminals don't need to "hack" into eBay's computers to get it. They try to find a way to get it from you—and that's why you need to be on guard for the signs that you're being targeted, as described in the sections that follow.

Knowing the Warning Signs

You're checking your e-mail, and you receive a message from eBay's support staff, with an e-mail address of support@ebay.com. The message, which bears the eBay logo, asks you to verify your account. Maybe there's been a problem with your account; the message may state that you are about to be suspended unless you verify your account. You're in a hurry and you don't want to think about it too much, you click the link supplied in the e-mail message, which certainly looks like one of the URLs you typically see in your browser's Address box:

```
https://scgi.ebay.com/saw-cgi/eBay|SAP|.dll?VerifyInformation"
```

You go to a web site that has a name like eBay-Verify.com. You are asked to fill out a form in which you verify your credit card number, bank name and account number, your mother's maiden name, and so on. Are you beginning to get suspicious? You should be. The message is a cleverly designed fake intended not to protect your safety or preserve your account, but to give your account and the rest of your identity to someone else. The success of such scams depends on a few people not being aware of the warning signs of eBay fraud. They include the following:

- You get an e-mail message purporting to be from eBay and asking you to solve problems with your registration information. eBay will never try to contact you by e-mail to ask for your personal information such as your credit card number or your password. All e-mail messages asking you for such information are fraudulent.

- You are asked to click a link that looks like one of eBay's, but that, if you inspect it closely, has a few subtle differences that identify it as fraudulent (see the following examples).

- You bid on an auction, and the seller asks you to end the sale early so you can be the winner. After agreeing to this, you are then asked to wire transfer funds to the seller's overseas account using Western Union's wire transfer service.

As you might expect, after you send the money, you never receive the item you purchased.

■ You view an auction listing and a tiny browser window opens briefly. It may be open only for a second—in fact, if you blink or look the wrong way, you might not even notice it. The window opens a connection to an external computer controlled by an attacker. The attacker is able to install a malicious piece of software called a Trojan horse or a virus, which can perform functions that track your computer use. The attacker can use the information sent back by the program to uncover passwords or other personal information needed to steal your identity.

The third type of attack is the hardest to detect, and is potentially the most malicious because it involves a direct attack on your computer. Thankfully, it is relatively uncommon.

> **TIP** *If you are worried that you may have viewed an auction listing in which a small browser window opened up quickly and then disappeared, scan your computer using an antivirus program. You can try out a program called QuickHeal (www.quickheal.com) free for 30 days, and then pay $30 if you decide to keep it. You can also install software such as the Google toolbar (www.google.com) that blocks pop-up windows. Or, adjust Internet Explorer's security preferences to prevent software from being installed without your knowledge: click Tools, click Internet Options, click Security, and change the security level to Medium, if necessary.*

Looking Out For Suspicious URLs

Fake URLs and web sites are unfortunately becoming an increasingly common type of auction fraud. Gullible members are induced to click a URL that has suspicious elements in it. A typical URL from eBay looks like this:

```
http://signin.ebay.com//aw-cgi/eBayISAPI.dll?SignIn&ssPageName=h:h:sin:US
http://cgi1.ebay.com/aw-cgi/ebayISAPI.dll?MyEbay
```

A technically savvy attacker will create a fake web page that appears to be from eBay and that presents you with a form you need to fill out with your personal information. The form is designed to resemble eBay's in every way, with the usual logo and colors, and a URL that is close to one of eBay's but that's not exactly the same. See if you can spot the differences in the following URLs:

```
http://signin.ebay.com//saaw-cgi/eBayISAPI.dll?SignIn&ssPageName=h:h:sin:US
http://cgi1.ebay.com/aw-cgi/ebay|SAP|.dll?MyEbay
http://www.ebay.com@someotherplace.com
```

In the first example, the URL includes "saaw-cgi" rather than the usual "aw-cgi" or "saw-cgi." In the second, you see ebay|SAP|.dll instead of ebayISAPI.dll. The third example uses the @ symbol to make it look like the site is actually eBay. Microsoft has released a patch for its Internet Explorer to prevent you from accessing sites that use such fraudulent URLs. Make sure you have downloaded and installed the patch by visiting www.microsoft.com/windows/ie/security/default.asp.

If you see any of these warning signs, be sure to contact eBay. Fraudulent e-mail messages should be forwarded to spoof@ebay.com. Other reports should be made using eBay's Contact Us form (http://pages.ebay.com/help/contact_inline/index.html). In the first box of the form, choose the option Report Fake eBay Emails (Spoofs) and Unauthorized Account Activity, as shown in Figure 6-2. In the second box, choose the type of specific activity you want to report.

6

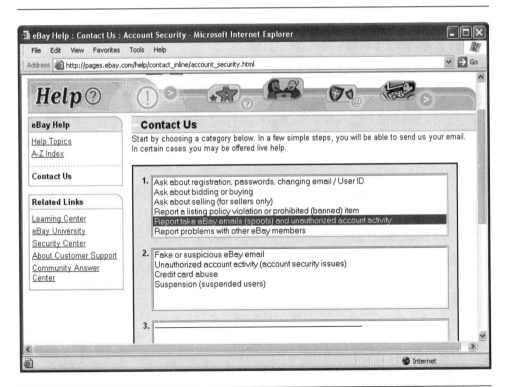

FIGURE 6-2   Fill out this form to report suspicious e-mails or other activity to eBay.

> **TIP** *eBay's own page full of instructions for what to do if you think you are a victim of identity theft can be found at http://pages.ebay.com/help/confidence/problems-identity-theft.html. You'll also find a complete list of URLs that eBay uses at www.pages.ebay.com/help/account_protection.html, so you can be sure which e-mails are coming from eBay and which are fakes.*

Avoiding Fraudulent Web Sites

Often, users are directed to web sites that have domain names with the term "ebay" in them. To inexperienced users, such domains have an air of legitimacy about them. The URLs might look like www.change-ebay.com or www.ebay-verification.com. A story on CNET News.com (http://news.com.com/2100-1017-966835.html) reported that the latter site attempted to get eBay members to give over a substantial amount of sensitive information, including their checking account number, social security number, the PIN of their debit card, and even their driver's license number. Such sites might only exist for a matter of days before they scam a few eBay members and then shut down (or are closed down by the service that hosts the site).

Avoiding Loss Due to Fraud

Typically, people who practice fraud on eBay steal someone's identity in order to fraudulently put up items for sale. They create legitimate-looking descriptions of items for sale, and collect money from the high bidders. But they never ship what was purchased (often, it never existed to begin with; the descriptions and photos can easily be lifted from other web sites). But other things can go wrong if someone hijacks your eBay account, such as:

- Someone can attempt to make purchases, if they have your credit card number as well as your personal information.

- Bidders can engage in "shill bidding," where they bid against one another to drive up the price of an item and make legitimate bidders pay more to a seller. They are usually the seller, using another User ID, or a friend or relative of the seller. They then disappear with the high bidder's money.

- They scam a bidder. A common scam involves getting a bidder to immediately wire transfer money to them using Western Union, before the sale ends. The lure is that they will get the item at a bargain or, often, bidders are asked to pay an extra fee and then promised a refund. Needless to say, the refund and the merchandise never arrive.

Some strategies for avoiding these pitfalls are described in subsequent sections.

Picking a Good Password

In one type of fraud, criminals use software that scours eBay looking for User IDs that haven't had much activity of late. Members who don't use their accounts often are desirable because they are unlikely to notice when those accounts are used without their knowledge. Once they have a likely User ID, they attempt to "crack" the password by guessing it. Often, computer programs are used that can generate thousands of passwords in quick succession by going through all the words in the dictionary.

The way to avoid getting one's account stolen by having a password guessed probably seems obvious:

- Don't pick a password that is a word in the dictionary, whether it's a commonly used word or not.

- Don't pick a password that is easy to guess.

- Create a password that contains six to eight characters. The longer the password, the harder it is for someone to "crack."

- Create a password that contains both numerals and letters, and that mixes both lowercase and uppercase letters, such as eB9f57.

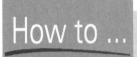 **Verify Your User ID**

One way to reassure eBay buyers and sellers who conduct business with you is to have your identity certified. For a $5 fee, you get a special icon that appears next to your User ID. The icon is granted after you submit your personal information to the ID Verify program.

ID Verify is eBay's way of verifying the identities of its members to other members. eBay itself does not perform the verification. Your information is sent to the well-known credit verification company Equifax. It checks your information against databases of consumers and businesses that are already in Equifax's computers.

6

NOTE   *If you have a credit card account or a loan, Equifax almost certainly has information about you and your credit rating in its files. You can request your own credit report for $9 at the company's web site at www.equifax.com.*

To get started with the program, go to the ID Verify page by clicking Services | ID Verify, or going directly to http://pages.ebay.com/services/buyandsell/idverify-login.html. Then follow these steps:

1. Click Sign Up Now.

2. When the ID Verify Accept Terms page appears, click I Agree.

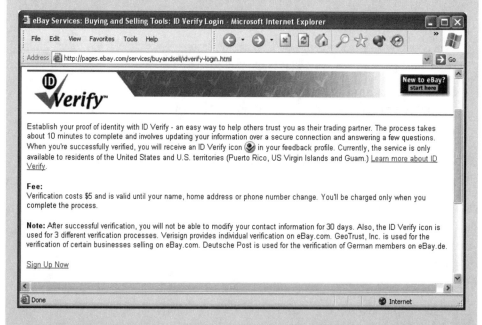

3. When the Sign In page appears, sign in with your User ID and password.

4. When the Verify Account Information page appears, enter the personal information requested, and then click Continue.

5. Follow the steps presented on the pages that follow in order to complete the ID verification process.

Once your information has been verified, you can check your own page in the Feedback Forum, where the ID Verify icon now appears, along with any other icons (feedback stars, the About Me page icon, or PowerSeller icon) you may have accumulated.

NOTE *You submit a wider range of information to ID Verify than you did when you registered with eBay, including your social security number and your driver's license number. If you're not comfortable with giving out such information (even though it is encrypted when you submit it), don't sign up.*

6

Unfortunately, all too many eBay users (and others who use passwords to log into web sites or make purchases) fail to follow these two simple rules. Instead, they assign themselves passwords that are obvious because they resemble their User ID. If their User ID is *insecure-user,* for instance, they might choose a password like *insecure* or *user,* or even *insecure-user,* the same as the User ID. If their User ID is *antiques-maven,* their password might be *maven.* If they have a User ID of *MrUser,* their password might be *MrsUser.*

Changing Your Account Information

If you feel that your eBay account information has been compromised, you should immediately change your password. You may also want to change other personal information. To do this, go to your My eBay page (click My eBay in the eBay navigation bar) and select the Preferences tab. Under Personal Information, click Change My Registration Information. You'll be asked to sign in; you'll then go to the eBay Change Registration form, where you can change virtually anything about your account: your e-mail address, your User ID, your name, and so on.

If you are only a buyer on eBay, you only need to update your address in the Change Registration form mentioned in the previous paragraph. If you sell on eBay, you'll need to update your address in two other places:

1. Return to My eBay, click Preferences, and click Change My Stored Shipping Information. The Update Shipping Addresses page appears, where you can change your shipping information.

2. Return to the Preferences tab. Under Seller Preferences, click Update payment/checkout preferences to include the new address.

   *If you use PayPal (eBay's payment service) to buy or sell items, you'll need to update your shipping information on your account with PayPal, too.*

Avoiding Common Problems for Buyers

Suppose you are browsing through sales on eBay and you notice something that's not quite right. You see someone selling something that you think is against the rules, or someone approaches you with an offer that you know is wrong. What do you do? It's easy enough to shrug it off and walk away. But remember that eBay can't be everywhere when it comes to policing the millions of sales that are offered on its worldwide sites every day. You should report what you see and let eBay's investigators determine what is going on.

Suppose you encounter a problem that occurs with one of your own connections. You should try to resolve the problem yourself, and then use eBay's procedures for setting things right, which are described in the sections that follow.

Dealing with Non-Selling Sellers

Much attention is given (in the eBay Community discussion boards, at least) to Non-Paying Bidders (NPBs). But you don't hear as much about another problem that's just as serious: Non-Selling Sellers (NSSs)—sellers who take someone's money and then do not ship what was originally purchased. Your alternatives are described in Table 6-1.

If you are *really* unhappy with a seller and want to pursue every possible means to either get compensation or make the person's life more difficult, you can do two other things. First, go to Basic Search and click the By Seller tab. Search By Seller, and search for the seller's completed auctions. Contact the winning bidders of those auctions to see if they are encountering similar problems with the seller. If they are, encourage them to pursue complaints of the sort described in the preceding table.

You can also go to small claims court and file a suit. You can then get a copy of the paperwork and send it to the seller. Be sure to specify a date by which you desire payment; this court notice can be intimidating and may get results when other options have failed.

TIP   *You can read eBay's own policy on Non-Selling Sellers at http://pages.ebay .com/help/policies/non-selling-seller.html.*

Time Frame	What to Do	Where to Find It
10 to 14 days after sending payment	Request contact details and phone the seller.	http://cgi3.ebay.com/aw-cgi/ eBayISAPI.dll?MemberSearchShow #ContactInfo
30 to 60 days before end of sale	File a fraud alert to report the member as a non-selling seller and have eBay contact the person.	http://pages.ebay.com/help/ confidence/isgw-fraud-alert.html
Up to 30 days after end of sale	Contact your credit card company and ask for a chargeback.	N/A
Up to 30 days after end of sale	Apply for up to $500 reimbursement if the item qualifies for PayPal Buyer Protection. Report the seller to PayPal; they may suspend his membership.	http://pages.ebay.com/help/ confidence/purchase-protection.html
30 to 60 days after end of sale	Post negative feedback for the seller.	Feedback Forum
After filing fraud alert, and less than 90 days before end of sale	Fill out a claim with eBay's Fraud Protection Program	http://pages.ebay.com/help/ community/fpp.html

TABLE 6-1   Approaches for Sellers Who Won't Sell

What to Do if You Change Your Mind

You've probably had the unpleasant feeling that occurs when you click something (such as your e-mail program's Send button) and you immediately regret it. "Wait! I didn't want to do that!" you think. In the case of e-mail, you can't "unsend" a message once it has been sent. But what about a purchase you make on eBay?

Technically, you can tell a seller you have changed your mind and don't want to follow through with a purchase. This is called "Buyer's Remorse." It can sometimes happen when young people in a family use their parents' eBay account to make a purchase. When the parents find out, they might well ask the seller to nullify the purchase. You've always got to be aware of the consequences in terms of negative feedback, however. Most sellers are not going to look kindly on someone who becomes the high bidder on one of their sales and then backs out.

True, some PowerSellers who deal in high volume can afford to accept returns of items that are not damaged—though you may be charged a 25-percent or more restocking fee if you do return something. You are almost certainly going to receive negative feedback as a result. The feedback comments can "taint" any future transactions you attempt on eBay.

If you plan to buy and sell on eBay for months or years to come, seriously consider following through and completing a purchase even if you have changed your mind. You'll avoid negative feedback, for one thing. For another, you can always turn around and resell the same item on eBay, and possibly make a profit besides.

The Item Arrives Damaged

As anyone who has seen the opening sequence of the movie *Ace Ventura: Pet Detective* can tell you, shippers don't always take care with the packages they deliver. The lead character in that movie, played by Jim Carrey, went out of his way to cause as much damage as possible to a package he was delivering.

Many sellers have a policy of granting refunds if something they send is damaged during shipment. You can also request that the seller pay an additional fee to insure what is shipped (see Chapter 9 for more on this and other aspects of shipping).

NOTE *Some eBay sellers intentionally put damaged merchandise up for sale. The items may or may not have been damaged during shipping, but are advertised as being damaged, and are offered to buyers as a "deep discount". To find damaged items, go to Advanced Search by clicking Search in the eBay navigation bar, and then clicking the Advanced tab. Enter the term damaged and, in the Words to Exclude box, enter shipping, "Not responsible." This enables you to find descriptions that include the term "damaged" while excluding the common phrase: "Not responsible for items lost or damaged during shipping." Check the box next to Search Titles and Descriptions. Then click Search to find such items.*

Avoiding Common Problems for Sellers

It might seem like sellers are in total control when it comes to eBay sales. While it's true that sellers control the auction terms, they can't really predict what their high bidders or buyers are going to do after the sale ends. Many problems can occur that can undo all the work you have put into a sale. Luckily, in each case you can take advantage of procedures put in place by eBay to help recoup your losses.

Buyers Who Disappear

One of the common problems sellers encounter with bidders or buyers is the inability to locate them in order to finalize a transaction. Sometimes, bidders suffer "buyer's remorse" and simply fail to straightforwardly admit it to a seller. Instead, they simply fail to respond or assure the seller that they will pay, and then never send payment.

If you have neither received an e-mail nor a payment from a buyer, you can request their phone number and address from eBay. (You can only get such contact information from people with whom you are completing transactions.) You do this by filling out the Contact Info section of the Find Members page (http://cgi3.ebay .com/aw-cgi/eBayISAPI.dll?MemberSearchShow#ContactInfo). This also gives the buyer access to your contact details so he or she can get in touch with you.

When you request the information, you will receive the bidder's name, city, state, and phone number. Table 6-2 details how to deal with a nonresponsive buyer.

Keep in mind that you have to issue a Non-Paying Bidder alert even if you are absolutely sure the buyer is not going to pay (if the buyer has told you as much, for instance). Only then can you get a credit for your Final Value Fee before you relist the item.

Time Frame	What to Do	Where to Find It
3 to 30 days after end of sale	Issue a Payment Reminder	Go to My eBay | Selling | Items I've Sold
10 to 14 days after sending payment, if you don't get a response to a Payment Reminder	Request contact details and phone the seller	http://cgi3.ebay.com/aw-cgi/ eBayISAPI.dll?MemberSearchShow #ContactInfo
7 to 45 Days	Issue a Non-Paying Bidder alert	http://cgi3.ebay.com/aw-cgi/ eBayISAPI.dll?NPBComplaintForm
Ten days after issuing the Non-Paying Bidder alert	Request a Final Value Fee credit	http://cgi3.ebay.com/aw-cgi/ eBayISAPI.dll?CreditRequest
17 to 90 days after end of sale	If buyer decides to pay, you can have warnings removed	http://cgi3.ebay.com/aw-cgi/ eBayISAPI.dll?RemoveNPB WarningShow
7 to 30 days after end of sale	Relist the item	Go to your My eBay page and select Selling
7 to 90 days after end of sale	Make a second chance offer to an underbidder	See the item description page

TABLE 6-2   Approaches to Nonresponsive Bidders

Buyers Who Won't Pay

A more serious problem than a buyer who simply won't contact you is one who refuses—or forgets—to send payment. Don't immediately assume the buyer is walking out on the deal if you don't see a message from PayPal or receive a check or money order in the mail a week or ten days after the end of the sale. There may be legitimate reasons why it's taking time for the money to get to you. The buyer might have to go to the post office to get a money order, or the buyer might be sick or out of town.

Calling the buyer directly and either speaking to the person or leaving a friendly message will often produce a response. Otherwise, filing a Non-Paying Bidder (NPB) report will usually get the job done. Being branded as an NPB is something that few

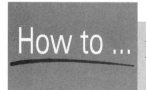

How to ... Deal with Problem Customers

One member I interviewed for this book ran into problems with a male buyer, but wisely responded in a professional way, keeping the situation from getting worse. (In her story, which follows, I've held back her name for safety purposes.)

"Most transactions on eBay go smoothly and without incident. The problems I typically experience as a seller are with NPBs—non-paying bidders. I have some auctions close for which I am never paid. When that happens, I just file for my Final Value Fee credits from eBay and relist the item. I once had a bidder that became verbally abusive when he found out I was a woman. He started making vulgar references to PMS and other "female" things, all simply in response to my polite and professional requests for payment. I later found he was suspended from eBay. In that case, I learned from other sellers how to block an e-mail address that was sending offensive language, and how to report the offender to eBay for abuse of the e-mail forwarding system."

You can use your e-mail program's controls to block an e-mail from a particular sender. In Microsoft Outlook Express, choose Tools | Message Rules | Blocked Senders List. When the Message Rules dialog box opens with the Blocked Senders tab selected, click Add. When the Add Sender dialog box appears, enter the person's e-mail address in the Address field and click OK (see the image that follows). Click OK to close Message Rules and return to the Outlook Express window.

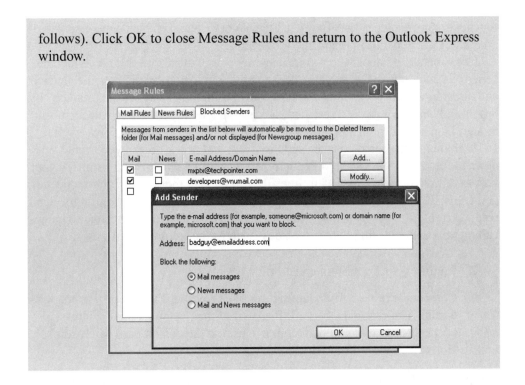

if any eBay members want. The report can be filed anywhere between 7 and 45 days after the end of the auction. Once you file, eBay sends out an e-mail to your auction winner. This notification can cause bidders to pay, because they can be intimidating. If a member accumulates three or more of these warnings, he or she will be suspended from using eBay.

If your buyer does pay, be sure to cancel your previous Non-Paying Bidder alert by submitting a Non-Paying Bidder Warning Removal (see Table 6-2 for the URL of this form). You're likely to get e-mail reminders from the buyer if you do not.

Buyers Who Just Behave Badly

You can't get along with everyone. Businesspeople get complaints all the time, and are used to angry or dissatisfied customers coming to them and demanding refunds for one reason or another. On eBay, it's difficult not to take such incidents personally—after all, it is a person-to-person auction medium.

Occasionally, it happens that you encounter one of those rare and nerve-racking series of e-mail messages or phone conversations in which buyers become abusive and threaten you for some reason. I have heard of members who were "stalked" by buyers and others who were threatened and called names (both were female members, though I am sure it can happen to males as well).

Such incidents should be taken seriously. But that doesn't mean you should sink down to the level of the other party and resort to name-calling of your own. Try your best to remain professional at all times. If you receive messages from the person, don't open them when you're angry. If the messages themselves make you angry, don't respond right away. Give yourself time to cool down. Instead of resorting to name-calling, respond with some practical steps, such as the following:

- Contact your law enforcement officials.

- Contact the other party's Internet service provider if the threat was made by e-mail. You can identify the ISP as part of the person's e-mail address: an address of *person*@hotmail.com means that the person used Microsoft's Hotmail service to send the threat.

You can read more about eBay's policy regarding e-mail threats at http://pages.ebay.com/help/policies/everyone-threats.html.

Sellers Who Steal Your Photos or Text

It's not at all uncommon to see auctions that use photos that originally appeared elsewhere. Sellers don't always take the time to take their own pictures. They copy them from Web sites that sell electronics, clothing, or other consumer items. Sometimes, they take photos from the auction descriptions posted by other sellers on eBay itself.

It's easy to copy images from other people's web pages, and seems harmless at first. In many cases, the owners of the photos don't complain if they are copied. But they could if they wanted to because such copying is technically illegal. Everything that is published on the web is automatically protected by *copyright laws.* Copyright is a legal term that describes the right of a published work's creator to control how it is copied. People are often surprised to learn that copyright protection applies whether or not the creator includes a copyright notice (such as "Copyright 2004. All rights reserved.").

In practice, most eBay sellers don't include an actual copyright notice with their photos or other parts of their auction descriptions. However, many sellers protect their images from theft by marking them with an identifying phrase called a watermark. The phrase is added with a graphics imaging program such as Paint Shop Pro or Adobe Photoshop Elements. One of the sellers profiled in this book, Lori Baboulis of NYC Designs for Less, "brands" each of her auction images with her company's name (see Figure 6-3).

6

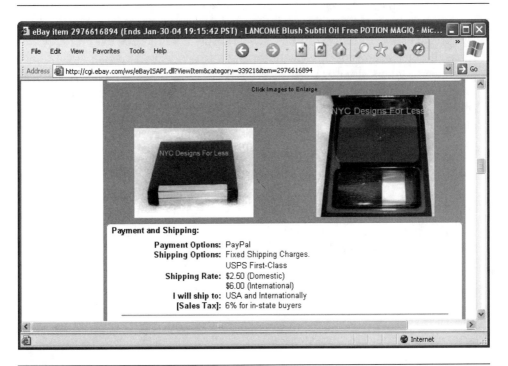

FIGURE 6-3 You can protect your images from being copied by adding a watermark.

Borrowing Is Illegal

Shannon Miller and Suzanne Ziesche, who run the highly successful eBay business Venus Rising Limited (http://www.venusrisinglimited.com), are protective of the images they include with their descriptions. In their auctions, they tell prospective bidders that they should be careful to choose the color they want. The photos of clothing and other items display the colors accurately and are critical to sales. Not surprisingly, they react strongly if they see a seller attempting to reuse one of their images or some of their auction listing text.

"We take a hard stance when it comes to copyright infringement in the form of either textual infringement or image theft," they say. "For new sellers, we do our best to send a courteous e-mail warning the seller that attempted use of the text or photo is illegal; we give the seller the opportunity to correct the mistake and illegal use. It is imperative that sellers respect the intellectual property rights of others, and keep an eye out for any infringing auctions that violate their rights. Sellers should take the time to thoroughly understand copyright infringement to ensure that they are not violating federal and state laws. Violations should be immediately reported to eBay Rules & Safety for auction removal. Doing so helps make eBay a safer community for all involved."

—*Shannon Miller and Suzanne Ziesche*

eBay and Other Protection Services

It can be confusing when trying to decide which one of eBay's various support areas is best for your needs. The different options open to you are listed in Table 6-3.

If You Want to...	Go to this eBay Page	Where to Find It
Report identity theft or fraudulent e-mail	Security Center	http://pages.ebay.com/ securitycenter/
Investigations	Report trading offenses	http://pages.ebay.com/help/ confidence/ programs-investigations.html
SafeHarbor	If you can't find what you need anywhere else, go here to find links to eBay's fraud and investigations areas and listing policies.	http://pages.ebay.com/help/ community/index.html

TABLE 6-3 eBay Help and Support Options

eBay's primary resources for protecting buyers and sellers who encounter trouble are described in the following sections.

Rules & Safety

If you ever run into trouble with a transaction or see something happening that appears improper or suspicious, turn to the Rules & Safety (also known as SafeHarbor) link at the bottom of each page.

It's a page full of policies, warnings, and disciplinary action you can pursue should you encounter someone who is not playing by the auction service's rules. The page is divided into two columns (see Figure 6-4). On the left are links that describe the rules that all members need to follow. On the right are links you can pursue if you need help.

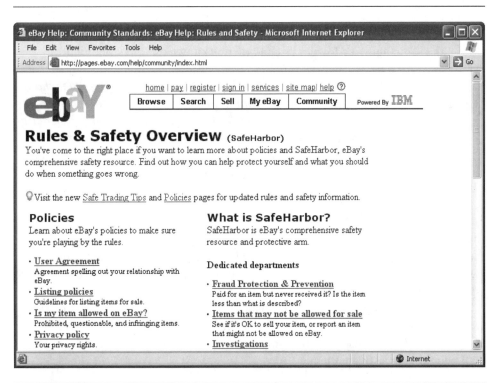

FIGURE 6-4   Rules & Safety, also known as SafeHarbor, is the place to turn to if you run into trouble.

The links take you to actual eBay staff members who handle complaints in the order in which they are received. If you send in a tip about someone who is selling a prohibited item on eBay, for instance, you would cause eBay to e-mail a warning message to the person.

You should turn to Rules & Safety if you encounter the following kinds of situations:

■ Criminals who intercept your eBay account information (specifically, your eBay User ID and password, or your PayPal account information) and who can then use it to direct payments to them, not you.

■ Someone who enters phony bids in an attempt to make something seem more popular than it really is.

■ Dishonest sellers who practice "shill bidding," in which they recruit friends or relatives to artificially drive up the bids on an item in an attempt to earn more money.

■ Sellers who approach a bidder on someone else's sale and try to offer a bidder the same item at a lower price, a practice known as "bid siphoning."

TIP   *eBay's policies on what constitute violations of its User Agreement change occasionally. It's a good idea to opt in to receive any updates when eBay's User Agreement changes. Go to your My eBay page, and click the Preferences tab. Scroll down to the Personal Information section of the Preferences tab and click Change My Notification Preferences. Sign in with your password, and then check the box next to User Agreement Changes.*

Federal Organizations

Internet auction fraud is just one of many commerce-related problems tracked by the Federal Trade Commission (FTC). The FTC's Bureau of Consumer Protection (www.ftc.gov/ftc/consumer.htm) allows you to file complaints related to e-commerce and the Internet, as well as identity theft.

In addition, the Internet Fraud Complaint Center (www1.ifccfbi.gov/index.asp), which was created by the Federal Bureau of Investigation (FBI) and National White Collar Crime Center, also accepts complaints from victims of fraud, and assigns staff people to investigate them.

Did you know?

eBay Insurance

Both buyers and sellers can benefit from insurance. For sellers, if a package is damaged in transit and they are forced to give the buyer a refund, some insurance can help keep the incident from being a total loss. For buyers, insurance can help if payment is sent but nothing is received in return. You can get insurance from a number of sources:

- **eBay**   eBay provides up to $200 worth of coverage for most items (less a $25 fee) through its standard purchase protection program. The final winning price of the item must be more than $25. See http://pages .ebay.com/help/confidence/isgw-fraud-claim-requirements.html for more information about what constitutes eligibility.

- **PayPal**   As stated in Table 6-1 in the "Dealing with Non-Selling Sellers" section earlier in this chapter, some items are eligible for PayPal Buyer Protection. The sellers of those items have to have feedback ratings of 50 or more on eBay, 98 percent positive feedback, and a Premier or Business account with PayPal. The program provides up to $500 of insurance. Find out more at www.paypal.com/cgi-bin/webscr?cmd=_pbp-info-outside.

- **One of the "Big Three" shippers**   UPS charges $.35 per $100 of insured value, while FedEx charges $.50 per $100 with a $2.50 minimum. If you ship with the United States Postal Service (USPS), you pay $1.30 for up to $50 of insurance and $2.20 for up to $100 of insurance.

- **A package insurance company**   Universal Parcel Insurance Coverage (U-PIC) ships packages at lower cost than the USPS. You pay 75 cents for up to $100 of insurance and $2.25 for up to $200. Find out more at www.u-pic.com.

- **Your credit card provider**   All of the big credit card companies—Visa, MasterCard, American Express, and Discover—offer "zero liability" policies to their customers for fraudulent purchases made over the Internet. This covers you if someone uses your card fraudulently, or if you pay for something with a credit card but then never receive it. However, if you paid through PayPal with your credit card and the seller fraudulently

6

accepts your money, PayPal, not the credit card company, must conduct the investigation, according to their user agreement.

With all those protections in place, it makes sense for buyers to purchase with a credit card through PayPal. Not so long ago, paying with a credit card over the Internet was regarded as a risky proposition. Improvements in security and in the way most organizations involved in e-commerce handle customer data have dramatically changed the attitude of the general public.

Yes, fraud is still a huge problem on the web. But on eBay, credit cards are regarded as a safe means of payment—safer, even, than sending a personal check or even a cashier's check. Why? The reason is simple: even if someone steals your credit card information and uses it to make a fraudulent purchase on eBay, you, the cardholder, aren't liable for any of it.

You may also want to contact your local law enforcement agency, as well as law enforcement officials in the area where the seller is located. Theft is theft, whether it occurs while you are out shopping in the mall or online.

Where to Find It

Web Site	Address	What's There
Appendix to Privacy Policy page	http://pages.ebay.com/help/ community/privacy-appendix.html	A list of the kinds of information eBay collects from members and the types of organizations that have access to it
Protecting Your Identity	http://pages.ebay.com/help/ confidence/problems-identity-theft.html	eBay's instructions for victims of identity theft
Security Center	http://pages.ebay.com/ securitycenter/	Links to parts of eBay's site that handle fraud, identity theft, and other complaints
eBay Buyer Protection Program	http://pages.ebay.com/help/ community/fpp.html	Steps that both buyers and sellers can take if they encounter fraud
Protection Claim: Eligibility Requirements	http://pages.ebay.com/help/ confidence/isgw-fraud-claim-requirements.html	Lists of requirements for buyers and sellers to file a claim under eBay's standard purchase protection program

Chapter 7

Winning Tips for Beginning Sellers

How to…

- Choose what to sell and prepare it for sale
- Register to sell and put your first items up for sale
- Open an eBay Store to help boost sales
- Create an About Me web page to advertise your current auctions

People come up to me all the time expressing interest in selling their first item on eBay. I try to tell them how simple it is to get started, but their eyes glaze over. The problem is twofold: first, it seems more difficult to get started putting items up for auction than it really is. Second, it really *is* more difficult to sell with great success, for the long term, than it is to put up three or four items once in a while. In this chapter, you will learn how to get started selling on eBay, and get some tips that will increase your chances of getting bids, too.

 This chapter assumes you are only going to sell occasionally on eBay, not that you are planning to be a full-time seller or start up a part-time or full-time business on eBay, as a growing number of ambitious entrepreneurs have done. If you want to turn to eBay for a regular source of income, see my book How to Do Everything with Your eBay Business, *also published by McGraw-Hill/Osborne.*

Deciding What to Sell and Preparing Your Merchandise

How do you get started selling items on eBay? Most people start by scrounging around their attics or garages, looking for things they want to get rid of. In most cases, they have absolutely no idea whether the items are valuable or not. Let's say you have found four items:

- A dingy old painting of a farm in the country
- The Elvis Presley album *Viva Las Vegas*
- A brown cookie jar shaped like a pig
- A 1969 newspaper with a headline about the first man on the moon.

You suspect that some of these things are worth something. You have no idea about the painting, however, and you aren't about to go to a fine art dealer for an appraisal, nor is the "Antiques Roadshow" about to come to your area in the near future. So, where should you start?

Learning Something about What You Want to Sell

Plenty of sellers put items up for sale with absolutely no idea what they are worth. They want eBay's members to determine what they are worth. For instance, I was told about a man in England who reached into his pocket and pulled out a one-pound coin. He put it up for sale on eBay on a whim. The coin must have been notable in some way, because a buyer in the United States ended up paying two hundred dollars for it.

I'm not saying that you have to take a course and study up on something like Chinese porcelain or early American folk art and become a know-it-all on the topic. I am saying that you need to find out a few important facts about what you are selling that will help attract interest. Many collectors depend on dates, model numbers, and identifying trademarks or other attributes to decide if they want to bid. The more such information you can provide up front, the fewer questions you'll have to field later on.

Creating a Good Presentation

In any store, the owners take care with what they are selling. They clean and arrange the merchandise in such a way that customers will be induced to pick them up, inspect them, and hopefully buy them. On eBay, you can't get anyone to actually pick up your item. Your goal is to get them to look and consider, read the description, and hopefully place a bid or make a purchase.

You don't necessarily have to create photos of what you sell. Wally Rockawin, a seller in Australia, wrote to tell me that he had just purchased a digital camera— this was after he sold more than a hundred things on the Australian version of eBay without any photos at all. Wally specializes in selling books on eBay. He says

> "Originally I took images of the books that I was selling. Then I switched to writing very good advertisements instead. I read many books on how to write good advertisements. There was a dramatic improvement in sales. The books I sell are not of the rare type but generally are good value for money; hence, a picture of the actual book was not necessary as I give very good, and truthful, information on the condition of the item. However, I will eventually buy a digital camera as they are becoming affordable (for instance, they are half the price of a year ago)."

7

If you decide to include photos, the first rule might seem simple and obvious: clean up your items before you sell them—polish the silver, take some glass cleaner to the glass, dust off the wood and porcelain.

Then, position your sales items in a place that has good lighting so they will be easy to see when photographed. Many regular sellers create their own home photo studio, complete with stands, backgrounds, special lights, and more. You don't need to do this.

The next rule is to take a good photo (or better yet, photos) of the item. Chapter 8 discusses digital images in more detail. The sections that follow concentrate on getting started as a seller on eBay.

Shopping Around for the Right Sales Category

It's also a good idea to do some research into the best category in which to list your item. You choose this when you fill out the Sell Your Item form, but giving some thought to the matter beforehand will ensure that you make a good choice. You may also want to consider listing the item in a second category along with the first. Picking a second category costs extra: your insertion fee is doubled, and upgrade fees to make the sale bold, highlighted, or featured are doubled as well. But many sellers (and eBay itself) report that items listed in two categories simultaneously get more attention than those listed in only one category.

For instance, suppose you have a collectible Elvis Presley "Love Me Tender" 45 RPM record to sell. The obvious place to sell the record is in the following category:

```
Entertainment > Music > Records > 45 RPM > Rock > Early Rock-n-Roll
```

However, you might get some more attention from collectors who specialize in "everything Elvis" by also listing the record in a second category:

```
Entertainment > Memorabilia > Music Memorabilia > Rock-n-Roll > Elvis > Music
```

You might wonder just how to determine what the best category choices are. Is there a way to search for category names on eBay, for instance? There is, but it's difficult to find: you see the search utility when you begin to fill out the Sell Your Item form and have the opportunity to choose a category (see "Choosing a Category" later in this chapter).

As you can see from the Elvis example, some subcategories are five levels down from the top level. The best way to "shop" for possible categories without filling out the Sell Your Item form is to do a search for items currently up for sale on eBay that are similar to yours. Make note of the subcategory in which the item is located; it appears at the top of the listing (see Figure 7-1). You may have to browse through several listings in order to get a few alternatives. Jot down your desired category or categories, and then move on to registering to sell and putting your first items up for sale.

Becoming an eBay Seller

Even if you already have an account on eBay, you have to register to sell as well. That doesn't mean you have to select a new User ID and password. It does mean you have to give eBay some information about how you are going to pay your seller's fees. You can then put your first item up for sale, as described in the sections that follow.

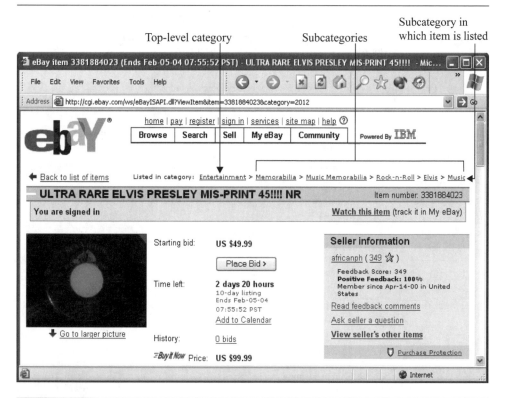

FIGURE 7-1 You can "shop" for categories by inspecting sales items that are close to your own.

Providing Your Seller Registration Information

The process of becoming a seller on eBay begins with some additional registration steps that you need to follow even if you already have a buyer's account. You need to put checking account information or a credit card number on file so eBay can use it to charge seller's fees. Table 7-1 provides a brief overview of the kinds of fees you can expect to pay. You also need to have your identity verified by your credit card company or your bank, or through the ID Verify program.

 You can find out more about the fees eBay charges and the formulas used to calculate those fees in Chapter 9.

Many sellers use the same account for selling on eBay that they use for buying. It's worth noting, however, that some sellers create different accounts for buying and

Fee	What It Means	How It Is Calculated	Example
Insertion Fee	A fee for listing an item for sale	For standard auctions, the fee is based on the starting price. For reserve auctions, it is based on the reserve price. For Dutch auctions, it is based on the opening value of the items for sale.	If the starting price or reserve price is $35, the insertion fee is 60 cents.
Insertion Fee (eBay Motors)	Fee for listing a vehicle on eBay Motors	Flat fee based on type of vehicle	Motorcycles: $30, other vehicles $40
Insertion Fee (eBay Real Estate)	Fee for listing homes or other real estate on eBay	Flat fee based on type of sale and length of listing	For a home auctioned off for 30 days, the fee is $150
Reserve Price fee	Fee for listing an item with a reserve price	Depends on reserve price	If reserve price is $100, the fee is $2
Picture Services	Fee for having eBay's own Picture Services host your photo on the Web so it appears with your auction	First image free; each additional is 15 cents	
Final Value Fee	Fee charged for selling an item on eBay	Complex; exact formula depends on type of sale	An item that sells for $800 has a Final Value Fee of $22.62.
Listing Upgrade Fees	Fee charged for highlighting an auction so it gets more attention	Flat fee; depends on type of highlighting chosen	For standard and reserve auctions, formatting the title in bold costs $1; highlighting with a color costs $5.

TABLE 7-1   eBay Seller's Fees

selling. Having separate accounts helps sellers who are well-known and who have a high profile, such as PowerSellers, shop and bid on eBay without being "recognized." If they are recognized, potential buyers might realize that the sellers are purchasing their inventory and intending to resell. They feel more comfortable going "incognito." You might also create two seller's accounts to have fees deducted from a checking account on one account, and fees deducted from a credit card on the second account.

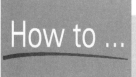

TIP   *For more information on the ID Verify program and how it can help protect your identity, see Chapter 6.*

How to ...   **Have Someone Do the Work for You**

You don't have to do all the work when you are getting started selling on eBay. If you plan to sell only once in a while and don't have the time or technical expertise to take digital photos or field e-mail questions, you may want to sell on consignment. Selling on consignment means you give your item to someone who sells for a living and knows the ins and outs of the system.

There are two different types of consignment sellers from which to choose: sellers who put items up for sale "on the side" but who don't have any formal designation as consignment sellers, and those who have been admitted to eBay's Trading Assistants program. Either way, the general idea is the same: you bring your item to someone who handles the photography, description, and management of the sale. When the item sells, you both share in the sale price. You don't make as much money as you would if you did everything yourself, but you don't go through as much work and you save considerable time and energy, too. If you don't have a computer or a digital camera, turning to a consignment seller may be the only way you have to put something up for auction on eBay.

The first kind of consignment seller is usually someone you know, or a friend of a friend. Such sellers might charge you 10 to 15 percent of the purchase price or high bid, as well as a fee for packing and shipping. You might be shopping an eBay Store and find a Trading Assistants logo. Jill Featherston has one at the bottom of her eBay Stores home page (http://members.ebay.com/aboutme/bargain-hunters-dream/), shown here.

7

If you don't know a seller yourself, turn to the Trading Assistants program to find one in your area. You find the program either by clicking Services and then Trading Assistants, or by going directly to http://contact.ebay.com/aw-cgi/eBayISAPI.dll?GetTAHubPage. At its annual conference in summer 2003, eBay estimated that there were 20,000 trading assistants around the world. In order to join the program, trading assistants must have a feedback rating of 49 or higher and more than 97-percent positive feedback.

Once they are certified, trading assistants have the ability to set their own terms of sale, and to specialize in certain types of items they know well. You might find that some trading assistants charge $1 per listing plus 4 to 5 percent of the final sales price. Others might charge 25 percent of any high bid. Do a search for assistants in your area and read their terms of sale. When you find one you want to use, you can contact them directly, negotiate fees, and bring the items over so they can be sold.

Filling Out the Sell Your Item Form

The basic, straightforward way to put items up for sale on eBay is to fill out a form that eBay provides called Sell Your Item. If you start to sell in quantity and need to manage your sales, you might use a tool like eBay's Turbo Lister, which can create

 **Set Up Your Account Information**

You should determine beforehand whether you want the fees to be deducted from your checking account or charged to your credit card. Have your checkbook and your credit card ready (so you can supply account numbers), and then follow these steps:

1. Click Sell in the eBay navigation bar.

2. When you are prompted to sign in, enter your User ID and password and click Sign In. At this point, one of two things happens:

   ■ If you have not yet placed a credit card number on file with eBay, a page entitled Create or Update Your Credit/Debit Card appears. Fill out the form and then click Submit. You'll be taken to a page entitled Create a Seller's Account, where you are prompted to sign in again. Enter your User ID and password and click Secure Sign-In.

   ■ If you already have a credit card on file with eBay, after you click Sell and sign in, you go to a page entitled Create a Seller's Account, where you are prompted to sign in again. Enter your User ID and password and click Secure Sign-In.

3. When the Seller's Account: Verify Information page appears, review your information to make sure it is accurate, and then do one of two things: click Continue if you want to use a credit card to pay your fees and verify your information, or click the ID Verify link near the top of the page to have eBay verify your information using ID Verify. (You'll have to pay a $5 fee for using ID Verify.)

4. If you choose to pay with a credit card, enter your credit card information and click Continue.

5. You are next asked to provide your checking account information on the Seller's Account: Provide Check Identification page. You need to provide this information even if you don't want to pay your eBay fees with your checking account; it's an extra security precaution to guard against the improper use of your credit card number if your account is "hijacked"

7

by a thief. Enter the information; eBay won't actually charge your checking account until you tell them to do so. Then click Continue.

6. When the Seller's Account: Select How to Pay Seller Fees page appears, check one of the two options to indicate whether you want to use your credit card or your checking account to pay your eBay fees. Then click Continue.

7. Click Authorize on the next page to have eBay use your chosen method of payment.

If you ever need to change your account information, click My eBay, click Preferences, and then click Change My Registration Information. You'll be prompted to sign in, after which you can fill out the eBay Change Registration form.

multiple sales listings at once. But to get started, use the Sell Your Item form as described in the sections that follow.

TIP   *If you have never sold anything before and are worried about getting your auction listing just right the first time, consider creating a test description. eBay provides a test category so you can try out a sale and see how it looks before actually putting something up for sale. When you are selecting categories, choose Everything Else > Test Auctions > General.*

Choosing an Auction Format

Once you have created your seller's account, click Sell in the eBay navigation bar, sign in with your User ID and Password, and you go to the Sell Your Item: Format page. Choose one of the following options:

- **Online Auction**   This term covers standard, reserve, and Dutch auctions.

- **Fixed-Price Sales**   Choose this option if you don't want to have shoppers bid on your item but would rather sell it for a fixed price.

- **Real Estate**   This category is increasingly popular; it lets eBay members put up homes, condos, timeshares, or property for sale. Real estate sales, like auctions, can last for ten days or less. You can also specify that you want the sale to last 30 or even 60 days.

After you make your choice, click Continue to move to the Step 1 of 5: Category page. When you click Continue, if this is the first time you have used Sell Your Item, you may see an alert message labeled Security Warning (see Figure 7-2).

Don't be alarmed: eBay prompts you to download a piece of software that enables you to add photos interactively and view them in the Sell Your Item form as they are added. Click OK to close Security Warning and automatically download the software. You can then move on to filling out the rest of the form.

Choosing a Category

After you have specified the type of sale you want to conduct, the first part of the Sell Your Item form requires you to choose a category in which to list your item. For those buyers who browse though categories, looking for specific types of items, the place where you locate it makes an important difference. In another sense, the category choice is less important, because anyone who does a keyword search for your item using Basic Search or Advanced Search will find it no matter what category it's in. Nevertheless, you should try to choose a category so it appears in a place where shoppers expect to find it. You have two options for choosing a category:

■ Look for similar items on your own and see where they are located.

■ Enter a keyword that describes your item in the box on the Select Category page (see Figure 7-3), and then click Find.

7

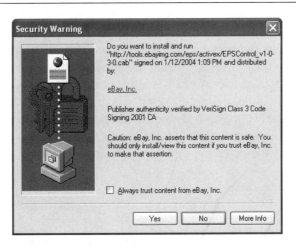

FIGURE 7-2   In order to add photos interactively, you need to download this software from eBay.

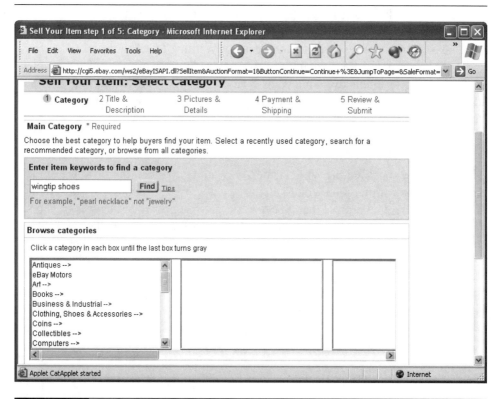

FIGURE 7-3   If you're unsure of a category, enter a keyword and eBay will suggest categories for you.

If you know what category you want, click the top-level category in the box on the left. A set of subcategories appears in the box next to it. Click the subcategory, and a set of the subcategories beneath it appears in the next box. Keep selecting subcategories until no more appear. Even if you think you know what category you want, you should probably do a search just to make sure. eBay returns a set of suggested categories that are ranked according to popularity. For instance, a search for "wingtip shoes" turned up the following results:

```
Clothing, Shoes & Accessories > Men's Shoes > Oxfords 42%
Sports > Sporting Goods > Golf > Shoes, Sandals > Men > Other Brands 18%
Clothing, Shoes & Accessories > Men's Shoes > Other Shoes 10%
```

The percentage ranking indicates, on a scale of 1 to 100 percent, how many sellers with items similar to yours list those items in a particular category. The results indicate that 42 percent of all sellers of wingtip shoes list their item in the category Clothing, Shoes & Accessories > Men's Shoes > Oxfords. You don't have to list your item there, however, and you can choose more than one category to list it in.

You can choose a second category by entering a keyword in the search box in the form at the bottom of the page, and then clicking Find. For instance, a search of categories for the term "Elvis" turned up a number of categories that weren't found by browsing items for sale, as described in the section "Shop Around for the Right Sales Category" earlier in this chapter. The results ranked by percentage. For instance, the results shown in Figure 7-4 indicate that 18 percent of all Elvis-related items are contained in the category Entertainment > Memorabilia > Music Memorabilia > Rock-n-Roll > Elvis > Other.

Keep in mind that, when you choose a second category, your insertion fee and fees for upgrading features such as bold and highlighting are doubled. When you are done, click Continue. The page labeled Sell Your Item: Describe Your Item appears.

7

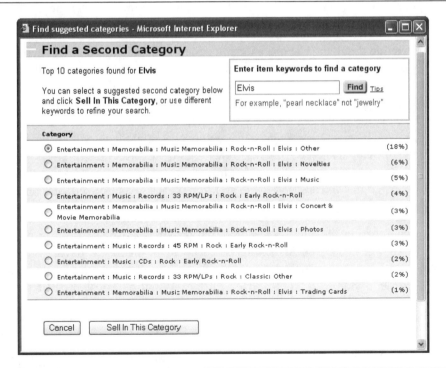

FIGURE 7-4   eBay ranks suggested categories based on the likelihood that your item will be found there.

Fine-Tuning Your Description

The heading and the description are probably the most important part of an auction listing. (I say "probably" because it can be argued that photos or No Reserve prices are just as important. But if no photos are included, the description is certainly most important.) What characteristics in a description make it effective and encourage people to look, investigate, and hopefully bid? Here are some suggestions:

- **Create a good heading** The auction heading is what people will see in response to a search on eBay. But unless you pay $19.95 for a Featured Plus! upgrade, which causes your title to be presented at the top of a list of search results, your title will be buried in the pack along with others. Keep the heading to no more than five or six words if possible. Don't use ALL CAPS since it is overused and will make your heading look like everyone else's. Simply using upper- and lowercase will make it differ from many others. But try to add keywords that will turn up as a result of a search, so you'll maximize its chances of being found. (An auction title can be no more than 45 characters in length.)

- **Provide details** The more details you provide, the more interest you'll generate. Shoppers on eBay love to read as much as possible about the things they are considering buying. The more details you provide, the longer they'll stay on your auction listing page, and the more likely they'll click the Place Bid or Buy It Now button. Try to get shoppers to visualize how they might use that blender, how snuggly that winter coat might feel, or how they might look driving that convertible car down the street. Also, be upfront about any flaws your item has, such as bumps or cracks. It's better to put out such information up front, so buyers aren't unpleasantly surprised later on.

- **Consider adding a subtitle** A subtitle is a second set of words that accompanies the auction title and that provides a little extra information. A subtitle costs 50 cents extra, but it's a way of making your sale stand out from others that surround it in a list of search results. For instance, in a listing entitled "Men's Florsheim Size 12 Black Wingtip Shoes" the title takes up 37 of the maximum 45 characters. A subtitle might add "Never Worn, Mint in Box."

After you type your heading and subheading, you enter the listing details in the box labeled Description. You can type the text directly in the box. Or, you can type it in a word-processing application, and then copy and paste the text into the Description box. You can also type your description and format it at the same time using HyperText Markup Language commands.

If you need some help with HTML, click the link HTML Tips in the yellow column on the right-hand side of the page. It's beyond the scope of this book to go into great detail on how to use HTML to format auction descriptions. But here are some simple suggestions:

To make a large heading, enclose the heading text with the HTML commands <H1> and </H1>:

```
<H1> 1968 Ford Mustang GT Convertible </H1>
```

To highlight some text in bold, use the <B> and </B> commands. To format text in italics, use the commands <I> and </I>:

```
Highly collectible 1968 Ford Mustang Convertible with the sought-after
<B> 323 V6 engine </B>and <I> white convertible top. </I>
```

You can also format auction descriptions using programs like eBay's Seller's Assistant, which is described in Chapter 12 along with other auction listing tools. When you have entered the text, click Preview Your Description just beneath the Description box. A browser window opens with your description displayed. The HTML examples mentioned earlier are shown in Figure 7-5.

It's important to take a moment to read through your description to check for spelling errors. Even a single misspelling makes you look unprofessional—or, at the very least, makes it seem that you were in a hurry and didn't take care about your description. When you're done, click Close Window to close the preview window. Make corrections in the Description box if they are needed. If not, click Continue to move on to the next part of the form.

TIP *If you see a misspelling or other error in your description, you can edit it as long as no bids have been placed. Once a bid has been placed, you can no longer make changes. You can, however, make an addition to your description in which you include the corrected information.*

Going Once, Going Twice: Scheduling Your Auction Wisely

The next page in the form, Step 3 of 5: Pictures & Details, lets you specify the ground rules for the sale and add images as well. First, you specify the length of the sale.

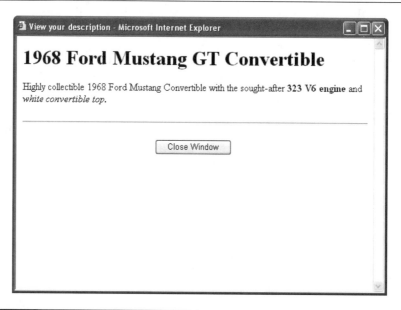

FIGURE 7-5   You can review any HTML formatting and proofread for mistakes using this preview feature.

When it comes to scheduling auctions, you've got two things to decide: how long the sale will last, and when it should start and end. For standard and reserve auctions, eBay gives you six different options for the length of the sale. Some pros and cons of each are listed in Table 7-2.

Length of Sale (Days)	Pros	Cons
1	Great for unloading items that need to be used immediately, like concert or travel tickets	Short time frame limits the number of buyers the sale will attract
3	Short enough to sell time-sensitive items, but long enough to attract more bidders than a one-day sale	Can't be used to sell items that need to be used in one or two days
5	Enables you to start a sale during the week and end it on a weekend	Will not attract as much attention as a seven- or ten-day auction
7	Easy to schedule; commonly used	Won't give you as much exposure as a ten-day sale; sales that start midweek will end midweek
10	Most likely to attract the highest number of shoppers	More page views does not necessarily mean more bids; extra fee required

TABLE 7-2   Options for the Length of eBay Auctions

The Best Time for a Sale

What's the best time to schedule a sale? I asked several experienced eBay sellers for opinions and advice.

"It really depends on the item you're selling," says Jill Featherston (User ID: bargain-hunters-dream). "If I am auctioning a high-dollar antique or collectible, I list for ten days and run it from Thursday night to the following Sunday night. Most of my regular auctions run seven days, from Sunday night to Sunday night."

"I still have the best luck with the traditional end date of Sunday for my auctions," says Emily Sabako (User ID: tradrmom). "I like Sunday for the number of bids as well as the fact that I can then schedule my week around the packing from the bulk of my closed sales. I also use Buy It Now on pretty much everything and probably 15 to 20 percent of my sales are from Buy It Now."

"Auctions generally see the most traffic on their last day, as most people refine the search to show "items ending first," says Roni Neal (User ID: roniheart). "Most of my auctions end Friday, Saturday, or Sunday between 9 P.M. and 10 P.M. EST. For sellers who offer children's clothing, weekdays between 10 and 3 might be best because that is when Mom is online while kids are napping or at school. Best thing to do is trial and error. Also, check completed auctions for the items you are selling and see what time the highest priced ones ended."

"We have found the following times serve as good guidelines," say Shannon Miller and Suzanne Ziesche of Venus Rising Limited. (Times are in PST, which allows our customers from further locales to purchase or bid two or three hours later in their local time):

- Monday through Thursday, 4–9 P.M.

- Friday, 12–5 P.M.

- Saturday, 10 A.M. to 8 P.M.

- Sunday, 10 A.M. to 6 P.M.

"Be careful to never begin any auction past 1 A.M. PST," they add. "eBay performs site maintenance every Friday between approximately 1 and 3 A.M. PST. Otherwise, bids will be nonexistent during the final hours or minutes of the sales."

You also choose when the auction will start. By default, the sale starts when you submit your information to eBay after filling out the Sell Your Item form. You can also specify that the sale starts at a specific time (for an extra 10-cent fee). You might want to do this if you are creating the listing at a time when traffic is relatively low (for instance, midnight), and you want the sale to end in the afternoon on a Saturday or Sunday, when more visitors are likely to be available.

Setting Prices for Your Sale

Next, you need to specify the financial parameters for your sale: your starting bid, your reserve price (if you want to specify one), and your Buy It Now price (again, optional). The starting price indicates where you want the bidding to start. In one sense, the starting price is symbolic: it's traditional to start the bidding out at some

Starting Prices and Reserves

Is it better to set a high starting price or a high reserve? In my opinion, a high starting price discourages bidders. I've heard others argue that reserve prices also discourage bidders. Here are some other opinions:

"In our experience and with our products, customers have expressed impatience and frustration with reserve auctions," say Shannon Miller and Suzanne Ziesche of Venus Rising Limited. Customers who are interested in an item prefer to bid from a clearly stated and reasonable starting bid price as opposed to an auction with a hidden reserve. Our customers also appreciate the Buy It Now option we include in every auction for immediate purchase and shipment."

"I never use a reserve," says Lori Baboulis of NYC Designs for Less. They are too frustrating because you have no idea how high you have to bid to win the item. Instead, I will use a Buy It Now format so people can buy at the price you accept."

"As an occasional buyer, I do not care for reserve auctions so I do not use them when I sell," says Roni Neal. "I list my items at the bottom line I am willing to accept as the opening bid. This could range from $1 to $100."

Virtually all of the sellers interviewed for this book shared the anti-reserve opinion.

dollar amount rather than zero. In another sense, the starting price is important: in a standard (no reserve) auction, the insertion fee is based on the starting price. The higher the starting price, the higher the fee. Many sellers choose a starting price of $9.99 because an insertion fee of 30 cents is charged for starting prices that are less than $10.

Many sellers specify a high starting price to ensure that they get at least that amount for the sale. If a starting price of $100 is specified, anyone has to bid at least $102.50 (the bid increment at $100 is $2.50). This also means the seller has to pay a $2.40 insertion fee. By keeping the starting bid at less than $10 and specifying a reserve price of $100, they get the same result: no one can win the item unless they bid $100 or more. But there's a catch: they also pay a $2.40 insertion fee, because on a reserve auction the insertion fee is based on the reserve.

You can specify a Buy It Now price whether or not there is a reserve price. The point of having a reserve price is that bidders might go over the reserve price and you'll get even more than you initially hoped. Someone who purchases at a Buy It Now price ends that possibility. Therefore, the Buy It Now price should be higher than the reserve.

7

Specifying Your Location

In the next part of the Step 3 page of Sell Your Item, you specify where the item is located. You are required to list a city. Should you specify a region? There's no reason not to. By doing so, you increase the chances that your item will be found by someone who is looking for items in a particular part of the country. Many shoppers do this if they are looking for heavy equipment or especially fragile or precious items that they prefer to pick up in person.

Adding Pictures

In the next part of the form, you add images to your auction. Images are such an important part of eBay auctions that they are discussed in detail in Chapter 8. It's worth noting, though, that the Add Pictures part of this page is divided into two tabs. Each of the two tabs represents a choice for hosting your image: the eBay Picture Services page enables you to move digital image files from your computer to eBay.

The Your Own Web Hosting tab lets you make a link from the auction description page you are creating to an external (non-eBay) hosting service. Rather than moving your photos to eBay, you move it to a hosting service with which you have established an account.

Adding Graphic Interest with Listing Designer

Listing Designer enables you to add considerable graphic interest to your auctions. For an extra fee of only 10 cents, you can add a theme to your listing. You enclose your description in a border with a bright color or lively design. The theme you choose also determines the font and background color of the listing. You can choose from five themes:

- **New**   These themes cover holidays and special occasions (for instance, Anniversary, Christmas Tree, and Hanukkah). The New category includes designs like Disco, Haunted House, and Travel.

- **Categories**   These themes correspond to some of eBay's own categories: Collectibles, Computers, Jewelry, Motors, and more.

- **Events**   These themes include special occasions such as Anniversary, Baby, and Wedding.

- **Seasonal/Holiday**   These themes include Father's Day, Fourth of July, and Valentine's Day.

- **Other**   These themes illustrate design ideas such as Flower Power, Mosaic, and Nightlife.

Once you have selected a general theme, the options in the box beneath the Select a Theme drop-down list change. Those options let you pick the specific colors and graphics that you want to apply. When you choose an option, you see a preview of the colors and graphics in the small box to the right (see Figure 7-6). Next, you choose a layout for images and text. A preview of the selected layout appears in the Listing Designer section of Sell Your Item as well.

When you're done, click Preview Your Layout to see your auction description with the design you have selected.

Listing Upgrade

The section beneath Listing Designer enables you to choose a listing upgrade: a way of highlighting and gaining more attention for an auction so that it stands out from other, similar sales. The options are shown in Table 7-3.

Some examples of the highlighting options are shown in the page of search results in Figure 7-7.

Another upgrade option, Gift Services, adds a gift icon to the auction title when it appears in a list of auctions; you can mention gift-wrapping and other services

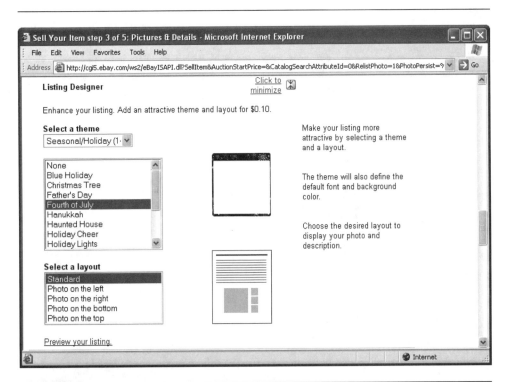

FIGURE 7-6   Listing Designer is an economical way to add design elements to your auction.

in the item description, as an extra inducement for a shopper to buy the item from you. The fee for designating the item as part of the Gift Services program is 25 cents.

Another way to enhance your auction description is to add a counter to the listing. A counter is a utility that records the number of visits that are made to that auction listing. A counter sits on an auction page (or on any web page) and records the number of times the page has been viewed. It doesn't tell you who is viewing those pages,

Upgrade	What It Does	Fee
Bold	Presents auction title in bold typeface	$1
Highlight	Encloses auction title in colored band	$5
Featured Plus!	Positions auction title at the top of category and at the top of search results	$19.95
Home Page Featured	Item is listed in Featured Items category and has a chance to "rotate" into the featured eBay home page listings	$39.95

TABLE 7-3   Listing Upgrade Options

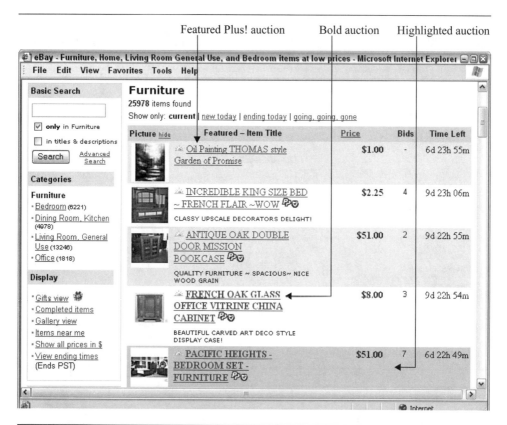

FIGURE 7-7 Inexpensive listing upgrades can help your sale stand out from the crowd.

or whether each of the visits recorded is by a unique viewer. A counter that records ten visits, for example, might only record visits by two individuals—one who has seen the page nine times and one who has visited just once.

A counter that indicates to visitors that a page has been visited a high number of times tells them there must be a lot of interest in the item, and suggests that they may want to place a bid themselves. On the other hand, if a counter has a low number, it may turn people away. If it has a high number of visits but just a handful of bids, it might even suggest that there's something wrong with the item being sold—or that bidders are biding their time and preparing to bid at the very last minute.

The Sell Your Item form gives you the choice of two counters: one in the style of the auction service Andale (www.andale.com), and one in the common "Green LED" style. You can also specify a hidden counter that only you can see (see Figure 7-8).

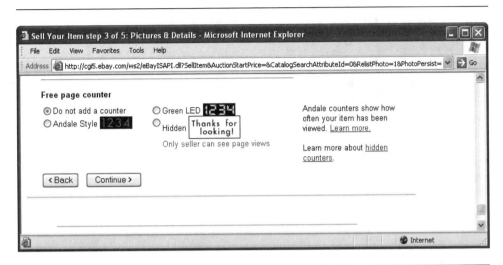

FIGURE 7-8   You can add a free counter to your auction description.

Once you are done, click Continue to move to the next page of the Sell Your Item form.

Putting the Buyer in Charge of Payment Options

The next page of the form is entitled Sell Your Item, Step 4 of 5: Payment. This is where you select payment and shipping options for your customers. These, too, are essential parts of selling on eBay, and are discussed in more detail in Chapter 9. The important thing to remember at this point is that you need to give buyers several options for payment.

Many buyers feel an extra level of security if you accept credit card payments through eBay's electronic service, PayPal. Some won't even bid unless they know the seller includes PayPal among payment options: the buyer is protected by his or her credit card provider's fraud policies, and by PayPal's own policies.

Improving Your Profits

By cutting some costs and increasing exposure for your merchandise, you can improve your overall profits from your eBay sales. The following sections describe ways in which you can gain more attention, encourage more purchases, and otherwise make your experience as an eBay seller more profitable, both literally and figuratively.

Opening the Doors on an eBay Store

In order to make the most profits on eBay, you need to get maximum exposure for your merchandise. One of the best ways to increase exposure is to open an eBay Store. An eBay Store is a web site that eBay lets you establish, and where you can sell items at a fixed price. The cost is only $9.95 per month for a basic subscription plus nominal listing fees. In contrast, setting up your own online web-based store with a web-hosting service might cost $50 a month or more.

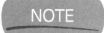
You need a minimum feedback of 20 and an ID Verify listing to open an eBay Store. The fees include the $9.95-per-month charge, a 5 cents-per-item listing fee, and a Final Value Fee of 5.25 percent for items priced at $25 or less.

Should You Open an eBay Store?

eBay claims that sellers who open eBay Stores see their sales increase substantially. I asked the sellers who were interviewed for this book (those who have eBay Stores) whether they found that to be the case, and in what way running a store helped their overall sales plan.

"I do think having an eBay Store boosts business," says Jennifer Karpin-Hobbs (User ID: morning-glorious). "I have noticed an increase in my bottom line since getting the store. The key is promoting it yourself in as many ways as possible. You need to draw buyers into your store, since the store listings do not appear in a general eBay search. For me, that kind of promotion means running lots of regular auctions with links in the descriptions designed to draw buyers looking for similar items into my store. If someone is bidding on a scarf, for example, I set up links that connect them to more scarves, jewelry or other complimentary items that the buyer may be interested in browsing. In addition, I include my store link in every e-mail message I send out, and it's on all my packing slips, as well."

"An eBay Store does help your business and is worth the minimal monthly fee, I believe," says Lori Baboulis of NYC Designs for Less, whose store is shown next. "Store sales do not happen overnight, but what does? With a lot of hard work and persistence, it will pay off."

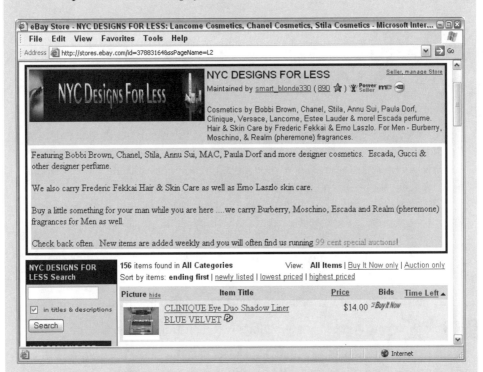

7

As far as increasing store sales, Lori advises: "Place prominent links in all your auction listings (such as "click here for more widgets in my eBay store") and you will start to see some results. Stores are excellent for sellers with multiple quantities of items. They are also great for organizations that sell a variety of items since an eBay Store allows you to put items in categories. Stores also encourage repeat buyers because they have one spot to search through all your items at their leisure. New buyers are great, but repeat buyers are free! One of the reasons I was able to take my part-time eBay business to full-time was a strong repeat customer base from which to draw. I do believe that this was aided significantly by my eBay store, which gives me a platform to showcase my entire inventory in one place."

Once you've got the preliminaries covered, go to the eBay Seller Landing page (http://pages.ebay.com/storefronts/seller-landing.html), and click the conspicuous OPEN STORE NOW! button.

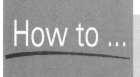

How to ... Create an eBay Store

Log in with your password, if you aren't logged in already, and click Sign In. Read the statement that says you are subject to the same user agreement that governs your auction sales. Then click Continue to connect to the Store Content page, where you begin to create your store.

The Store Content page presents you with a form that you fill out to locate your store and describe it to potential customers.

1. First, you select one of 14 main categories for your store. Pick the category you use most for your auctions—or choose Everything Else.

2. Enter your store's "brand name" in the Store name box.

3. Type your address in the Seller's Payment Information section.

4. Write a short (250 characters or less) description of your store in the Store description area. (You can add more information in Step 9 if you run out of space.)

CAUTION *You don't get much room to sell your store—each field in the Store Content page is limited to a small number of characters. If you really want as many words as you need to create your own store, opt for your own web site instead. Otherwise, type your content in Microsoft Word and count the number of characters using the program's Word Count feature (it's under the Tools menu).*

5. Fill out some additional information about what makes your store unique in the Store specialties box (you only get 200 words this time).

6. In the Custom store categories area, enter the types of sales categories under which your merchandise will be sold. Supposedly, these choices are optional. However, when you want to sell an item, you have to list it

under one of the categories you have already defined here. Do yourself a favor and come up with some categories under which your merchandise will be listed.

7. Specify your payment methods and ship-to locations, as well as your sales tax specifications.

8. In the Store Customer Service & Return policy box, type in any money-back guarantee, customer service numbers, return policies, or SquareTrade memberships you can boast. You have to enter 90 characters or less here, and the field is required.

9. Be sure to take advantage of the opportunity to sell yourself and your store even more in the Additional Store Information box. You get 200 more characters to tell people how long you've been selling on eBay, how long you've been in business, and so on.

10. Optionally, if you haven't created an About Me page, you get the chance to do so after the Additional Store Information box. The advantage of creating an About Me page here is that, when users click on your "About Me" logo, they'll be taken to your eBay Store, just as they would if they clicked on your "Stores" logo.

11. Choose colors for your eBay Store. Be sure to pick an accent color of some sort—black and white just looks too stark and uninviting for an online store.

12. Choose graphics for your store. If you already have an About Me page or a web page, you can simply choose one of your existing image files for your store. Otherwise, you have two choices: create a logo for your store, or use a predesigned eBay graphic. The predesigned images are overused and don't distinguish your store in any way. I strongly suggest that you create a logo as described later in this chapter.

Give yourself a pat on the back: you've created your store and now you can start selling on it.

7

TIP   *You can always change your store's category or description by clicking the Seller, Manage Store link on your store's home page.*

Listing Your Sales Items

Once you've made the decisions needed to create your eBay Store, you'll probably find listing items for sale a breeze, especially if you are already adept at putting up items for auction on eBay. The principles described in Chapter 3 for creating auction listings and Chapter 8 for creating good images apply. But there's one big difference: you don't have to worry about setting reserve prices or starting bids. You also don't have to worry about monitoring bids as they are placed. There aren't any bids at all; rather, you set a fixed price and the item is listed at that price for 30 days.

There are downsides to selling with an eBay Store. For one thing, the items you sell aren't retrieved by users who use eBay's popular Search page. They only appear in response to a Seller search. There's also no guarantee you'll get enough business to make the store worthwhile, and it takes work, time, and commitment. If you're already spending 10, 20, or 30 hours a week on your auctions, expect to add several hours more for your store. You've got to put new items up for sale regularly and ship items out quickly, just as you do with auctions.

Sold! Connecting Your Auctions to an About Me Page

One of the ways you can attract increased attention for your auctions is to make connections to them on a web page that eBay lets you create—an About Me web page. An About Me page is a web page that you can set up for free on eBay's web site. It promotes eBay as a community and gives you another place to advertise your sales listings.

When you create a page, you gain a new icon, a "me" logo that appears next to your User ID. If someone double-clicks your "me" icon, they'll be taken to your About Me page. Jill Featherston has a PowerSeller icon, a "me" icon, and an eBay Stores icon next to her User ID (see Figure 7-9).

Deciding What You Want to Include

What sort of information can you include on your About Me page? The best way to brainstorm for ideas to this question is to browse through the other About Me pages that eBay members have created. You might enter information like the following:

- Your User ID, your real name, or the name of your business
- Your most recent feedback

- A set of links to your current auctions

- Something about what you do on eBay—whether you sell on eBay full-time, and, if you don't, what you do for your "day job"

- What makes you a good seller and someone that buyers should trust

At its simplest level, an About Me page contains a little personal information about a member, what they collect or what they sell, and their level of knowledge or experience in a particular area. Many About Me pages are used to display photos of members and examples of the feedback they have received either as a buyer or a seller.

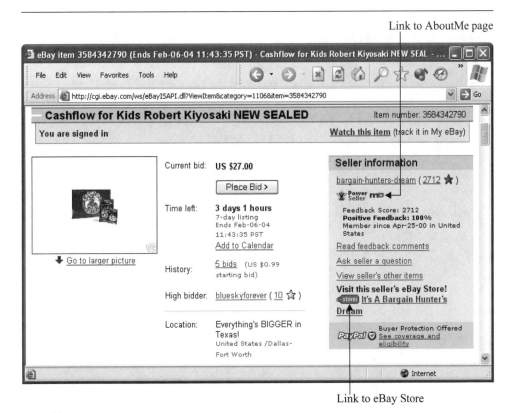

Link to AboutMe page

Link to eBay Store

FIGURE 7-9 When you create an About Me page, you get a link to the page next to your User ID.

Wally and Carole Rockawin, who sell on eBay under the User ID carole_wally, publish a short bit of biographical information on their About Me page (http://members .ebay.com/aboutme/carole_wally/), followed by examples of the most recent feedback they have received (see Figure 7-10).

For sellers, the big advantage of having an About Me page is the chance to publish links to your auctions along with information about why you are a reputable seller. Roni Neal (User ID roniheart) includes a photo and information about her family on her About Me page (http://members.ebay.com/aboutme/ roniheart/), along with links to each of her current eBay auctions. She even formats her links in the form of a web page feature called a table to give them more graphic interest (see Figure 7-11).

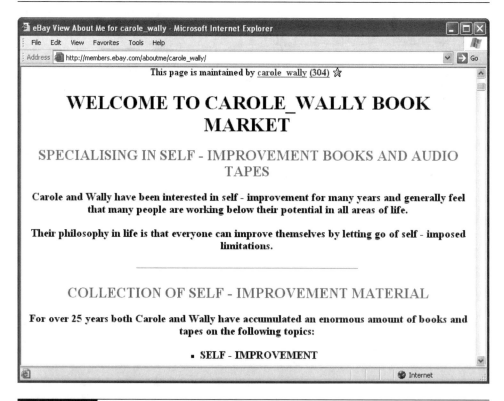

FIGURE 7-10   Many About Me pages provide personal background about buyers or sellers.

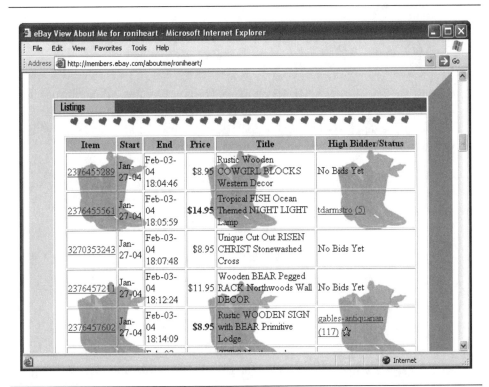

FIGURE 7-11   About Me pages give sellers a chance to present links to their current sales on eBay.

Still others use their About Me page to promote their eBay Store. Their About Me page is, in fact, a part of their eBay Store. If you click the eBay Stores logo or the "me" logo next to their User ID, you go to the About the Seller page in their eBay Store. Venus Rising Limited's About Me page (http://members.ebay.com/aboutme/venusrisinglimited/) is part of their eBay Store (http://stores.ebay.com/id=16897808), for example.

Creating Your Own About Me Page

One of the big advantages of About Me pages is that they are easy to produce. It only takes a few minutes. In fact, it's about as time-consuming as putting an auction listing online with the Sell Your Item form. Thus, there's no excuse not to create such a page: you become a part of the eBay community, and you increase the chances that someone will bid on one of your sales.

 **Create Your Own About Me Page**

You don't need to know HTML (HyperText Markup Language), the formatting language used to create web pages, nor do you need any special software. You just have to decide what you want to include on your page and a photo if you have one. Once you're ready, just follow these steps:

1. Make sure you're connected to the Internet, start up your web browser of choice, and enter the URL http://members.ebay.com/aw-cgi/eBayISAPI.dll?AboutMeLogin to go to the About Me login page.

TIP *You can also find the About Me login page by clicking My eBay and signing in with your User ID and password to go to your My eBay page. Click Preferences, and then click Create and Edit My Page.*

2. Read the instructions, and then click Create and Edit My Page.

3. When the About Me–Step 1 page appears, review the web page layouts available to you. Then click the button next to the arrangement you want: Two-column layout, Newspaper layout, or Centered Layout. The first two options are shown in Figure 7-12.

TIP *You might choose the two-column layout if you want to address a variety of different subjects, such as you, your family, your hobbies, and your business. The newspaper layout works well if you want to present various bits of information about the same topic (the different items you sell online, for instance). The centered arrangement is a good choice if your content—such as a brief description of your store—is short and sweet.*

4. When the About Me – Step 2 page appears, you fill out a form that helps create your page's contents. Choose a title for your page and add some information in each of the boxes. Also, select the option that indicates how many eBay feedback comments you want the page to contain. When you're ready, click Preview Your Page to see your page and make sure it looks the way you want it to.

5. If you don't like your page's layout, click Start Over to try one of the other two options. You'll be asked to confirm that you want to delete it by clicking Delete, and then you'll return to the About Me – Step 1 page where you can pick a different layout. Otherwise, if you're happy with your work, you can click Edit Some More, Save My Page, Edit Using HTML, or Start Over.

Once you click Save My Page, your page goes on the Web where everyone can see it. Be sure you're the first one to view your own About Me, so you can catch any mistakes you may have made. If you need to edit your page, return to the About Me Login page.

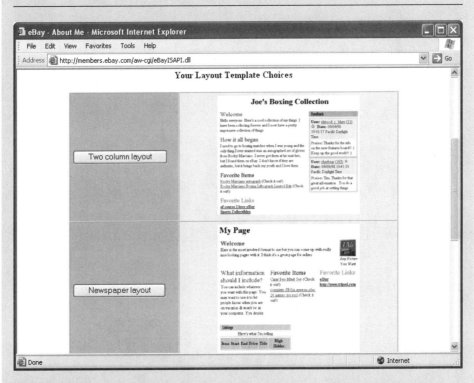

| FIGURE 7-12 | Pick the About Me layout option that matches your range of subjects. |

Where to Find It

Web Site	Address	What's There
Trading Assistants	http://contact.ebay.com/awcgi/eBayISAPI.dll?GetTAHubPage	Information about eBay's Trading Assistants program
Seller Landing Page	http://pages.ebay.com/storefronts/seller-landing.html	Resources for members who want to open or manage an eBay Store
About Me Login Page	http://members.ebay.com/aw-cgi/eBayISAPI.dll?AboutMeLogin	The first step in creating an About Me page

How to...

- Understand the qualities you need for eye-catching auction images
- Capture digital images of your merchandise
- Find a web site to host auction images
- Add images to your eBay sales descriptions
- Adjust images for optimal file size and appearance

When you scan a list of search results of category listings on eBay, what do you look at first? Chances are, your eye is drawn first to the images on that page. The title and the description hold your attention and prompt you to investigate. But what really gets you to place a bid? Have you ever bid on an auction for which there were no photos at all? Such auctions do occur on eBay all the time, and they do attract bids. But the inclusion of one or more good images is an essential element of a winning sales description.

The need to take good photos and present them in an attractive way can be intimidating to new sellers. The good news, however, is that it's getting easier all the time to obtain photos that are in the form of computer files (in other words, digital images) you can add to your auctions. This chapter describes what kinds of images you need to get, your options for taking them, and how to edit them so you can create sales descriptions that encourage bids.

What Makes a Good eBay Image?

eBay images are *digital* images. That doesn't mean you draw them with your finger (your digit). Digital images are also not the type you get back on photo paper or in the form of slides. Rather, they are images that consist of the digital information that computers can interpret. The first requirement for including an image with your auction listing, then, is to obtain images that are in the form of computer files. But any old computer file won't do.

In order to keep up with the many sellers who are becoming proficient at taking and editing digital photos, you need to do your best to present clear, sharp images that show an object in its most attractive light. The qualities your image needs to have are described in the following sections.

JPEG, GIF, and Other Image Formats

The colors and shapes in a computer image are saved in tiny bits of digital information called *pixels*. Each pixel in an image contains one or more bits (literally, data bits) that a computer program like a web browser can interpret. The amount of information that is saved, and the way it is saved, is determined by a formula that is part of an image format. Because your eBay images need to be in a format that a web browser can display, they need to be saved in one of three possible image formats:

- **Joint Photographic Experts Group (JPEG)**   This format compresses the digital information in an image to keep the file size small; it is especially designed for photos intended to be displayed on the Web.

- **Graphics Interchange Format (GIF)**   This format is best for use with line drawings rather than photos.

- **Portable Network Graphics (PNG)**   This format compresses files better than JPEG but is not yet in widespread use.

Another formula, Tagged Image File Format (TIFF), is good for saving digital images you want to print on photographic paper, but TIFF images aren't optimal for the Web because the colors cannot be accurately displayed by web browsers. Plus, the TIFF format produces large files.

Which format should you choose? It's really no contest. At this writing, eBay's own photo-hosting service, eBay Picture Services, only supports JPEG images. If you plan to save money and gain control over which images you include by using a hosting service other than eBay, you can save the images in PNG format. But JPEG is still the most popular format for images on the Web, so this chapter will assume that JPEG is what you're using.

NOTE   *JPEG compresses image files, but it provides you with several different levels of compression from which to choose. The higher the level of compression, the smaller the image file. But at maximum compression, you lose some information in the image, and the image doesn't appear as sharp as it can if you use a lower level of compression. If you're not sure which level to choose, try Medium compression to keep the file size small while maintaining image quality.*

8

Resolution, Contrast, and Other Image Qualities

Why are some digital images sharp and easy to look at while others appear rough and "pixelated" (in other words, you can see the individual pixels in the image)? One of several possible reasons is that the sharp ones contain more pixels. More pixels means more information, which means more detail. The more pixels you squeeze into a compressed space, the smaller those pixels have to be. The smaller the pixels, the sharper and more detailed the image appears.

Other reasons include a poor-quality scanner or digital camera, or an original image that is of poor quality. Yet another reason is the JPEG compression method, which eliminates some image information. The amount of digital information, in the form of pixels, that are contained in an image is described by the term *resolution*. Resolution, contrast, and other desirable qualities of eBay auction images are described in the sections that follow.

Resolution

For digital images, resolution is usually described in terms of pixels per inch (ppi) or dots per inch (dpi). You've probably heard the term "megapixel" used to describe the quality of a digital camera. "Megapixel" means a million pixels. A camera that has a 5-megapixel capacity has the capability to squeeze 5 million pixels into a single image, resulting in an image so sharp that it begins to rival the quality of many conventional cameras.

It's great to have a digital camera that has a multi-megapixel capacity if you can afford it. The high quality will come in handy if you want to print photos on glossy photographic paper and put them on your wall. But it's important to keep in mind that you don't need such quality for the images you hope to display on eBay or other web pages.

For one thing, images containing millions of pixels would likely be 300K to 800K in size, if not more. For another, all that information would be wasted on most computer monitors. Some of the huge, flat-panel monitors can display millions of pixels at once. But you can't count on most eBay shoppers having such high-tech toys.

After you have captured a high-quality digital image, you need to *downsample* that image for the Web at a low resolution: say, 72 dpi. The low resolution keeps the file size of the image small. Small file size for digital images is a desirable quality and is explored in more detail in the next section.

TIP

It's a good idea to scan a digital image at a higher resolution such as 300 dpi or take it with your digital camera at a resolution such as 5000×5000 pixels, then reduce the resolution to 72 dpi in the image-editing program that comes with your digital camera or scanner (or with another graphics editor). You can use the high-resolution version for personal photos, and the low-resolution version for the Web.

Contrast

Contrast is the difference between the light and dark areas in an image. Images that have a substantial amount of contrast, such as photos taken outdoors on bright sunny days, will scan better than images taken in a dimly lit basement. If you're not scanning, you want to make sure your eBay auction photos are adequately lit and that they have a sufficient amount of contrast as well.

Many sellers photograph their merchandise outdoors in order to let Mother Nature provide the lighting. Bright sunlight makes most objects easy to see, but it can create shadows in objects that have complex shapes. If you can, try to take your outdoors photos on a bright, cloudy day, which will provide you with good lighting while reducing, or even eliminating, shadows.

The image shown on the left in Figure 8-1 is an example of one with good contrast and lighting; the one on the right is too dark.

Cropping and Other Ways to Reduce File Size

Usually, things that are bigger in some way are automatically assumed to be better. When it comes to eBay, big bids are in, and big profits are good. Photos with big file sizes are *not* good, however. In order to understand why size makes a difference in this case, you first need to understand the difference between an image's physical size and its file size.

Physical Size

An image's physical size is its height and width, in inches or in another unit of measurement. Most eBay buyers and sellers will tell you that bigger is better in terms of photos: a bigger image lets you inspect more of the item being sold, after all. But if one of your images is wider than the viewer's browser window, it won't appear in its entirety at first glance.

In order to completely view an extra-wide image shown in Figure 8-2, the viewer has to click the scroll bar at the bottom of the browser window. This probably doesn't seem like a lot of work—and of course, it's not. But it doesn't look professional,

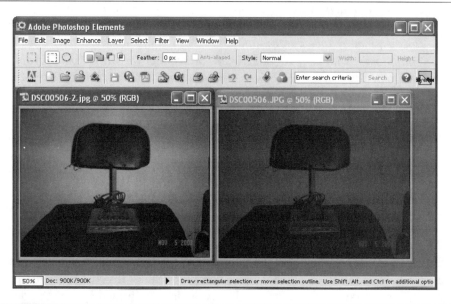

FIGURE 8-1   Make sure your auction images have good contrast and lighting; consider taking your photos outdoors.

and it's inconvenient to shoppers who don't have a big enough monitor to display the image fully.

It's important to remember that all shoppers don't have 19- or 21-inch monitors. They may have one of the newer flat-panel monitors but, because they cost more than conventional monitors, they might only have a 15- or 17-inch model. What size should your image be, ideally?

In Figure 8-2, I've drawn a maximum width measurement that seems manageable to me for a 17-inch monitor. The measurement assumes, of course, that the viewer has his or her browser window maximized to fit the width of the monitor, which may or may not be the case.

File Size

The file size of a digital image is the amount of memory it consumes on a storage disk. For images that are intended to be viewed on the Web, file size is a critical consideration. When someone views an image in a web browser, the JPEG, GIF, or PNG image is downloaded from the server on which the image file is hosted. The file goes into the user's computer, where it is put in a storage area called the web browser cache.

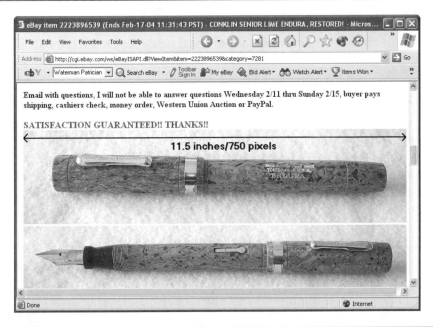

FIGURE 8-2   Limit your images to a height and width that will fit in most viewers' monitors.

The speed (or slowness) with which the image appears in a browser window is a function of the size of the image and the speed of the user's Internet connection. The smaller the file size, the faster the image will appear in the browser window. If you keep the image file's size small enough (say, 10K to 30K), it will appear quickly even over a relatively slow dialup modem connection.

Images that are 100K or more in size are generally undesirable because they will take too long to appear online. Compressing the files, as described earlier in this chapter in the section "JPEG, GIF, and Other Image Formats," will make files smaller so they can be transmitted more quickly. You can also reduce the file size in an image-editing program through cropping or by reducing the resolution, as described in "Tips for Editing Your Images" section later in this chapter.

Capturing Digital Images

The preceding sections described some of the qualities that enable an auction image to effectively enhance a good description. There is no substitute for scanning the images in the categories in which you plan to sell. See whether other sellers take photos outdoors or indoors. If inside, do they mount the object on a stand? Are there many close-up views? Once you have an idea of the kinds of images you need, it's time to actually create those images, as described in the following section.

Options for Capturing Images

When you take an image with a digital camera or scan a printed photo or drawing, you *capture* that image. Capturing an image means that you convert it from its original form—a real three-dimensional object, or tones on a piece of paper—into those bits of digital information called *pixels*. How do you capture those pesky pixels? You need access to a device that will gather them for you. Your options are described in the following sections.

Letting the Photo Lab Do the Work

If you don't want to buy a digital camera or scanner, you don't have to. Take pictures of your auction merchandise with your conventional camera. When you order prints from your photo lab, check the box that provides an extra copy of your photos on CD-ROM. When you get your photos back, you get both prints and the CD-ROM. The prints can go into your photo album (or, if you're like me, a very crowded cardboard box). The compact disc can go into your computer, and you can copy the photos you want to use in your auctions.

The advantage of letting the photo lab do the work is convenience: you don't have to purchase a camera or scanner and learn how to use it. But there's a big disadvantage: price. Those photo CDs can cost as much as $10 each. If you hold auctions regularly, you can quickly end up spending as much on photo developing as you would on an inexpensive digital camera.

In the long run, a digital camera or scanner is much more cost-effective. For the short term, before you purchase a camera, turn to a photo lab. Table 8-1 lists some suggestions of low-cost photo-developing services that will provide you with CDs.

Photo lab	Cost for CD	URL
Shutterfly	$9.99 for up to 50 photos	www.shutterfly.com
Photothru.com	$8.40 for 24–27 prints; CD included	www.photothru.com
Snapfish	$4.99 for a set of prints; photos also posted online for free	www.snapfish.com

TABLE 8-1   Photo CD Options

 *The phrase "posted online," as mentioned in the listing for Snapfish, means that your photos are placed on the Web where you can view and copy them to your computer. You can also share them with family members and friends. You can make a link to your Snapfish-hosted image from one of your auctions. It's free to set up an account with Snapfish, too.*

Using a Digital Camera

For an ever-increasing number of eBay sellers, the most practical and affordable option is to use a digital camera to photograph sales merchandise. The camera saves the image directly to computer disk. In other words, you don't have to mail your film to a photo lab, you don't have to wait a day or even an hour to get your pictures back. In just a matter of minutes, you can transfer your photo files from your camera to your computer.

Digital cameras, like the one shown in Figure 8-3, are becoming more affordable all the time; you can take as many photos as you want and transfer them to your computer in a matter of seconds.

8

FIGURE 8-3 Digital cameras give you instant results at an increasingly affordable price.

Perhaps the most important piece of equipment you can obtain in conjunction with your digital camera is not a light, a memory stick, or a tripod. It's a special macro feature that either comes built-in with a camera or needs to be added in the form of a macro lens. A macro setting or macro lens is indispensable for close-ups of small objects, as well as details of larger objects. It's the best way to get images as sharp and clear as those seen in Figure 8-4.

TIP   *Some high-quality digital video cameras can capture still images that are high enough in resolution to put on the Web. In the past, still images captured with a digital video camera were fuzzy and of generally poor quality.*

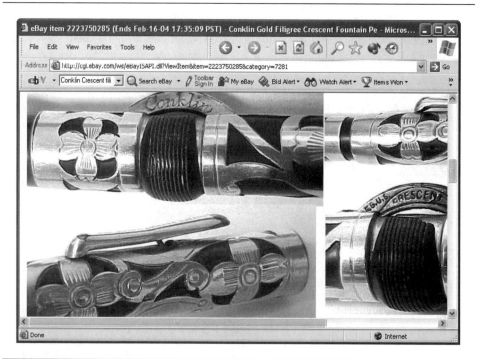

FIGURE 8-4   A macro lens will help provide sharp close-ups that can encourage shoppers to bid.

Voices from the Community

The Benefits of Digital Cameras

I don't know if there are any studies of how eBay sellers take photos of their sales items, but my gut feeling is that a clear majority use digital cameras. What kind of digital camera should you buy? Luckily, prices have decreased dramatically. What kinds of cameras do the experienced sellers interviewed for this book choose, and what qualities do they propose you look for? Here are some suggestions:

Roni Neal: "I have a Fuji Finepix S5000, but you can do just as well with much cheaper cameras. Any digital camera will work well, but you must have macro capabilities."

Suzanne Ziesche and Shannon Miller: "The best investment a seller can make, in terms of images, is the purchase of a good-quality digital camera. It is not necessary to invest a large amount of money in such a purchase, as many great cameras are available at reasonable prices. A minimum 2.0 megapixel camera is recommended, preferably with a 'Plug-and-Play' USB interface that enables quick and simple file transfer."

Emily Sabako: "I realized that my two main competitors for my most expensive line had much better photos than I did, so I went out and bought a Canon G3 PowerShot for around $500. I just think your camera is your business and it has paid for itself ten times over. Your camera must have good macro capabilities and a good light sensor."

Jennifer Karpin-Hobbs: "I have a Nikon digital camera, and I take indoor photos with a simple background (such as a lace tablecloth beneath a plate) with a fill flash. I try to show as much detail as possible. When the weather is nice, I take items outside and photograph them on the porch in bright shade, to eliminate harsh shadows."

Scanning Your Images

Sometimes, a digital camera is not the best tool for capturing images of your merchandise. Wally Rockawin, the Australian seller interviewed for this book, uses a scanner. Why? He sells books on eBay. Books, postcards, magazines, posters, and photos are all perfect subjects for scanning.

A scanner is a piece of hardware that connects to your computer and that works much like a photocopier. The scanner scans the object placed on a glass bed with a special lens. But instead of outputting the image to paper like a photocopier, the output goes to your computer, where you can preview it using software provided with the scanner. You can then save the image to disk so you can use it in your auctions.

Scanners (like the flatbed model shown in Figure 8-5) are less expensive than digital cameras—you can find them at Buy It Now prices of $40 to $60. You can also rent time on a scanner at a branch of Kinko's Copies. Or you can borrow a friend's scanning device. Simply take a conventional photo of an object with a camera and scan the image to convert it to the computer file.

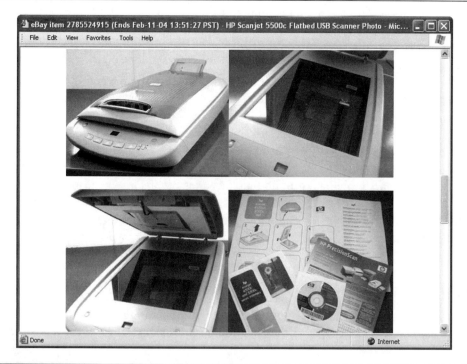

FIGURE 8-5   Scanners are better than digital cameras when it comes to capturing books, cards, or other flat objects.

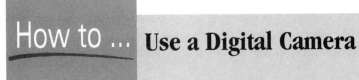 **Use a Digital Camera**

While scanners are pretty much office-bound, digital cameras can be carried around easily and used to capture candid scenes outdoors or in. Many digital cameras make taking a photo a simple matter of pointing and shooting.

1. Before you start, you may need to decide what media you are going to use to store your image. Some digital cameras let you choose between saving images in the camera's internal memory or on a small flash memory card (a small device, about half the size of a stick of gum, that can store your photos and easily transfer them to your computer). Once you have specified which storage method you're going to use, equipped the camera with a battery, and given your camera's instruction manual a read-through, you're ready to get started.

2. Almost all digital cameras give you the option of either looking through the Liquid Crystal Display (LCD), the miniature screen that lets you preview images, or the viewfinder (the little window on the back of the camera). Use the LCD whenever possible because it's more precise. But remember that the little framing square that's supposed to indicate what's going to be in the final image isn't perfect. Rather than framing everything so it's right up to the edge of the frame, leave some extra room around the edges (see the illustration).

8

3. Once you have the image framed the way you want, you can take the image and preview it. You can then simply throw out the image if it isn't quite right.

> **TIP** *Most digital cameras don't let you focus manually. They use a focal area in the middle of the image that controls the focus. If you don't have your image centered quite right, it might not be in focus. Reposition it and reshoot if you're in doubt—or consult your camera's manual to see if you can turn off auto-focus lock so your subject does not have to be in the middle of the frame in order to be in focus.*

4. Save the image to your chosen storage media.

5. Transfer the image to your computer. The option you choose depends on your camera as well as your selected storage method.

Once you have the image on disk, you can open it in your graphics-editing program of choice. This enables you to crop the image and adjust qualities like contrast and brightness, as described in "Tips for Editing Your Images" later in this chapter.

> **CAUTION** *One source of digital photos is not discussed in this section because it's not recommended. Don't simply try to reuse someone else's photos, even if they are something that is identical to your own item. You can end up with an angry e-mail from the person who originally took the image, as well as negative feedback.*

Arranging and Lighting Your Merchandise

You've probably seen photos of auction items that look like they were taken in a cluttered basement or garage. The item sits in the foreground, barely distinguishable from the lawn rakes, tools, brooms, boxes, and other debris filling up the background. For some rare and beautiful objects, a "busy" background won't detract from the value or discourage bidders. But borderline objects that aren't especially rare or valuable need all the help they can get. Positioning them alone against a solid background can make a big difference.

 **Use a Scanner**

Every scanner comes with software that you install on your computer and that enables you to preview and control how the scanning is done. Sometimes the software works as a stand-alone application; other times, the software acts as a plug-in: it works within another graphics application such as the powerful drawing and editing program, Adobe Photoshop. After you install the program, start it up, turn on your scanner, and follow these steps:

1. Make a preview scan of your image. Position the image on the scanning bed, close the cover, and press the Preview button in your scanning software. The scan should appear in the software in a matter of minutes. Previewing lets you see the image before you make the final scan.

2. Adjust contrast and brightness before making the scan, if you need to. Use the Crop tool to select the part of the image you want to use in the final scan—in most cases, you're not going to use the entire space available, but only the area that is taken up by the photo or other object you're scanning.

3. Select an input mode. An input mode tells the scanner how you want the information in the image to be captured. For most auction images, you'll choose the Color option. However, if what you're scanning is a black and white photo, you can reduce the file size dramatically by choosing Grayscale mode. On the other hand, if you're scanning line art, a signature, a cartoon, or another drawing, use Line Art mode.

4. Set the resolution. Since you're scanning auction images for the Web, choose a higher resolution such as 300 dots per inch (dpi). Then you can downsample the image to 72 dpi.

5. Make adjustments. All scanning software comes with brightness and contrast controls that you can move to see if the image improves. You can do this later using image-editing software, but why not save yourself the work by making improvements at the scanning stage?

8

When you're done with all the preparation work, you can press the Scan button and finally scan your image.

> **TIP** *It's a good idea to calibrate your scanner before you start making scans. Calibrating means that you match the scanner to your monitor so that your image previews are accurate. The exact procedure differs from scanner to scanner. But in general, you make a test scan of an image. Next, you use your scanning software's calibration controls. The exact menu options vary depending on the software used.*

Should you use a photo lab, a scanner, or a digital camera for your auction images? It isn't necessarily an either-or proposition. If you can find a scanner for $50, a digital camera for $250, and get your conventional images on CD or posted on the Web for free when you get prints made, you haven't made a huge investment. You then have the flexibility to choose an option based on your budget and your needs.

If you only plan to put a few auctions online once in a while, you can take photos with a conventional camera and have a photo lab convert your images to digital files. When you want to capture flat objects such as magazines, use your scanner. For everything else, use a digital camera.

> **TIP** *eBay's Photos/HTML discussion board is a good place to get advice from eBay sellers on what digital cameras to use and how to use them. Click Community in the eBay navigation bar, then click Photos/HTML under the Community Help Boards heading to find this group.*

Creating a Home Photo Studio

If you plan to photograph a lot of auction items in the comfort of your home, consider setting up a miniature photo studio in a spare room or a corner of a room. A studio should have a table on which you can place your merchandise. (Larger items can go in front of the table.) For small objects such as watches, earrings, and other jewelry, buy a display stand. You don't have to look far to find some at reasonable prices: just search eBay itself (see Figure 8-6).

One of the best things you can buy for your home photo studio is a solid- colored drape or sheet that can function as a background. You don't want shoppers to be distracted or to make judgments on you based on stains or cracks in your walls. Be sure to get at least two different colors of backgrounds—a dark one for lighter objects, and a light one for darker objects. The greater the contrast between the object and the background, the greater the likelihood that it will sell.

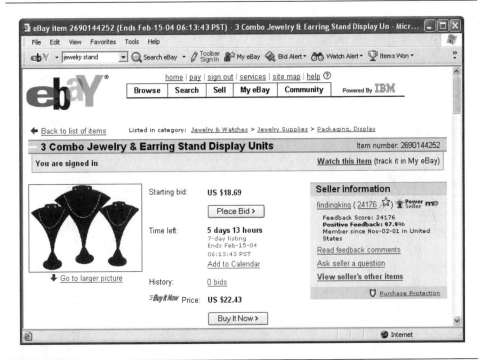

FIGURE 8-6   Buy stands for jewelry and other small items on eBay itself.

Lighting Your Merchandise

You can tell when a photo has been lighted using an overhead kitchen light and the feeble flash from a digital camera. Such images are almost inevitably dim and plagued by shadows. The problem is that the built-in flash on a digital camera comes from only one direction and is apt to leave shadows around the edges of what you're photographing. Two or three good studio lights with umbrellas to diffuse the light, like the devices shown in Figure 8-7, will do the trick.

What can happen if you fail to diffuse or balance the light shining on the object you want to sell (especially if it's an object with an especially shiny or reflective surface)? No disasters will occur. However, you will probably have to answer questions from curious bidders.

An example is shown in Figure 8-8. The text indicates that the seller has received a number of questions as a result of the too-bright flash pointed directly at the guitar for sale. The bright light has distorted the color and revealed some fingerprints that appear to be flaws.

FIGURE 8-7   Professional studio lights will pay off in the long run.

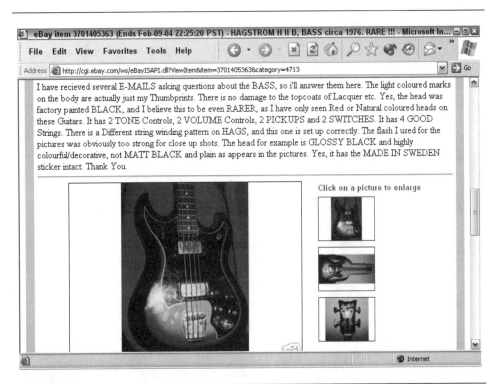

FIGURE 8-8   Be careful when you use a flash to light shiny or reflective surfaces, otherwise light "flares" may result.

Finding a Host for Your Images

Everything you see on the Web comes to your browser from a computer that has been equipped with server software, and which functions as a web server. Most web sites (except those that are hosted by on someone's home computer) are contained on servers that are located at big Internet service providers and are connected to the Internet round the clock over fast connections.

If you want your auction images to appear on the Web, you need to move them from your computer to a company with a web server that will provide you with disk space. Such a company functions as a web host. When you place your image on the space provided by your host, you make a link to it from your auction description when you fill out the Sell Your Item form (see Chapter 8). Some suggestions on where to find a host, and what makes a good host, are described in the sections that follow.

eBay Picture Services

The first hosting option for many eBay users is eBay itself. eBay provides all sellers with the ability to *upload* (a computer term that describes the process of moving a file from a computer to a server on a network) photos easily onto its own servers right from the Sell Your Item form. The form even gives you an interactive way to crop and reorient images (if you use the full-featured version of Picture Services as described next).

Yet, many sellers turn to other photo hosting options when they begin to add images to their auctions. Why? Here are two common reasons:

■ eBay Picture Services lets you add one photo to an auction for free. After that, each image costs 15 cents. Suppose you put 25 items up for sale each week, and each sale has five photos. That's 125 photos, 100 of which cost a total of $15. Spread that over 50 weeks or so, and you've paid $750 annually to eBay for photo hosting.

■ You may already have space available on a server where you can store your images. If you have an account with America Online, you can create up to seven usernames, and each of those usernames is entitled to 2MB of space for web pages and photos. Virtually all ISPs provide web server space to their customers along with their Internet access. You don't have to pay anything for this storage space.

Still, eBay Picture Services is a convenient and cost-effective way to get at least one image online, along with your auction descriptions. If you're just starting out and you only want to include one or two images with a listing, eBay's two versions of Picture Services represent a good choice.

eBay Basic Picture Services

When you first connect to the Sell Your Item form (a process described in detail in Chapter 7) and you get to the Step 3 of 5 pages, you scroll down to the section labeled Add Pictures, which is where you identify the photos you want to add to the auction description you are creating. By default, you view the basic version of eBay Picture Services (see Figure 8-9).

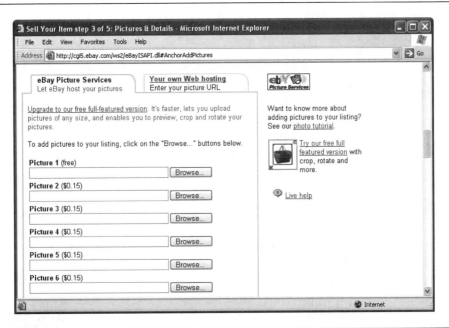

FIGURE 8-9 eBay's basic Picture Services lets you choose and add photos without any fuss or complexity.

Basic Picture Services is easy to use:

1. Click Browse next to Picture 1. The Choose File dialog box opens.

2. Click the Look In drop-down list at the top of the dialog box and locate the image file you want to add to your auction.

3. Click Open. The Choose file dialog box closes, and the path leading to the file on your computer (for instance, C:\My Documents\My Pictures\ imagefile.jpg) appears in the box labeled Picture 1.

4. Repeat Steps 2 and 3 for any other images you want to add to this auction (Picture 2, Picture 3, and so on).

When you're done, you can go on to select any special features, such as slideshows, supersize images, or Gallery images.

The Gallery and Other Special Features

Once you have identified the images you want to add to your auction, you can select special ways to present those images. Under the Picture Layout heading (just beneath the Add Pictures section), you can specify whether to create a slideshow of your images or to "supersize" them. Click the Slideshow or Supersize links in the yellow column on the right-hand side of the Sell Your Item form to see examples of these treatments.

A more eye-catching and important extra feature is a Gallery image. This is an image that you choose for special attention. It can be one of the images you added earlier or a completely different one. The Gallery is a collection of images that auction sellers submit of items they're currently offering for sale. Buyers can browse through the images and click one in which they're interested; clicking the image takes them to the auction sales page where they can read a description and place a bid if they so choose.

The Gallery doesn't display all the images that accompany auction listings—only the ones for which sellers pay the extra 25-cent fee for extra exposure in the Gallery. (You can splurge and pay $19.95 to place your image in a featured area of the Gallery as well.)

TIP *You can create a link to your own Gallery page that you can include on your web site or About Me page. Be sure to replace the eBayUserID string with your own user ID:*
<a href=http://search-desc.ebay.com/search/search.dll?MfcISAPICommand=GetResult&query=eBayUserID&srchdesc=y&ebaytag1=ebayreg&ebaytag1code=0&ht=1&SortProperty=MetaEndSort&sc=1&st=2> Click here to view my Gallery auctions </a>.

Perhaps the best thing about Gallery images is the fact that they are added to your auction titles when those titles are listed in search results or when people browse through categories in which your sales are listed. In my opinion, Gallery images always attract more attention for the auctions in which they appear (see the illustration).

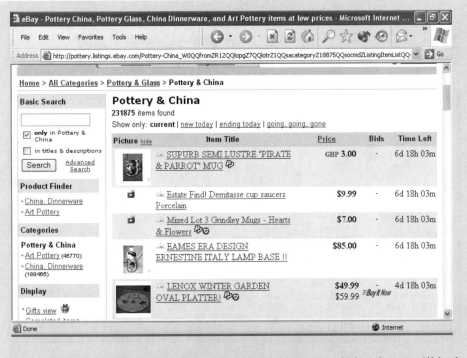

Because so many other sellers add Gallery images to their sales, you'll look out of place if you don't have one. Unless your item is rare or valuable on its own, you should strongly consider adding a Gallery image. Browse through some auction listings yourself to see if they catch your attention compared to the sales that don't have miniature images next to the title.

Picture Services: The Full-Featured Version

You get access to a wider range of functions when you use the full-featured version of eBay Picture Services. You choose photos and upload them to eBay, just as you do with Basic Services. But you can make adjustments such as the following:

To get access to the full-featured version of Picture Services, click the link Try Our Free, Full-Featured Version in the yellow column on the right-hand side of the Sell Your Item form. The Add Picture section of the form reloads with a new layout— a series of squares. Click the Add Picture button under the heading First Picture–Free. The photo is copied from your computer and appears in the square (see Figure 8-10).

Click here to crop image   Click here to rotate image

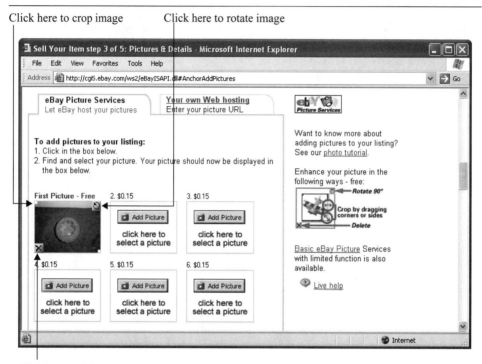

Click here to delete image

FIGURE 8-10   The full-featured version of Picture Services lets you crop images before listing your auction.

NOTE   *You can also copy files from your computer to the Add Pictures section of the Sell Your Item form by dragging the image file's icon into the appropriate image square.*

If you want to crop the image, click the arrow in the upper right-hand corner of the image and drag it toward the center. A cropping rectangle appears (see Figure 8-11). Drag it inward until the image is cropped the way you want.

NOTE   *The full-featured version of Picture Services works only with Windows systems; the basic Picture Services works with Macintosh or Windows.*

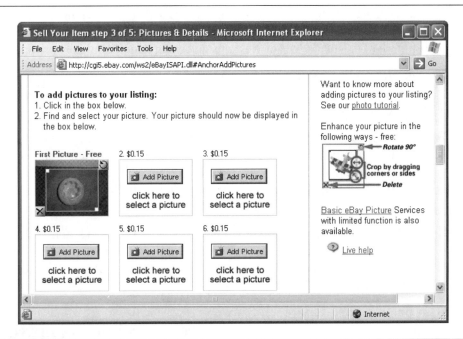

FIGURE 8-11   You can crop a photo in the Sell Your Item form without having to use a graphics editor.

Other Image-Hosting Services

It pays to shop around when looking for a web server that your auction images can call home. After all, if your images don't appear reliably and quickly, your bidders might well leave your sale and bid on someone else's items. Another consideration is the software you use to get your images from your computer to the web storage space. You may have to use a particular program that does the transfer by using a special set of instructions called File Transfer Protocol (FTP).

Other services (such as AOL) provide such software for you. If you use one of the auction management packages mentioned in Chapter 6, you don't have to install special software, either; the transfer utility is provided as part of the service's user interface. The following list describes some of the types of web hosts you can use to make your auction image files available online:

■   **Your own ISP**   The first place to turn is to the company that gives you access to the Internet: your Internet service provider (ISP). Providing users with access to the Internet and hosting web sites are two different functions, certainly, but the same organization may do both. Many ISPs provide you with use of at least 10MB of web site space at no additional cost to you.

- **America Online (AOL)**   AOL enables subscribers to create and publish their own web pages or to place simple image files on the Web. It's quite popular with sellers on eBay and other auction services.

- **A web-hosting service**   The same web-hosting services that publish your web sites give you space that can be used for posting images and web pages alike. One of the least expensive, Deadzoom (www.deadzoom.com), gives you 10MB of hosting space and one gigabyte worth of data transfer per month for $5 per month.

- **An auction management service**   Most services that help you manage your auction sales, such as ManageAuctions.com (www.manageauctions.com) and AuctionHelper.com (www.auctionhelper.com) make it easy to upload your image files.

- **A photo-hosting service**   A few web sites specialize in providing space where eBay and other auction users can publish auction images to accompany sales listings. Deadzoom.com (www.deadzoom.com) costs $5 per month for 10MB of server space, which is more than enough for thousands of auction images. No eBay Motors images are allowed, however. A few free services also exist: Auction-Images (http://auction-images.com) gives you 1MB of space for free (eBay Motors images are not allowed here as well, however).

After you create a digital image and add it to your host site, you add that image to your sales description by specifying the URL for the image on the eBay Sell Your Item form. All ISPs provide customers with instructions on how to figure out their web page URLs. Call the Customer Service section of your ISP, or check the company's FAQ. A common convention is to assign a URL that looks like this:

```
http://www.yourISP.com/~yourusername/filename.jpg
```

After posting an image online, verify that it actually appears on your page. The commonest cause of a broken image or question mark icon appearing with your description instead of the image itself is an incorrect URL. If you're typing the URL from scratch, you must get it right exactly: A single blank space, capital letter, or typo in a URL can prevent a web browser from locating the image and displaying it onscreen.

Tips for Editing Your Images

Often, images aren't good if you capture them straight from your scanner, digital camera, or other input device. Instead, after you save your image in JPEG or PNG format, you can then edit (or, in photographic terms, *retouch*) the image in a graphics program to improve its appearance.

Personally, I like a program called Adobe Photoshop Elements, which, I'm happy to say, comes bundled with many digital cameras. If you get this software along with your camera, you've got a great deal. The following sections describe the kinds of things you should adjust with Photoshop Elements or another graphics program.

Adjusting Contrast and Brightness

The *contrast* of an image is the degree of difference between its light and dark tones. *Brightness* refers to the vibrancy or energy of the colors or shades of color in the image. Images displaying adequate levels of contrast and brightness are easier to view on a monitor.

Photoshop Elements includes menu options that adjust a photo's contrast and brightness automatically. Elements also provides you with controls for making manual adjustments, such as the dialog box shown in the following illustration.

Resizing Images

Resize images so that they're smaller than originally scanned and fit well on the eBay auction web page. (Look through your graphics program's menus to find a resize option.)

Generally speaking, an image that's two or three inches wide and perhaps four to five inches tall is a good size. File sizes of 20 to 30K or less are also desirable.

Cropping to Focus on What's Important

Cropping refers to the practice of cutting out unnecessary details and keeping a certain area of the image on which you want to focus. It makes the image size smaller so that the photo fits better in a web browser window. By making the image smaller, you also make the file size smaller. An image that's, say, 12K in size appears onscreen much faster than does one that's 100K in size.

In virtually every graphics program, the process of cropping works the same. You click the Crop tool, position your mouse pointer just above and to one side of the image, click and hold down your mouse button, and drag your mouse down and to the opposite side of the image. Release your mouse when the subject of your photo is outlined with the marquee box.

Where to Find It

Web Site	Address	What's There
Snapfish	www.snapfish.com	An affordable service that provides you with digital versions of your conventional photos
ManageAuctions.com	www.manageauctions.com	A service that manages auctions and hosts auction image files
Deadzoom.com	www.deadzoom.com	An economical service that many eBay members use for image hosting

Chapter 9

Finalizing Sales

How to...

- Accept electronic payments from your customers

- Offer "Anything Points" to potential buyers

- Establish a credit card merchant account

- Protect what you pack to insure your transaction

- Ship your merchandise quickly and cost-effectively

When sellers first start out on eBay, they put their attention into the parts of the sale that matter most: getting bids and receiving payment. Payment is one of the most important parts of a transaction. But in some ways, it's not an activity that sellers can control. Once they set up a payment option, it's up to the buyer to follow through with handing over the money. Because of this, eBay, along with its payment service, PayPal, have taken some important steps toward making the payment process run smoothly.

It's easy to overlook the activities that happen after payment is received—namely, packing and shipping. This is a process over which sellers can exert a good deal of control, and the way they are handled can make the difference between a successful transaction that generates positive feedback from the buyer, and a ruined deal that ends up in returned merchandise, a refund, and neutral or negative feedback. This chapter examines the important activities that occur after a sale is made—checkout, payment, packing, and shipping—and gives you an overview of how to ensure, to the best of your ability, that everything runs smoothly so both you and the buyer end up satisfied.

Accepting Online Payments

Chances are you've held a garage sale at least once in your life. If you have, you know how simple the payment process is. You sit behind a card table with a little cash box next to you, and people literally come to you with their money as they purchase, or perhaps haggle over, one thing after another. At the end of the day, you've hopefully got a tidy sum you can sock away in the bank or use at a nice restaurant.

Making the move from conducting in-person sales to online auctions isn't quite as simple. When you sell on eBay or on your own web site, you don't have personal contact with your customer. You can't look people in the eye, watch them sign a charge slip, or inspect their identification. You can, however, rely on various services to help you receive the payments you want and deserve. eBay, PayPal, credit card merchants, and other online payment services all have it in their interest to make the Internet a safe place to do business.

It's important to remember that the vast majority of people you encounter on eBay are not out to "get you." Most transactions go through smoothly, without problems. If they didn't, eBay just wouldn't run smoothly and it wouldn't be so popular. If you follow the safety procedures set up by these organizations and are aware of the ways in which unscrupulous individuals may try to defraud you, the chances are good that you'll have smooth sailing as an eBay seller.

Should You Accept Checks?

Computers and the Internet are making paper obsolete, in many cases. It's natural to ask, then, whether you should receive payment from bidders and buyers is in the form of a piece of paper—a check or money order. It's hard to beat these two options for simplicity and reliability. When you're just starting out, you should definitely include them among your payment options. But you have to remember to choose them.

In Step 4 of the Sell Your Item form (shown in Figure 9-1), the option for PayPal (the payment service that's affiliated with eBay) is checked. But the options to accept

9

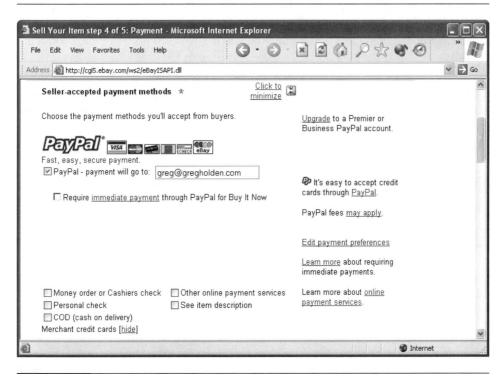

FIGURE 9-1   Be sure to select the options for checks and money orders; they aren't preselected.

checks or money orders are unchecked. You should check them to keep things easy and reliable for yourself and your customers.

Accepting personal checks can make you more attractive to bidders. Doing business on the computer was what attracted them to you in the first place, so they are likely to be grateful that they avoided standing in a line in a post office or currency exchange to buy a money order. But you don't want to be the one left in the lurch when the law of averages dictates that it's time for someone to try to float a bad personal check.

The most obvious solution is to not send out your item until the personal check clears the bank and you're sure you have your money. That's a common provision to make in auction terms. You might also consider stating that you'll accept personal checks only from buyers who have positive feedback ratings of, say, more than 100.

Cashier's Checks and Money Orders

Cashier's checks are one of the most secure forms of payment you can receive. As soon as the customer obtains one from a bank, the money is debited from his or her account—in other words, you don't have to wait for such a check to "clear" when it arrives. However, cashier's checks are pricey. They carry a service charge that ranges from $3 to $5, so you can't blame your customers if they don't want to send you a cashier's check. Because of this, you should be sure to provide other options as well.

Money orders, too, usually carry a service charge when obtained from a bank. The fee can be anywhere between $1 and $3. However, money orders can be obtained less expensively from a wide variety of sources. In fact, if you look around your own neighborhood, you're liable to find currency exchanges and stores that issue money orders. Some of these options are listed in Table 9-1.

Money Order Source	Fee for $20 Money Order	Fee for $100 Money Order
Western Union BidPay.com	$2.95	$5
United States Post Office	$0.90	$0.90
Payko	$3.99	$8.89
c2it by Citibank	$0.40 in U.S. ($10 international)	$2 in U.S. ($10 international)

TABLE 9-1   Fees for Money Orders

Getting Started With PayPal

Based on my own experience and on what other eBay users tell me, PayPal is the type of payment that most sellers look for when they are trying to decide whether to bid on an eBay auction or make a fixed-price purchase. For buyers, this electronic payment service satisfies the need for speed: they don't have to go to the bank or post office to get a money order, they can instead transfer money with just a few mouse clicks and receive shipment quicker than they would otherwise. Some important aspects of working with PayPal are described in the sections that follow.

PayPal started out as a small payment service that was separate from eBay, but like eBay, it grew largely by word of mouth, and buyers and sellers have come to trust it and use it widely. In fact, the service became so popular that eBay purchased PayPal and used it to replace its own payment service. All this should reinforce your convictions that PayPal is reputable and can make your transactions more secure.

NOTE *Many eBay members strongly dislike PayPal. They object to the fees PayPal charges, and they cite complaints made by PayPal customers who contend that PayPal fails to pay out refunds or investigate fraud complaints. Before deciding to use PayPal yourself, you may want to find out what all the fuss is about by visiting web sites such as PayPalSucks (www.paypalsucks.com).*

9

Did you know?   Anything Points: As Good as Money?

You're probably familiar with frequent flyer miles: If you use an airline, you earn miles that can be used on subsequent flights. Anything Points is a similar type of incentive program that eBay created to give buyers an extra inducement to push that Place Bid or Buy It Now button. If you join the Anything Points program, you can offer this extra benefit to buyers.

When buyers purchase something from a seller who offers Anything Points, a certain number of points is stored in the buyer's PayPal account. (The program is only available to buyers who use PayPal to pay for items.) The points can then be used for future purchases on eBay that are made with PayPal.

The exact number of Anything Points that a buyer can earn is determined by the seller. Each seller offers a certain number of points per dollar. The number of points you earn is based on the final sale price. For instance, if a seller offers two Anything Points per dollar and the final sale price is $50, you earn 100 Anything Points. "So what?" you ask. Those points can save you money later on. Each point earns you one cent toward a purchase on eBay. That might not seem like a lot, but if you accumulate 1000 points, you can buy something for $10 through PayPal, using your points, and essentially get it for free.

In order to claim your points and use them toward future purchases, you need to open up a free Anything Points account with PayPal. (Actually, you should open an Anything Points account even if you already have a PayPal account.) You do this by filling out a form on the Anything Points home page (http:// anythingpoints.ebay.com/), shown next.

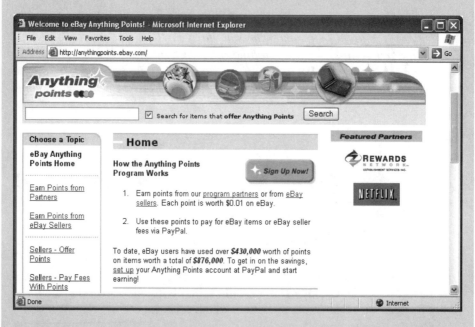

Sellers also need to register on the Anything Points site to offer Anything Points. To do so, click the Offer Manager link on the home page and sign in with your username and password. The Offer Manager page appears. That's all you need to do to register. To actually offer points, you click the Offer Points tab in

Offer Manager and enter the item number of the item you have currently for sale to which you want to add the points. Once you have added Anything Points to an item, a special logo and photo are automatically added to the auction description. An example is shown next.

You don't have to offer Anything Points on everything you sell, by the way. You also may want to choose carefully how many points you actually offer because you are charged one cent per point. For example, if you offer 3 points per dollar on an item that sells for $100, the buyer earns 300 Anything Points, and you have to pay a $3 fee to eBay.

Credit Cards and PayPal

One of the best advantages of using PayPal, for both buyers and sellers, is speed. If a buyer has a credit card on file with PayPal, he or she can transfer payment in a matter of minutes after the auction ends (provided the seller gets payment and shipping costs to you quickly enough). The seller can get paid right away, and the merchandise can be out the door in a matter of hours. Sellers who accept PayPal often add the following note to their sales descriptions:

```
PayPal payments can be made immediately at the end of the auction.
Please include your eBay auction number and your eBay username with
payment.
```

PayPal is best known as a service that allows buyers to transfer auction payments to sellers using their credit cards. (Buyers can also make automatic deductions from their checking accounts, as described in the upcoming "eChecks and PayPal" section.) The system requires that both buyer and seller have PayPal accounts. The process works like this:

1. A buyer establishes an account with PayPal. The account includes the name and address of the buyer as well as payment information. If the buyer wants to use his or her credit card to send payments, the number and other account information is put on file with PayPal.

2. When the buyer purchases something at auction, the total cost is sent either through eBay's automated Checkout system or by the seller.

3. The buyer logs on to PayPal using his or her predetermined password and username, and then authorizes the transfer to a seller.

4. PayPal charges the buyer's credit card (or debits the buyer's checking account) and transfers payment to the seller's PayPal account.

Sellers never work directly with the buyer's credit card information. They don't have to go through the effort of setting up a merchant account that would otherwise enable them to handle credit card payments. They also don't have to worry about verifying the buyer's identity. PayPal functions as a go-between, moving the payment from buyer to seller. For its services, PayPal charges a fee to sellers (see the "How to Set Up a PayPal Account" section later in this chapter); buyers aren't charged.

eChecks and PayPal

PayPal buyers don't necessarily have to have funds charged to their credit cards when they make payments. They can also receive eChecks. The term "eCheck" is short for electronic check. It simply means that, instead of having purchase money charged to a credit card account, it is deducted from the buyer's checking account. The process should be familiar to anyone who uses debit cards.

People who accept eChecks should make buyers aware of the extra time needed to process them. If you've used a debit card to make a purchase, you may have discovered that you can use the card even if your account does not have sufficient funds. eChecks can "bounce" just like regular checks. For that reason, sellers typically include a note like this in their auction description:

```
An eCheck is also acceptable but must first clear prior to shipment
of goods. This will delay the shipment.
```

The threat of eChecks bouncing should not discourage you from accepting them. Just use your common sense, and wait five days to a week to make sure the eCheck clears before you ship out the item. You'll know when the eCheck has cleared, because only then will the money be released to your account. PayPal requests an eCheck from the buyer's bank immediately upon request. But it can take four to five days before the bank actually releases the funds.

PayPal Account Options

If you're a PayPal seller, you can accept credit payments for auction sales on an e-commerce web site. That's a big plus for buyers and, given the choice, many will choose a seller with this option over one without it. You register for free after your first payment comes in. Before that, all you have to do is leave the PayPal box checked on the Sell Your Item form.

When you register, you'll need to choose one of two types of accounts: a Personal Account or Premier/Business Account. If you sell and want to receive money via PayPal, the choice is simple. You definitely want the Premier/Business Account because Personal Accounts may not receive credit card payments.

NOTE *Business Accounts are similar to Premier Accounts, but they enable a company to do business under its corporate name, and they allow more than one employee to log in under the account.*

In order to receive credit card payments, sellers are charged either a Merchant Rate or a Standard Rate. When you start out, you'll most likely pay the Standard Rate. In order to qualify for the lower Merchant Rate, one of the following must apply:

- You have been a PayPal member in good standing for the past 90 days and received an average of $1000 in payments per month over the previous 90 days.

- You have received a competitive offer from an established merchant account provider such as First Data Merchant Services or Metavante Corporation.

■ You have proven yourself to be a long-standing eBay seller who deals in high volume, and you include your eBay User ID and password on your Merchant Rate application.

To keep yourself qualified for the Merchant Rate fees, you need to maintain a volume of $1000 a month with PayPal and keep your account in good standing (that is, you have unresolved chargebacks due to customers using credit cards fraudulently). The difference between the Standard Rate and Merchant Rate fees at this writing is shown Table 9-2.

You can subtract a sizeable 1.5 percent from either the Merchant or Standard Rate if you qualify for Preferred Rate. To qualify for the 1.5 percent Preferred Rate discount, sign up for a PayPal ATM/Debit Card and advertise PayPal as your only online payment option—not Western Union Payment Services, Yahoo! DirectPay, or other payment services. As a Premier/Business Account customer, you can gain access to your PayPal funds with PayPal's ATM/Debit card.

 *Keep in mind that PayPal's fees change from time to time and may be different by the time you read this. You can get the current fees at www.paypal.com/cgi-bin/webscr?cmd=p/gen/fees-receiving-outside.*

One particularly nice thing about PayPal is that it accepts credit cards such as Discover and American Express that aren't always accepted with with conventional merchant accounts. Normally, you have to make arrangements through those credit card companies themselves to be one of their merchants, rather than through your financial institution.

PayPal Buyer Protection

One of the reasons why PayPal is a desirable option for many buyers is the fact that it offers buyer protection. This is a type of purchase insurance that buyers can obtain

Currency in Which You Are Paid	Standard Rate	Merchant Rate
U.S. Dollars	2.9 percent + $.30	2.2 percent + $.30
Canadian Dollars	3.4 percent + C $.55	2.7 percent + C $.55
Euros	3.4 percent + EUR .35	2.7 percent + EUR .35
Pounds Sterling	3.4 percent + £.20	2.7 percent + £ .20
Yen	3.4 percent + ¥40	2.7 percent + ¥40

TABLE 9-2 Premier/Business Account Rate Fees

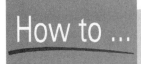 **Set Up a PayPal Account**

You can configure your PayPal account so your money is transferred directly to your checking account. You can do this by check (there's a $1.50 charge for each check), or have it held in your PayPal account. You set up a PayPal account as follows:

1. Go to the PayPal home page (www.paypal.com).

2. Click Sign Up For Your FREE PayPal Account.

3. When the PayPal Account Sign Up page appears, click the option you want (Personal or Business Account), and choose your country of residence from the Choose a Country drop-down list. Then click Continue. (These steps assume that you have chosen a Personal account—this option enables you to choose a Premier account so you can accept credit card payments.)

4. Fill out the information requested on the Sign Up form. When you get to the Premier Account section, click Yes.

5. Finish the form by reading the user agreement, filling out the security information, and clicking Sign Up.

After you sign up, PayPal verifies your identity based on the information you submitted. You will be able to accept PayPal payments right away during the verification process, but while your account is being established you won't be able to withdraw funds until your identity is verified.

9

in addition to eBay's own $250 worth of fraud protection. PayPal's buyer protection covers items that were

- Not received at all or that turned out to be significantly different than the original description

- Purchased on eBay

PayPal Buyer Protection is only available for users in the U.S. and Canada. Under this program, you are only entitled to two Buyer Protection refunds in one calendar year. The important thing to remember about this program is that it is not available for all items on eBay that can be paid for with PayPal. The protection is only available if sellers meet certain requirements, including the following:

- At least 50 feedback comments received on eBay

- At least a 98-percent positive feedback on eBay

- A Premier or Business PayPal account for accepting payments

- You are a verified PayPal member with an account in good standing in the U.S., UK, or Canada

You can read the full set of requirements (there are more than the ones just listed) at www.paypal.com/cgi-bin/webscr?cmd=_pbp-info-outside. If buyer protection is available, you will see the icon shown in Figure 9-2 at the bottom of the Seller Information box. To find out more about the program, click Services, click eBay Security Center, and then click PayPal Buyer Protection.

CAUTION   *If you get an e-mail from PayPal asking you to verify your personal information, don't respond. PayPal will not ask for specific personal information such as a credit card number by sending an e-mail message.*

FIGURE 9-2   eBay sales descriptions that include this logo offer buyer protection.

Considering Other Payment Services

PayPal isn't the only payment service around. Some sellers make use of other payment services because they are unhappy with the fees PayPal charges, or because they have found PayPal's level of customer service to be unsatisfactory. There are alternatives, and two of the services used by eBay auction sellers are described in the following sections.

Western Union Auction Payments

A few anti-PayPal sellers will not use PayPal at all. Rather, they accept checks, money orders, and Western Union's money order payment service. This service, Western Union Auction Payments, was formerly known as BidPay, and still has the URL www.bidpay.com.

Western Union Auction Payments is simple to use: sellers don't have to register with Western Union to receive money orders using the service. Registered sellers can set up accounts where they can review records of past orders and have their address verified by Western Union Auction Payments. However, buyers *do* need to register with Auction Payments so they can send you money orders. They use the Western Union Auction Services web site to choose a credit or debit card in order to make a payment. They add any shipping fees you have specified to the amount of the money order. They also pay transaction fees, as described in Table 9-3.

Western Union Auction Payments uses the U.S. Postal Service to send you its money orders. Once you get a confirmation e-mail from Western Union saying that the money order has been mailed to you, you have the option to either ship the merchandise immediately or wait until the money order actually arrives.

Money orders are shipped to sellers by first-class, and the shipping cost is included in the Western Union Auction Payments fees. However, buyers who are in a hurry to receive their merchandise can send you a money order by Priority Mail

9

Face Value of Money Order	Transaction Fee
$23 ($18 payment plus $5 shipping)	$2.95 (for $10.01 to $30 money orders)
$33 ($28 payment plus $5 shipping)	$3.95 (for $30.01 to $50 money orders)
$230 ($225 payment plus $5 shipping)	$10.12 ($4.95 + 2.25 percent of the face value of the money order for money orders ranging from $100.01 to $700)

TABLE 9-3   Western Union Auction Payments Transaction Fees

for an extra $6, and by Express Mail for $15. If you become a registered Western Union Auction Payments seller, you can add the service's logo to your auction listings, as shown in the following illustration.

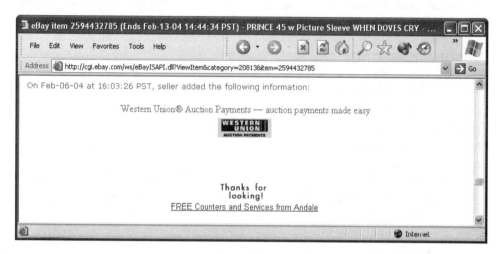

NOTE *Western Union Auction Payments limits its transactions to $700 or less, including shipping fees.*

Moneybookers.com

Moneybookers.com, a London, England–based payment service, enables buyers and sellers in a variety of countries to send payments to one another. Both buyer and seller need to have accounts established with Moneybookers, however. It's free to establish an account, and free for the buyer to deposit money in his or her account from a bank account. To send you money, the seller pays 1 percent of the transaction fee or a minimum of €.50.

However, it's worth noting that while it doesn't cost anything to have money transferred into your Moneybookers.com account, it does cost money to withdraw it to a bank or other account. You'll pay a flat fee of €3.50 (the U.S. equivalent at this writing is $3.81) to withdraw a check from your account. Sellers who accept Moneybookers.com add a logo (such as the one shown in Figure 9-3) to their auction descriptions.

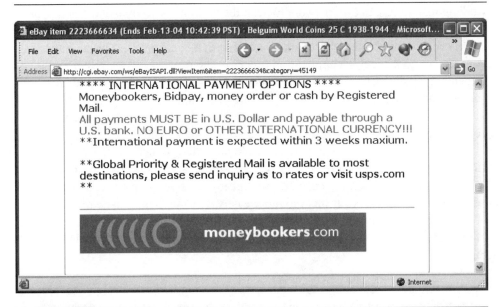

FIGURE 9-3   Moneybookers is especially good for international transactions.

CAUTION   *It's not a good idea to accept cash from your buyers because of the danger that it can be stolen from the mail. I know that some sellers do accept cash, however, especially from overseas customers who find it difficult to deal with escrow services. If something happens and payment is lost, it becomes your responsibility to explain to the customer that the money never arrived, which can easily lead to a dispute that can put your all-important reputation in jeopardy. It isn't that difficult for customers, even those who are overseas, to obtain a money order, and you should insist that they do so. Also avoid Cash on Delivery (COD), which carries hefty fees from the delivery services that offer it.*

Obtaining a Merchant Account

The alternative to payment services like PayPal, for sellers who want to give their customers the option of making a purchase with a credit card, is to establish a way of accepting credit card payments through a merchant account. A *merchant account* is a special account that a commercial operation (a merchant, in other words) sets up with a financial institution. The merchant account enables a business to receive credit card payments from its customers. Your financial institution processes the order, working with the credit card network to debit the customer's account and credit yours. Along the way, the financial institution charges fees for the processing.

In order to establish a merchant account with a bank or other organization, you need to go through an application process. The process can be rather involved. Depending on the institution, you may need to fill out forms, pay an application fee, and provide evidence that your business exists. Your application will probably need to be approved by a committee. Once your application is approved, you need to complete a second step—setting up your own payment system.

The process of setting up a merchant account and a payment system is complex. However, it gives you an advantage if you sell merchandise through your own web site or through a brick-and-mortar store. Setting up a single payment system will help you keep track of your income more easily. For purchases made through eBay or your web site, you can direct customers to the same payment form. An example of one form used by a company that sells both on eBay and on the Web is shown in Figure 9-4.

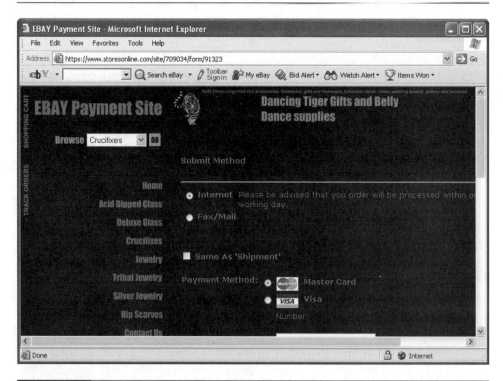

FIGURE 9-4   If you process your own credit card payments, you can direct high bidders and other online customers to the same form.

Turning to a Financial Institution

The traditional way to obtain a merchant account is through a bank or other financial institution. You apply to the bank and provide documents that show that you are a legitimate businessperson. You also pay an application fee, which can amount to $300 or more. The bank's officers review your request for several weeks, after which time they hopefully grant you approval.

You then purchase an input device that lets you send your customers' credit card numbers to the credit card network. This might be a Point of Sale terminal that lets you do "card swipes," plus a printer that can print out the receipts your customers sign. You can find inexpensive versions of such terminals on eBay for less than $50 (see Figure 9-5).

Other Payment Services

Setting up a merchant account and learning how to process your own credit card transactions adds complexity to your eBay sales. As you might expect, a number of companies offer services that claim to be an easier way to accept credit card

9

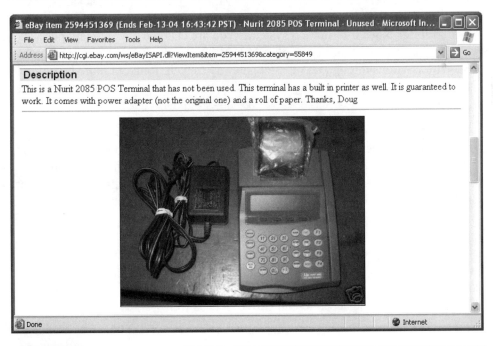

FIGURE 9-5   You need hardware like this or software to enter your customers' credit card data.

payments. Banks tend to be more expensive than companies that specialize in providing merchant accounts to online merchants. Companies like 1st American Card Service (www.1stamericancardservice.com) or Merchants' Choice Card Services (www.merchantschoice.com) don't charge an application fee. But they do charge Internet fees, discount fees, and so on.

A number of other services are available that streamline the process of accepting credit cards. Some suggestions are described next:

- **Yahoo! PayDirect (http://paydirect.yahoo.com)** This service enables you to receive payment for auctions, other purchases, dinner you bought for your friends when they were short of cash—anything. The fee structure is similar to PayPal's: you can sign up for free for either a Personal Account or Professional Account. The Professional Account, however, is the only one that allows you to receive credit card payments. In order to receive money, you have to pay a fee that ranges from 2.2 to 2.5 percent of the transaction + 30 cents.

- **Costco Internet Card Processing** Costco, the warehouse store my children and I visit regularly, offers a variety of membership packages. If you obtain an Executive Membership, you can obtain credit card processing status through Nova Information systems. You are charged 1.57 percent per Visa or MasterCard transaction plus 21 cents. Not only that, but you can process transactions through an Internet gateway as well. Find out more by going to www.costco.com, clicking Membership, and clicking Merchant Credit Card Processing.

- **VeriSign Payflow Link (www.verisign.com/products/payflow/link/index .html)** Once you obtain a merchant account from a financial institution, you can use Payflow Link as a gateway service to enable you to process credit card transactions online. You add a link to VeriSign's web site that enables customers to fill out forms in order to make purchases. The service costs $179 to set up, with a monthly fee of $19.95.

In addition, if you sign up for an account to sell online with Microsoft bCentral (www.bcentral.com), you pay $24.95 for monthly hosting. For an additional $24.95, you can sign up for Commerce Manager, which enables you to sell on eBay and in other marketplaces and accept credit card orders as well.

Verifying Payment Information

If you accept credit card payments only for Internet-based transactions, you don't need to purchase and set up a Point of Sale (POS) terminal to communicate with the credit card network. That's because people aren't going to be sending you their actual credit cards to swipe, and you aren't going to be printing out receipts for them to sign.

Both of these activities—receiving the actual credit card, and having the customer sign the card in front of you so you can compare his or her signature to the one on the card—are safeguards for you, the seller. They enable you to verify that the person making the purchase is actually the cardholder and not someone who has stolen the card.

How do you process transactions and verify the cardholder's identity in an Internet transaction? You're at a disadvantage because you have never seen the person with whom you are dealing, and you don't get a signature to ensure someone's identity. In that case, you need to use credit card processing software to do the verification for you. The software compares the card holder's billing address to the shipping address that the customer gives you. iAuthorizer (www.iauthorizer.com) performs verification and processing (see next), as does ICVerify (www.icverify.com).

If the billing and shipping addresses are different, that doesn't necessarily mean the card is being used fraudulently. Someone might be purchasing a gift for someone else; or the card-holder might have moved recently. But if the addresses vary dramatically (for instance, if the billing address is in Oregon and the shipping address is in Bolivia) you should call the card-holder to verify that the transaction is legitimate. If there's no problem, the cardholder will be glad you checked. If there is a problem, you save the cardholder a fraudulent purchase, and yourself a chargeback fee.

Sending a Payment Reminder

The preceding sections describe different ways in which you can receive payment from eBay buyers. But what happens if the payment is slow in coming? You may have to send a payment reminder to someone who hasn't yet paid for your auction items. However, that doesn't mean you need to lose your courteous, professional approach. Being nice when things aren't going perfectly is a surefire way to get positive feedback from grateful customers, in fact.

Be businesslike and firm when you send your reminder; keep in mind that payment may have been lost in the mail, the high bidder may have fallen ill or gone out of town, the neighbor's dog may have eaten the check on the way to the mailbox, or any number of legitimate reasons.

9

Be sure to specify a timeframe for receiving your response within the reminder e-mail. You might say the following:

Dear Buyer,

Last week you won a set of Polly Pockets dolls on one of my eBay auctions. The payment due date for this auction passed yesterday and I have not received a check or other payment notification. Perhaps the payment has gotten lost in the mail or you haven't been able to get to this matter yet.

I'd appreciate it if you could e-mail me within 24 hours to let me know what's going on, and whether you want to follow through with the transaction. Otherwise, I would like to relist the item if you don't want it any more.

Best wishes,
Greg Holden

Packing

Packing and shipping aren't the things you consider first when becoming a seller on eBay. They're about as exciting as other activities related to selling, like accounting and taxes. But they're very important just the same. A poorly packed item that is broken in transit or something that gets lost can effectively destroy a sale and damage your reputation as well.

Overpacking Like a Pro

A former coworker used to repeat to the point of distraction, "Presentation Is Everything." For the eBay buyer, opening the package is as exciting as Christmas morning. It's up to the buyer to make sure the result is a smile instead of a frown.

When you're packing, pretend that your customers are looking over your shoulder, and that you're going to hand the package to them in person. A strong box is the first requirement. Don't run the risk of the big moment collapsing because of a squashed container. Everyone likes to snuggle into a cozy bed, and your item is no exception. Make sure it is nestled into plenty of packing peanuts and surrounded by bubble wrap. Even items that were originally designed to go together should be separated for traveling. Avoid clashes by creating cardboard compartments. Take a hint from those Russian nesting dolls and put a box in a box if your item is fragile.

Voices from the Community

Sales Success Depends on Careful Shipping

You probably won't be surprised to hear that the successful sellers interviewed for this book are committed to fast and careful shipping.

"I believe in shipping in a timely manner," comments Roni Neal. "I ship packages usually within one day after payment is received. I ship at the U.S. Post Office (USPS) six days a week."

"For packages under 12 pounds and to most locations, USPS Priority Mail rates are typically only $1 or $2 higher than parcel post rates," say Shannon Miller and Suzanne Ziesche. "Priority Mail packages have a relatively quick estimated delivery time of two to three days, and typically this is much faster than parcel post. Priority Mail can be an excellent shipping method and a way to ensure happy customers."

"It's important to get a postal scale so you can figure your shipping costs correctly," says Lori Baboulis. "Also, print your postage online. The USPS offers it online for free, so you can print shipping labels with postage affixed. It also offers free delivery confirmation for Priority Mail packages and 13-cent delivery confirmation for first class packages. Delivery confirmation is quite important because PayPal requires a delivery confirmation tracking number in cases of claims of nondelivery. For postage, I use stamps.com for $15.99 per month and it's a much-needed business expense. The stamps.com service also allows me to purchase insurance for the package with no forms to fill out and no waiting in line at the post office. I just print out my postage/shipping labels, affix them to my packages, and drop them off. This is a real time-saver when you start shipping in excess of 20 packages a day."

"I try to pack and ship all my customer's items within two days of receiving payment," says Jennifer Karpin-Hobbs. "I ship three times a week, and I know eBay buyers really appreciate receiving their item quickly. I also pack breakables as if they were going to be stomped on by an elephant! I use a lot of bubble wrap, and I feel it's important to over-pack so the item gets to its destination in one piece. I use nice tissue paper, clean, unused boxes, and I decorate the outside of the packages with Victorian stickers. I include a packing slip in every box. I treat all shipments with care, whether the item sold for $1 or $1000. I know my buyers can see the thought I put into the presentation, and I have a number of repeat customers."

9

Getting Your Packing Materials for Free

I'm a dumpster diver who likes to see myself as ecologically sensitive rather than cheap. Whatever your motivation, be on the lookout for clean plastic bags and don't be too quick to recycle newspapers. They are basics for keeping your items safe and dry. Another way to use plastic bags is to inflate them with air, which will also save you money when it comes time to pay for shipping by weight.

Scrounge for recycled packing materials. Some budget-conscious sellers look for paper, bubble wrap, and peanuts wherever they can be found—even in the trash. If you can find a location that receives breakable items, you'll probably also find a lot of peanut packing material that is free if you haul it away. It's tacky to reuse boxes that are obviously worse for the wear. But many are in good shape even if they've been used once—especially if they've been the box within a box—so keep your eye out.

 *Many sellers use the U.S. Postal Service's Priority Mail service so they can take advantage of the high-quality Priority Mail boxes that the USPS provides free for you to pick up at a postal facility or by calling 1-800-610-8734.*

Picking the Right Fastening and Cushioning Materials

Boxes are important but, if your merchandise flies around inside the container or the container breaks open in transit, damage can occur. Make sure you obtain secure materials to protect your items, such as:

- **Goo Gone**   You may want to cover old labels over with fresh paper if you are recycling boxes. But in case you want to completely remove old mailing labels at some point, this stuff is great at removing adhesive residue from stickers and labels.

- **Bubble wrap**   This is a plastic product that contains little bubbles of air that protect what you pack. Bubble wrap can be expensive if you buy it in small quantities. Shop around on eBay and at online packing supply houses and buy the biggest roll you can afford so you don't have to buy it again for a while.

- **Packing peanuts**   These little white peanut-shaped items are handy for packing irregularly shaped objects in boxes. Storing them can be a pain, but consider hanging them in trash bags around your garage or basement.

- **Shipping tape**   You'll need clear tape that's two or three inches wide to seal boxes if you use a shipping method other than Priority Mail (in which case you can use their free packing tape). Be sure to cover the mailing label with the clear tape to protect it from the rain.

- ■ **Plastic bags or newspaper** Use these to wrap the merchandise inside the box. The plastic bags, in particular, will protect an item from any moisture that seeps inside.

- ■ **Bubble envelopes** If you ship out flat merchandise such as magazines or posters, these Bubble Wrap–lined envelopes are terrific for protecting your goods. Look for 3M's Inflata-Pak inflatable packing; you can find it for sale inexpensively on eBay.

A trip to the local office supply store will suggest many other kinds of tubes, triangle-shaped containers, and specialty boxes you can use to ship odd-shaped items.

> **TIP** *Double-pack if necessary. For especially fragile and precious items, put a box within another box for extra protection.*

Also consider including a note with your merchandise. Some sellers include notes pointing out any flaws that were on the merchandise before it was shipped, so it's clear to the buyer that that particular damage did not occur in transit. Others include a business card, a printed packing slip or invoice, and an extra gift to encourage subsequent sales, build goodwill, and ensure positive feedback.

Shipping

Most eBay sellers settle on one of the big shipping services to handle all of their needs: Federal Express (FedEx), United Parcel Service (UPS), and the United States Postal Service (USPS). If they use FedEx or UPS, they find it simpler to get one set of shipping statements, for one thing. For another, having to travel to only one facility at a set time each day or each week simplifies the whole week's activities— which can be pretty busy if you are selling dozens of items each week, and some of your time is spent shopping to build up your inventory.

Using eBay's Checkout Option

Shipping costs vary depending on where the buyer lives. Often, sellers either have to charge a flat shipping fee, or calculate exact shipping after they determine the buyer's location. Rather than having to calculate your shipping and handling totals in your end of the auction e-mail message, you can expedite the transaction by entering the details in the Sell Your Item form when you prepare to put your sale online. That way, your customers can use eBay's Checkout feature to calculate the charges themselves when the sale ends (see Figure 9-6).

Getting Your Merchandise Out Quickly

One of the things that ensures positive feedback is the ability to ship your merchandise quickly. One of the things that raises the likelihood of negative feedback, on the other hand, is taking a week or more to get your merchandise out to the shipper. It's hard to travel to the shipping office or postal facility every single day, of course, but try to do so more than once a week.

One way to save time spent shipping is to buy and print out your own postage. Stamps.com (www.stamps.com) lets you print out your own postage from the comfort of your own home.

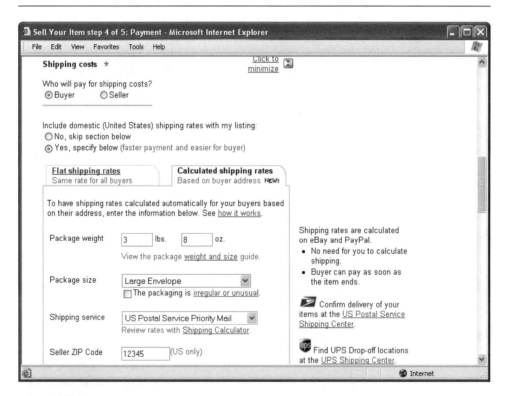

FIGURE 9-6   Help your customers by entering shipping and other charges when you create the sale.

Choosing the Shipper that Delivers for You

There are a variety of well-known shippers available to you as an eBay seller. The "Big Three" shippers—United Parcel Service, the United States Postal Service, and Federal Express—all give you a variety of options for getting your package from one place to another. They all offer important services such as package tracking, delivery confirmation, and insurance. The company you choose is the one you find most convenient for your needs and the one that complements your budget. Brief descriptions of the most common shippers used on eBay follow.

United States Postal Service

As American as the flag and apple pie, USPS is as close as your neighborhood postal substation. You don't need to have an account to order supplies, buy stamps, and ship out your packages, but you *can* get your shipping supplies for free if you use Priority Mail, which is ideal for one- and two-pound packages. Another good deal is using Media Mail if you're shipping books, cassettes, videos, or computer readable media. So shop around for services, but don't overlook the obvious.

If you ship using Express or Priority mail, call 1-800-222-1811 for a pickup; a flat rate of $4.95 per pickup applies, but there is no limit on the number of packages per pickup. (Ask about size and weight limitations, however.)

> **TIP** *If you get regular visits from a USPS mail carrier, you can always drop off a package with that person as long it has the correct postage affixed. In case you don't have mail delivery, a promising new Carrier Pickup program being tested by the USPS at this writing allows mail carriers to pick up packages from you at your home and ship them out the day after you request a pickup. It sounds too good to be true, but it's for real; the catch is that you have to pack the merchandise and affix the appropriate postage yourself. It's only being tested in a few locations around the country. Hopefully, if the program works out, it will be offered on a more widespread basis. Find out more at www.usps.com/shipping/pickup.htm.*

United Parcel Service

If you're going to be selling with any sort of regularity, you really don't want to be standing in line at the UPS shipper with the rest of the unwashed masses. The first thing to do is get a simple Internet account at www.ups.com/bussol/solutions/internetship.html. That way you can print out your own bar-coded labels.

9

Now that you have that capability, it makes sense to arrange for a driver to pick up even an individual package or two for an extra $4 or so each. Of course, if you're ready to make the UPS driver your best friend, you'll get a daily stop for $7 to $16 a week.

Federal Express

The first advantage of Federal Express is that you can use software called Ship Manager to print out labels. Set up your account through the FedEx web site at www.fedex.com. Another advantage is that you can have the shipper collect your charge (even cash) from the buyer when the delivery is made.

So don't hesitate to compare costs, keeping in mind that good, cost-effective options were created when FedEx (after acquiring Roadway Package Service [RPS]) began including FedEx Ground and its subdivision, FedEx Home Delivery.

Providing Your Customers with Shipping Costs

It's a good idea to give buyers a couple of shipping options rather than just one, so they can feel they have a choice in the matter. Very few eBay sellers give customers the option of sending packages overnight. FedEx Home delivery, UPS residential, USPS Priority Mail, and USPS and ground mail are among the most popular options.

Table 9-4 compares shipping costs for a package being sent from my ZIP code in Chicago (60657) to one in Los Angeles, California (90011). The UPS and FedEx prices incorporate $100 worth of insurance. Delivery confirmation is not included, however.

Delivery Service	2 lbs	5 lbs	10 lbs	20 lbs
USPS Priority Mail (2 days)	$28.75	$5.40	$11.00	$16.30
USPS Bound Printed Matter (six days)	$2.38	$3.46	$5.26	N/A
USPS Media Mail (six days)	$1.84	$3.10	$4.84	$7.84
USPS Parcel Post (six days)	$4.49	$8.64	$14.17	$20.05
UPS Ground (four days)	$4.65	$13.09	$15.28	$22.38
UPS Three-Day Select (three days)	$8.65	$20.45	$27.66	$41.77
UPS Second Day Air (two days)	$11.88	$23.80	$35.07	$54.56
FedEx Home Delivery (four days)	$5.82	$6.77	$8.35	$13.41

TABLE 9-4   Shipping Costs Comparison

It can be difficult, if not impossible, to give exact shipping costs in auction listings because, usually, the cost varies depending on the distance being shipped. Sellers who live in the central United States have an advantage, particularly if they ship by Priority Mail, because the distance to the various perimeters of the country is more or less similar. But someone who lives in Seattle might run into dramatically different costs to ship to California, as opposed to Florida.

As you can see from the preceding table, while Priority Mail is convenient in terms of packaging and economical for 2-lb. or 5-lb. packages, don't overlook the relatively new FedEx Home Delivery service (see Figure 9-3), which takes a couple of days more but provides an excellent value for larger packages. On the other hand, if you are shipping books, Printed Book Rate is a good choice. For media such as DVDs, videotapes, or CD-ROMs, the Postal Service's Media Mail is a good value, as well.

> **NOTE**   *You can use a variety of online calculators to quickly determine the most economical way to send your package. The USPS's Online Calculator can be found at http://pages.ebay.com/usps/calculator.html, the UPS Service Center online calculator is at www.servicecenter.ups.com/ebay/ebay.html#qcost, and FedEx's Rate Finder is available at www.fedex.com/ratefinder/home ?cc=US&language=en.*

9

Where to Find It

Web Site	Address	What's There
eBay Anything Points program	anythingpoints.ebay.com/	Information on Anything Points and how you can offer them to prospective buyers
PayPal	www.paypal.com	An electronic payment service owned by eBay that allows buyers and sellers to transfer payment online
Western Union Auction Payments	www.bidpay.com	A payment service run by Western Union that provides an alternative to PayPal
U.S. Postal Service Carrier Pickup program	anythingpoints.ebay.com/)	The home page for a pilot program that allows carriers to make next-day home pickups in selected locations
United Parcel Service	www.usps.com	A popular shipping service known as "Brown"
Federal Express	www.fedex.com	A popular shipping service that will pick up at your residence if you set up an account

Chapter 10

Managing Your Auction Sales

How to...

- Manage your current sales to provide good customer service

- Relist items that don't sell the first time around

- Solve problems that occur before and after the sale

- Get in touch with eBay when you need help

Once your sales merchandise is priced and put on display, you might think all you have to do is sit back and watch the bids come rolling in. But consider this: just how many store merchants do you see dozing in their chairs when you come through the front door? You are far more likely to see them on the phone, talking to customers, placing orders for supplies, or doing their bookkeeping. Commerce is an ongoing activity in which a sequence of sales-related activities is combined to actually make a sale.

eBay sales work the same way. After you successfully create your sales listings and put them online, you can't just sit back and rest on your laurels. Your sales descriptions may benefit by adding new information or making corrections (often, based on information provided by your own bidders). At the very least, you need to be available to respond quickly to questions posed by those customers. This chapter examines the many tasks that occur between the time the sale goes online and the transaction is successfully completed, and how you can handle them in a way that keeps your business running smoothly.

Managing Your Ongoing Sales

Consumers love a good deal. But they're not always into self-service. The hugely successful chain of discount stores that has swept the country, and whose name I probably should not mention, is known not only for low prices but for how friendly its underpaid employees are supposed to be.

On eBay, customer service mostly takes the form of checking your e-mail on a regular basis and responding to inquiries in a professional manner. It also involves providing more information as it becomes available, and promoting your sales to induce bids and purchases.

Editing Auction Descriptions

Once your eBay auction description goes online, the first person to view it should be you. Even if you previewed your description at the end of the Sell Your Item form before you actually put the sale online, it's always a good idea to double-check by taking a quick glance at your sale as soon as it appears. Time does make a difference: eBay allows you to edit a description until the first bid is received. After someone has placed a bid, you can't edit the description because it would be unfair—those who place bids after you make the change will be bidding based on different information than those who bid before editing.

After bids are made, you can only add information to an auction. This isn't necessarily a bad thing, and it doesn't mean that people would be less likely to bid. In fact, additional information shows that you are on top of things and that you are interested in making your description as accurate as possible. Plenty of sellers add information for reasons like the following:

- They have new photos.

- They want to call attention to payment methods.

- They offer "Anything Points," as described in Chapter 9.

- They accept electronic payment services other than PayPal that aren't included on the Sell Your Item form.

- They have new information.

Sometimes, the new information comes from bidders themselves. The seller is informed that the object being offered is rarer and more valuable than originally thought. In this case, the new information should help with attracting bids, so you should be sure to add it. To add information to one of your own auctions or to revise existing information, follow these steps:

1. Click My eBay in the navigation bar.

2. Click the Selling tab.

3. Do one of the following:

   - Click Revise My Item if your item has received bids *or* ends within 12 hours. If you have not received any bids and the sale does not end in 12 hours, you'll be able to revise the original description. If you have received bids or the sale ends in more than 12 hours, you can add new information to your description in a section that is separate from the original description. Any changes you make appear under a heading such as "At [time of addition], seller added the following information."

   - Click Add to My Item Description if your item has not received bids and if it does not end within 12 hours. This enables you to add more information to your original description.

If you have received bids and the sale ends in less than 12 hours, you can't make any changes to the description.

4. Enter the item number in the Item Number box and click Continue.

5. Make your changes in the form provided.

You can make all changes to a sales description once it is online. Timing and presence of bids determine what changes can be made and when you can make them. Table 10-1 provides a few examples of what you can do while the sale is still continuing.

Encouraging People to Buy It Now

If you have done your research and are reasonably certain about the value of the item you are selling, a Buy It Now price might just get you quick results. A Buy It Now option gives buyers another reason to make a purchase. Often, if they have been looking for that special something for an extended period of time, a Buy It Now option just might be the thing they're looking for. When someone clicks the Buy It Now button, they make a commitment to buy the item right away.

Buy It Now has both pros and cons for sellers. On the pro side, they can get what they want for the item and receive their money right away, without having to wait for the end of the auction. On the con side, you never really know if you would have gotten a larger amount for an item if bidders had been allowed to compete until the day and time the sale was originally scheduled to end.

From my own experience, I can tell you that Buy It Now works if you are offering something that someone has been seeking for a while. If the buyer knows how much he or she is willing to pay and the Buy It Now price fits into that budget, it makes sense to click the Buy It Now button to avoid competing with other bidders and possibly being outbid.

Revision	When You Can Make the Change
Change original description	Before first bid is received, as long as sale does not end in 12 hours or less
Add to description	Up to 12 hours before the sale ends
Add Buy It Now price	Before first bid is received, as long as sale does not end in 12 hours or less
Make the sale bold or highlighted	Any time before the sale ends

TABLE 10-1   When to Revise Auction Descriptions

Andale (www.andale.com) provides its customers with a service in which they track past eBay auctions and tell buyers that the Buy It Now price for the current item is a reasonable one (see Figure 10-1).

Fielding Questions from Shoppers

While you have an item up for sale, your main customer-service task is to be available to answer questions from prospective and current bidders. The important thing here is to be professional at all times, even if buyers irritate you or ask obvious questions. Remember—the quality of your response tells buyers something about the level of customer service you are likely to provide as a seller. Answering questions quickly and completely is one of the most effective ways to ensure that you'll get glowing feedback if those shoppers go on to make a purchase from you.

Even though you are undoubtedly busy with family and other responsibilities, you need to make an effort to check your e-mail every day. It can be difficult to do this. Getting a wireless e-mail account along with your wireless phone service can help; so can installing a computer in or near your living area, if you work at home, and keeping the sound on so you can hear the audible signal when an e-mail message comes in.

10

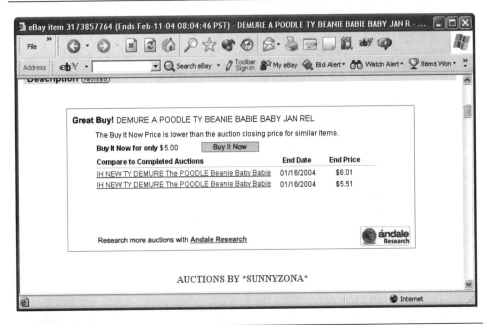

FIGURE 10-1   This feature box justifies your Buy It Now price based on recent sales.

Being Thorough and Professional

Whenever you respond to an e-mail message from a prospective or current buyer, put on the hat of a businessperson. Be patient and thorough in your response, no matter how hurried or harried you are at the time. Don't lose sight of your ultimate goal: the desire to make money for your sales efforts; remember that the level of customer service you provide through e-mail will help you achieve that goal.

Suppose you get a question about a car you have up for auction on eBay Motors. The shopper asks if the car has been well-maintained. Which of the following responses do you think is most likely to result in a bid or Buy It Now purchase?

1. "Yes."

2. "Yes, oil changes every 3000 miles, records available."

3. "Thank you for your inquiry. The car's tires were completely replaced a year ago; I kept records on this, as well as on tune-ups for the past three years. The car had a 30,000-mile maintenance check last April. The car is in great shape and ready to provide you with enjoyment for years to come. Feel free to write again with any other questions that come up. Don't forget to check my other auctions for auto-related sales such as repair manuals and halogen headlights."

It's no great mystery that answer number 3 takes longer to type, but is most likely to inspire trust in the seller as well as bids or purchases.

Handling Complaints with Patience

When you are busy with multiple responsibilities, and when it seems like the overwhelming majority of eBay sellers are courteous and wonderful to deal with, it can be irritating when someone voices a complaint and is clearly dissatisfied. Don't give in to the temptation to share in the buyer's anger.

If you get an e-mail that accuses you of doing something wrong, wait a couple of hours before responding. Take a walk or play with your kids for a while before you return to the message. It's important to remain professional at all times, and to remember that a single complaint isn't such a big crisis in the big scheme of things.

You might hate to do it, but it's often easier to simply refund an unhappy buyer's money rather than drag out a dispute over days and weeks. The time spent arguing is better spent getting the merchandise returned and relisting it on eBay.

You Can't Please All of the People, All of the Time

You can't please everyone on eBay. That's what the longtime sellers who contributed their views to this book believe. Just handle problems with patience, provide refunds when needed, and move on to more productive transactions, they say.

"Occasionally, everyone will get an unhappy customer," says Roni Neal. "I treat all people the way I wish to be treated, with respect. I am open to their points of view even if I do not agree with them. Listening to the other party is very important. Then, communicate your own point of view professionally. I always say I'm 'open to your suggestions' so they do not feel the dispute is one-sided. I try to resolve matters promptly, attentively, and with kindness."

"You have to look at each situation differently," comments Emily Sabako. "When you sell high-end items, usually you have a more sophisticated clientele, and you don't run into as many problems as you would selling, say, World Wrestling Federation memorabilia. In general, I refund the money when I receive the item back from the buyer. With my items, giving folks the benefit of the doubt has worked in my favor."

"I generally pull the person's contact information and give them a phone call," advises Jill Featherston. "Many times, points just aren't easy to make in an e-mail—no one can judge your voice inflection or your tone in an e-mail. Many of us are not skilled writers, so what we write can easily be misconstrued by the receiver. A phone call usually solves that."

Jill recommends that once you have your customer on the phone, you can take the following steps to turn a "bad" situation around:

1. **Listen**   Don't judge the person or get defensive, just listen. While you may not agree with what they are saying, they are voicing their perception of the transaction. A person's perception is their reality.

2. **Be respectful**   Even if your customer is cursing. Don't sink to that level. Ignore any impoliteness or rude behavior.

3. **Apologize**   Do your best to make it sound sincere.

10

4. **Tell them what you *can* do to fix the situation**   Never focus on what you *can't* do.

5. **Offer to fix the situation**   Whether that means sending them a replacement or a refund, do what you can to make it right.

"No matter what you do or how skilled you become at troubleshooting, you are not going to please all the people all of the time, but you should do your best to make sure that each of your customers is satisfied," Jill says.

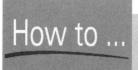 **End Your Auction Early**

Once you start an auction, you can exert control over many different aspects of the sale. You can end a sale before the originally scheduled ending time, too. But you should only do so under certain circumstances. Otherwise, you can get a bad reputation and even face disciplinary action from eBay itself. Here are some examples of acceptable reasons for ending a sale early.

- You lost the item or it was broken, so it can no longer be sold.

- You made a mistake in the starting price or the reserve price.

- The owner of the item, for whom you are selling on consignment, has withdrawn it so it is no longer available.

To end your sale early, follow these steps:

1. Click My eBay.

2. Click the Selling tab.

3. Click End My Auction Early.

4. Sign in with your User ID and password when prompted.

5. When the Ending Your Listing Early page appears, enter the item number of the sale you want to end, and then click Continue.

6. Choose between either selling the item to the current high bidder and ending the sale early, or canceling all bids and ending the sale early without selling to any of the bidders. (If the item has no bids, you won't see this form, and will instead skip ahead to step 7.)

7. Choose the reason why you are ending the sale early.

The sale will be removed from eBay, and any current bidders will be sent e-mail messages notifying them that the sale has ended.

CAUTION   *One common scam carried out by unscrupulous individuals occurs when a buyer convinces a seller to end a sale early and sell to them at an inflated price. Sometimes, the seller is told that he or she needs to wire transfer a certain amount to an overseas location. The buyer promises to transfer a larger amount in return, but this never happens. If you are approached with such an offer, report it to eBay's Rules & Safety area. To do so, click the Rules & Safety link that appears on the bottom of nearly every eBay page.*

10

Relisting Items

Don't be surprised if some of the items you put up for auction fail to attract bids. Millions of items are up for sale on eBay at any one time. Yours may only be one of several that are similar. Don't be discouraged: often, waiting a few days and/or making some adjustments to the sales description can help. Here are some suggestions:

- **Lower the starting bid**   If you set a high starting bid that happens to be a round number, such as $100, reduce it to $99 or even a lower figure—$99 looks substantially less than $100, while $199 seems more appetizing than $200, and so on.

- **Go with No Reserve**   Reserve prices turn bidders away. Try a higher starting bid with no reserve.

- **Take more photos**   Better closeups taken from different angles will make your object more attractive.

- **Rewrite the title**   A title with keywords that emphasize the object's rarity or desirability may get better results.

A Full-Time Endeavor

Jill Featherston says she has a "relist system" for items that don't sell on eBay the first time around. "If they do not sell the first time, they are immediately relisted with a 99-cent starting bid. There's a reason why I have the User ID "bargain-hunters-dream"! I do not sit on inventory; my goal is to move it *fast*. I am successful because I always have new items up, never the same thing week after week."

Featherston, who lives in Greenville, Texas, has been trading on eBay for four years. She's an active member of the eBay community, and belongs to five eBay Groups. "One in particular, PowerChicks, is a fabulous support network for female sellers. We brainstorm eBay issues and help each other be better sellers. I have come away with so many ideas that I simply would not have thought of on my own. Sometimes, you get stuck in the way you run your business. Most of us don't have employees or business partners; many times your spouse doesn't even fully understand what it is that you do on eBay. Not only can that be lonely, it's frightening. You need people (who understand the business) to bounce ideas off of."

Featherston's business has also been boosted by running an eBay Store. "Having an eBay Store saves me a couple hundred dollars a month in fees," she says. "Having 20 categories keeps me (more) organized. The Store Search function is indispensable. Since I've opened my eBay Store, about 15 percent of my customers purchase more than one item at a time. I know that comes from the ease in which they are able to navigate my listings and add on to their orders."

Featherston jokes that she's never really been a "part-time" seller on eBay. "I was hooked the second I registered, so it's always been a full-time endeavor!" Typically, she lists high-value antiques and collectibles for ten days and runs their auctions from Thursday night to the following Sunday night. Most of her regular auctions last seven days, from Sunday night to Sunday night.

"Those of us who run businesses on eBay take it very seriously," she says. "eBay is not a hobby for us, and shouldn't be treated like one. eBay offers a fantastic venue for us to get our wares seen by millions of potential customers, we do not take that for granted, as some of the part-timers might. I think there is a certain personality type, that 'takes' to eBay, and that's what we PowerSellers have."

Troubleshooting Transactions

Sellers and buyers alike have one big question on their minds when they start using eBay: will I be able to actually sell or buy something without getting swindled or cheated in some way? The fact that you can't see or personally talk to the eBay members with whom you do business lends uncertainty to transactions.

For sellers, the big uncertainty is that the high bidder or buyer will disappear without paying, or complain about receiving damaged goods. These problems do occur on eBay, but only a fraction of the time. There is probably no exact figure that applies to everyone. The instance of fraud varies depending on what you sell.

eBay itself claims that only a fraction of one percent of transactions go wrong in some way. I've heard figures of three to five percent from sellers. Whatever the truth, you have plenty of safeguards you can fall back on, and sensible practices that will help you protect yourself and your customers.

Your Buyer Is a No-Show

The bane of all eBay sellers is the Non-Paying Bidder (NPB)—a bidder who fails to follow through with a transaction and pay for what he or she has purchased. Such bidders are well known in the auction community. Typically, after the sale ends, the high bidder or buyer receives notice that he or she has won. Often, the buyer does not respond to the seller despite repeated attempts. Just as often, the buyer claims that he or she will send payment, but it never arrives, and the buyer simply seems to disappear.

If you run into a possible NPB, do the following:

1. Remember that the person is only a "possible" NPB. There's a chance that the bidder is ill, was called away by a family emergency, or is offline due to computer problems. Get the buyer's contact information from the Find Members form (http://cgi3.ebay.com/aw-cgi/eBayISAPI.dll?UserInformationRequest) and phone the person.

2. If you can't reach the buyer by phone, you can send the buyer a formal Payment Reminder by e-mail. Go to http://pages.ebay.com/help/sell/ bidders_payment_reminder.html to find out more. You must do this between three and 30 days after the sale closes. This is an optional step, however; instead, you can move on to step 3.

3. File a Non-Paying Bidder alert by filling out the form at http://cgi3.ebay .com/aw-cgi/eBayISAPI.dll?NPBComplaintForm. You must fill out this form between seven and 45 days from the end of the auction. eBay sends

10

an e-mail to both buyer and seller alerting them that the bidder has the potential of being designated an NPB. Hopefully, this will induce the buyer to complete the deal.

4.   If the buyer still refuses to respond or pay up, you can receive a credit for your Final Value Fee. You can then either relist the item or make a Second Chance Offer to an underbidder (someone who also bid on the same item but didn't turn out to be the high bidder). You make a Second Chance Offer by filling out the form at http://cgi3.ebay.com/aw-cgi/eBayISAPI.dll?PersonalOfferLogin. You should also file negative feedback for the buyer.

eBay states that after three Non-Paying Bidder offenses, the user will be suspended from using eBay. While it's true that the same user can re-register with a different User ID and password, eBay checks a user's name, address, phone number, or other aspects of his or her identity to discourage the person from having multiple accounts. It's important to follow the process through to its conclusion in order to make eBay a safer place for all members.

You're not alone, so don't take it personally. Deadbeat bidders are a common problem on eBay, though they're not as widespread as you might think. eBay has developed an FAQ to help you deal with deadbeat bidders at http://pages.ebay.com/help/basics/f-npb.html.

The Buyer Claims Non-Receipt

Every seller runs into problem buyers once in a while. While it doesn't happen all the time, you should be aware that some shoppers are actively trying to cheat sellers in one way or another. One of the most common ways for buyers to "scam" sellers is to falsely claim that an object was not received at all—that it was lost in the mail. The buyer demands a refund and, when it arrives, the buyer has essentially obtained an object for free.

The way to avoid this is simple: pay an extra fee for delivery confirmation. This fee is only 45 cents for a Priority Mail package. In addition, insurance is available for Priority Mail $1.10 for up to $50 worth of insurance, which includes package tracking. You can add such charges to your shipping fees as an extra handling charge, if you wish.

"As a seller, I have been quite fortunate," says Lori Baboulis. "Even though there are some CD-ROMs available claiming to provide instructions on how to 'scam' sellers out of money on eBay, I've only had a few buyers trying to claim that they never received what I sent. However, since I use Delivery Confirmation on every item that I ship, I am able to e-mail them proof of delivery. I never heard from any of them again after sending the tracking information."

You can get confirmation of delivery from the U.S. Postal Service if you send a package using Delivery Confirmation, Signature Confirmation, Certified Mail, or Registered Mail. The options are explained at www.usps .com/shipping/trackandconfirm.htm.

If Someone Leaves Bad Feedback

Sadly enough, it sometimes seems easier to talk trash than to make nice. But when you're a seller, it's not just your itty-bitty feelings that are at stake. If you have dreams of setting up an eBay Store or becoming a PowerSeller, words really can do more damage than sticks or stones.

So, putting personal issues aside, the first thing to do if somebody says something bad about it is to objectively determine if they have a point. If something went wrong with the individual sale, bend over backwards to make it right. If your way of conducting business could use an overhaul, clean up your act and thank them for bringing it to your attention.

If, however, you've been unjustly accused, see if they would consent to amending their comments to clarify the situation. And, although "the customer is always right," don't hesitate to provide a polite and factual rebuttal. More tips on making rebuttals are at http://pages.ebay.com/services/forum/feedback.html.

If you strongly disagree with bad feedback that has been left for you and you haven't been able to work out your disagreement with the other party yourself, turn to an arbitration service. SquareTrade a company that certifies businesses with a seal of approval for reputable practices, has partnered with eBay to provide dispute resolution services. One of its services is feedback arbitration. Follow these steps to take advantage of it:

10

1. Go to the SquareTrade home page (www.squaretrade.com) and click the eBay logo.

2. When the Online Dispute Resolution page appears, click the button marked Find Out How to Get Feedback Removed.

3. When the How to Remove Feedback page appears, scroll down the page to see a visual representation of the process (see Figure 10-2) and to read more about it. Then click the File a Case button to get the process started.

Simply filing a case with SquareTrade does not mean your feedback will automatically be removed. Even if you win your case, it must still be reviewed by eBay and approved before the feedback will be taken away. However, in some cases the person who originally left the feedback does not respond at all, and if this happens, the chances of your winning the case and having the feedback taken down are relatively good.

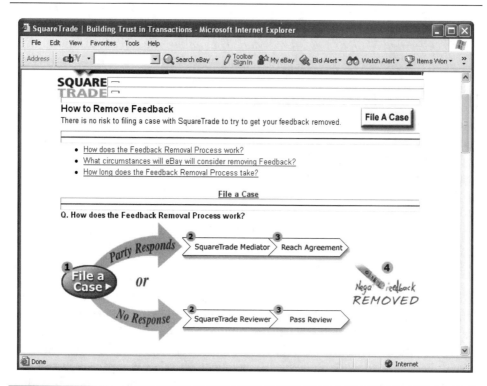

FIGURE 10-2   For a $20 fee, SquareTrade will arbitrate feedback disputes.

If the Goods You Sold Arrived Damaged

Here's another problem that "should" never happen. But it does. The fact is that, once your merchandise is given to the shipper, it's literally out of your hands. You can't absolutely prevent a package from being damaged by a careless handler. But you can minimize the chances considerably by doing the following:

■ **Use new or almost-new boxes that are sturdy enough to handle the clumsiest delivery person**   You can get fresh boxes from the U.S. Postal Service for free if you use Priority Mail. You can also get them cheaply from an office supply store, or from online outlets such as Uline (www.uline.com) or Mr. Box Online (www.mrboxonline.com).

■ **Using plenty of cushioning material**   Go for the sort described in Chapter 9. You can often find such material on eBay itself (see Figure 10-3 for an example).

■ **Obtain insurance**   All of the big three shippers provide it, as well as a third-party service called U-Pic (www.u-pic.com). But be sure you verify the insurance requirements for each shipper. For instance, UPS requires that you place three inches of packing material around an object, or it is disqualified from insurance.

If you have taken all of the preceding precautions and the buyer still reports that your merchandise was received with damage you did not disclose, either in your description, your photos, or in a note you included with the package, you should offer a refund—but only after the package is returned to you and you actually receive it back.

You can then file a claim with your shipper (it is the shipper's responsibility to do this, not the buyer's) for the cost of the refund and the return shipping. It can be time-consuming to get reimbursed, but all shippers stipulate that they will do so as long as your packaging was sufficient to begin with.

FIGURE 10-3   You can find packing material at affordable prices on eBay itself.

10

If Your Sales Don't Attract Any Bids

The section "Relisting Items" earlier in this chapter provided some concrete suggestions for things you can do to increase your chances of making a sale after you relist something that failed to sell the first time around. Here is a less simple suggestion: Take the time to make a name for yourself through your own web site or online store, moderating a discussion group, or answering questions on eBay's message boards or in Internet newsgroups. Your reputation and your reputability will make shoppers more likely to place bids.

Ask your best friend to be brutally honest in evaluating your auction descriptions and do whatever it takes to stand out from the crowd with clear and interesting information. Build up your positive feedback by purchasing or making other sales; your overall sales figures will go up when you reach figures in the hundreds, and take another jump when you break through the 1000 feedback level.

Do some research on Seller Central to find out what items are most popular in a given category on eBay. Click Services in the eBay navigation bar, and then click Seller Central. Once you get to the Seller Central home page, click Sell by Category. Click the In Demand link under the category that most closely matches the item you want to sell (see Figure 10-4). You'll get a list of the items that are used most often in searches conducted on eBay, as well as those that actually sold (or, in eBay language, "had high sell-through").

If the Check Bounces

Feedback can be satisfying in some situations, but that's not going to put money in your pocket. In this case, an ounce of prevention is worth a pound of cure. You can avoid the problem by requesting payment by cashier's check or postal money order. If you're part of Escrow.com, you'll be informed when the check clears. But even on your own you can wait until the money's in your bank before delivering the merchandise.

But okay, if that's all water under the bridge, chances are that it's an honest mistake. Most buyers will be only too happy to pay you—this time with a cashier's check or money order—for the item plus reimburse you for the fees charged by your bank for having a check returned. In the meantime, keep that bad check in a safe place in case there is a problem and you need evidence. If you're really dealing with a rotten apple, file a Non-Paying Bidder Form with eBay and then, if you don't receive payment in another ten days, file a Final Value Fee Credit Form.

NOTE   *It's advisable to add a phrase such as "A $___ fee will be charged for bounced checks" as part of your auction description. That way, you'll be on solid ground when you ask to have your fees reimbursed.*

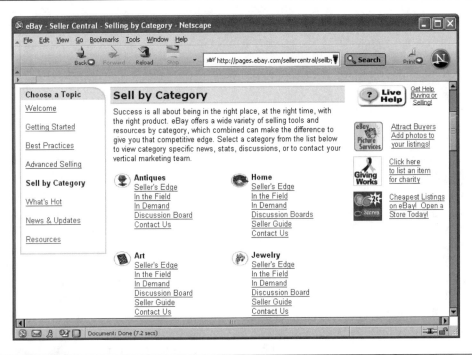

FIGURE 10-4   Seller Central provides data on items that are currently in demand in popular categories.

Contacting eBay for Help

Until you attend the annual eBay Live conference or a workshop conducted by eBay staff people, it's sometimes easy to lose sight of the fact that eBay is a real place inhabited by real folks. If you have a question you want to ask a member of eBay's Customer Support staff, you have a few options. The option you choose depends on the question or problem at hand:

■ If you suspect that someone is fraudulently using your User ID and password to conduct transactions without your knowledge, go to the Security Center (http://pages.ebay.com/securitycenter).

■ If you want to check one of eBay's user policies or report an item you have seen that is not allowed on eBay, go to SafeHarbor (http://pages.ebay.com/help/community/index.html).

■ If you encounter a trading offense, such as shill bidding (two or more bidders working together to artificially drive up the bidding on an item), go to the Investigations page (http://pages.ebay.com/help/community/investigates.html).

10

- If you want to suggest a new sales category on eBay (for instance, if the items you typically sell don't fall into a current category), go to the Customer Support area (http://pages.ebay.com/help/welcome/customer-support.html).

Before you fill out any of the support forms provided on these different pages, you should first turn to eBay's Help Center for some do-it-yourself support.

eBay's Help Center

You should also visit the Help Center if you have a question about a glossary term or a procedure. You might find that the answer to your question has already been published on eBay itself—and frankly, if the answer is there, you'll find it more quickly than by waiting for eBay to respond to one of your direct inquiries. It's easy to reach the Help Center. Just click the question mark icon (?) or click Help in the eBay navigation bar, and the eBay Help page will appear.

You can navigate the Help area in a number of ways. Click A–Z Index if you want to browse an alphabetical listing of topics. Enter a term in the Search box if you want to search eBay's database of web pages on procedures and topics.

Is there a way to contact eBay directly, either by e-mail or in person? You can't just call eBay on the phone. However, you can use the Live Help function or send e-mail to the customer support staff by filling out the proper form.

Live Help

All of the contact options mentioned in this section involve some sort of delay: you submit a question in writing, by e-mail or filling out a form, and you wait for a response. One other option enables you to communicate with eBay staff in real time. It's called Live Help, and it's accessible from the eBay home page. Click Home in the navigation bar, and then click Live Help. The chat window shown in Figure 10-5 opens.

First, select the topic that applies to your inquiry from the drop-down list at the bottom of the chat window. Then, type your message or question in the box just above the drop-down list. When you are done, click Send to send your message on its way. Wait a minute or so, and before long, a response will be sent back to the chat window where you can read it and respond by typing another message, if you need to.

The Contact Form

If you have a question about bills you receive from eBay, or if you aren't receiving the end-of-auction notices you usually get from eBay, you should contact eBay directly using the Contact Us form (http://pages.ebay.com/help/contact_inline/index.html).

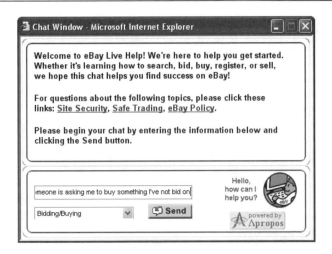

FIGURE 10-5   Communicate with a support person by typing a message in this chat window.

The form works much like the page of the Sell Your Item form that enables you to choose a category for sale (see the "Shop Around for the Right Sales Category" section in Chapter 7). First, in the box labeled 1, choose a general topic that represents the kind of question or problem you need addressed. When you choose a topic, a new set of more specific topics appears in the box labeled 2. Choose a topic in box 2, and a set of specific topics appears in box 3 (see Figure 10-6).

Did you know?   eBay Radio

Another way to connect with eBay on a "live" basis is to listen to eBay Radio. eBay Radio is a broadcast that is streamed on the Internet live every Tuesday between 11 A.M. and 1 P.M. PST. Go to www.wsradio.com and click eBay Radio to listen live. You can listen any time of the week, not just Tuesday, however; previous shows are archived, and you can click available titles to listen to the discussions. To do so, you will need an audio application such as RealAudio or Windows Media Player installed on your computer, though. You can download a copy of RealAudio's player from www.real.com. Microsoft Internet Explorer has Windows Media Player built in and can play audio files within the browser window, so you don't have to install the application yourself.

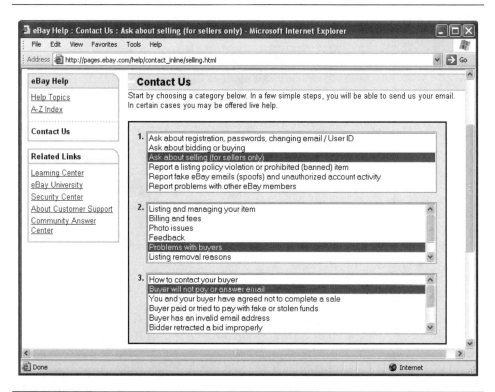

FIGURE 10-6   The Contact Us form helps you specify your issue or concern before you contact eBay.

Select a topic in box 3, and then click Continue. A new Contact Us page appears, which may present a series of Help topics. If you want to contact eBay, click Email, sign in with your User ID and password, and then click Sign In. A form appears where you can type in the message you want to send eBay. An example is shown in Figure 10-7.

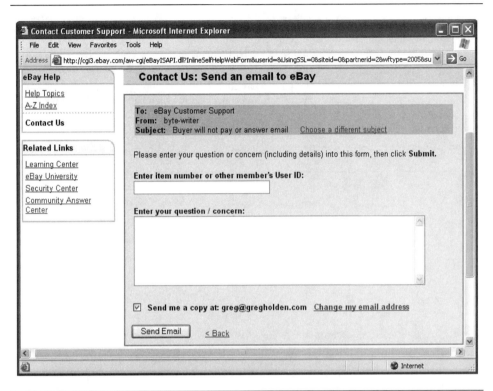

FIGURE 10-7 Fill out this form to submit an e-mail question to eBay's support staff.

Where to Find It

Web Site	Address	What's There
Andale	www.andale.com	Research data, Buy It Now comparison features, and other services for eBay members
Payment Reminder form	http://pages.ebay.com/help/ sell/bidders_payment_ reminder.html	Form you can use to send a formal payment reminder to buyers who haven't paid three to 30 days after the end of a sale

10

Web Site	Address	What's There
Non-Paying Bidder Alert form	http://cgi3.ebay.com/aw-cgi/eBayISAPI.dll?NPBComplaintForm	A form you can fill out to have eBay send an alert message to a buyer who has not yet paid
Feedback Forum	http://pages.ebay.com/services/forum/feedback.html	Links you can click to make a rebuttal or add information to feedback someone has left for you
Security Center	http://pages.ebay.com/securitycenter	Tools for reporting fraudulent use of your eBay account

Chapter 11

Insiders' Tips: Selling for Profit

How to...

- Attract more attention to your sales by adding features
- Develop your business's brand through your sales listings
- Increase your sales capacity through automation
- Install and use auction management software
- Advertise yourself and your auction listings
- Create a business web site to help boost eBay sales

eBay makes it possible for virtually anyone to put anything up for sale. But there are some tricks and some smart business practices that help sellers achieve a higher rate of success than others. What separates sellers who are frustrated at not receiving bids for their merchandise and barely breaking even from those who turn a profit?

The answer differs depending on what you want to sell and how often you want to sell on eBay. But you don't have to discover the answer on your own. Luckily, you can find out from successful sellers who have gone before you and learned from their own mistakes. This chapter describes some sales approaches that many sellers have followed in order to boost eBay bids, sales, and profits.

Adding Special Features to Your Listings

The most important feature of any eBay auction listing is the object being sold, of course. The description and title are also important, as are the photos you present. But some special features can be added to your listings to help you get more attention and increase the chances that people will bid and hopefully buy. Some suggestions are mentioned in the sections that follow.

Embedding Keywords

It used to be that when a merchant was featuring a special sale, he or she would hire a spotlight or, at the very least, have jugglers or clowns outside the store to lure in passersby. If you want potential customers, the first thing to do is provide them with a trail of breadcrumbs so they can find you. On eBay, the "breadcrumbs" are keywords that you add to the body of an auction description. You have to choose your words carefully but, if you pick the right ones, you can make your sales more visible than they would be otherwise.

Using Keywords that Apply

Suppose you are invited to a costume party with a 1970s theme and you need to find a pair of old Levi's jeans in your size. You go to the search box on one of eBay's pages (or in eBay's add-on browser toolbar), enter the keywords "Levi's bell-bottom," and press ENTER. Wouldn't it be better if you could find the same pair of pants by entering any of the following terms:

```
Levi's jeans
Levi's pants
Levi's 1970's bell-bottom
Levi's classic jeans
Levi's flare pants
```

It would help you find the pants more easily if you had these options, and it would certainly help the seller get more attention for the pants because they would be included in a far wider range of results than a simple search for "Levi's bell-bottom." Now, you can't include such words in the title, which has to be relatively short, but you can include some in the subtitle, if you pay extra for one (see Chapter 7 for instructions on how to choose a title and subtitle and other features of the Sell Your Item form). Your space is limited, however.

Thus, your job is to include as many of these keywords in your auction description as possible so the sale will pop up in a search that includes both titles and descriptions. For example, you might create a description like the following (keywords are highlighted in bold).

```
Classic Levi's 1970's Bell-Bottom Jeans
Hoping to recapture the past with a pair of classic pants from the 1970's? These
original Levi's bell-bottomed jeans will do the trick. These size 36-31 pants are in
excellent condition with moderate fading around the knees and a generous flare around
the bottom. They will go perfectly with other 1970's clothes I am presenting in other
sales, such as a denim shirt, Earth shoes, and extra-wide ties.
```

Notice the use of "bell-bottom" in the title and "bell-bottomed" in the description to ensure that the sale will come up in response to a search for each of those terms. Also note the inclusion of keywords that describe other sales of related items. The more keywords you include, the better your chances of having your sale appear in search results. The tricky part is including keywords that are actually relevant to what you are selling, not to someone else's items, as described in the next section.

11

Avoiding Keyword Spamming

Most people search for keywords when they are looking for an item or even when they just have a few minutes to kill and want to amuse themselves. If you include those keywords in your auction title or description, your auction will be viewed more often. The most popular keywords will attract the most attention. Knowing this, some sellers go so far as to include brand names that don't even relate to the item being sold to attract extra attention.

The classic example—and one that is specifically prohibited by eBay—occurs when a not-so-famous or not-very-desirable brand is described with a title that includes some very famous and desirable brands. On the other hand, some well-known brands are joined with the word NOT to some other well-known brands just to gain more attention. Here are just a few examples I found at random on eBay when I searched for the word "NOT."

```
2 Pair Old Navy Jeans NOT Gap/Levi's
New Gallery Clock 25" Not Howard Miller
Pair of Pentagon 10 Subwoofers Not Sony Xplod
```

It can be argued that it's actually helpful to include the word "Not" in these auction titles. After all, if someone is really expecting to find a Howard Miller clock and they click the second title in the preceding list, they won't be surprised that the clock is another brand. But that's not why such titles are frequently used on eBay. In many cases, the authors are practicing keyword spamming or, as eBay has described it more recently, search manipulation—the inclusion of keywords that don't apply to the object being sold just so those auctions will turn up more often in eBay search results.

eBay's policy is to withdraw any auctions that use keyword spamming. Yet, you see them frequently on eBay because so many sales occur at any one time, and because eBay can't be everywhere at once.

NOTE   *eBay's Verified Rights Owners program (VeRO) helps protect the copyright and trademarks of businesspeople. In the program, individual eBay users "police" auctions, looking for violations of their own (and others') copyright or trademark. The point for you, as a seller, is to be aware of recent efforts to avoid infringement and make sure your descriptions don't include keywords or brand names that might get you in trouble. Find out more at http://pages.ebay.com/help/confidence/vero-rights-owner.html.*

The use of "Not" is only the most obvious instance of what eBay considers keyword spamming. But any combination of words that represents a well-known brand name may be considered keyword spamming, and auction sellers can be suspended for doing it, even without consciously trying to do so. For instance, sales have been withdrawn in which the words "shabby" and "chic" occurred in the same sentence. The theory is that the use of the terms closely resembles the trademarked brand name Shabby Chic. If you are selling a Ralph Lauren shirt, for instance, it's okay to include the following:

```
Size 15-35 Ralph Lauren shirt
```

It's not okay to say the following:

```
Size 15-35 Ralph Lauren shirt, Giorgio Armani-style
```

You also can't compare items in your titles, like this:

```
Size 15-35 Ralph Lauren shirt, better than Gap or Perry Ellis!
```

In any case, make sure that the keywords embedded in your product description will get your item noticed—but not removed.

> **TIP**   *eBay held a workshop on Search Manipulation & Keyword Spamming in February 2004. The comments by eBay staff people who participated made it clear that eBay is taking a stronger stance on the misuse of keywords. You can read the archived proceedings at http://forums.ebay.com/db2/ thread.jsp?forum=93.*

11

Tracking Auction Success with a Hit Counter

How many times have you gone into a store only to be greeted by a "Hi, I'm glad you're here"? There may be security reasons for the person standing at the entrance with a big smile on their face, but there is a good chance that they are also counting bodies. The number of people who visit a store after a big ad runs in the newspaper versus a commercial on the local television station is definitely of interest to them.

Tracking business is a big part of marketing. I know because I used to write recruitment literature for a major university that was designed to attract high-school students. One measure of my success was the amount of inquiries versus the number of applicants versus the number of students who actually accepted the offer of admission. So, try out different ways of presenting products and then keep track of the numbers. They will tell you a story and it will be worth your while to listen.

As stated in Chapter 7, eBay's Sell Your Item form enables you to add one of two different types of counters to your auction listings. You have your choice of a counter that others can see, or one that is only visible to the seller. The former can actually turn people off if there isn't a lot of activity, so I suggest that secrecy is a good policy here. Just keep in mind that hits should only record the amount of visits, not whether or not a person viewed your item more than once. You can also add a free counter if you sign up for one with the auction service Andale (see Figure 11-1).

TIP *If you have a hidden counter, you can view it by clicking the View My Counters link at the bottom of the Selling tab on your My eBay page. In order to get a hidden counter, you have to sign up for an account with the auction service Andale. Andale (www.andale.com) is popular with many eBay sellers because it offers a free counter as well as a Counter Pro version that includes statistics on the best time to start your sales, based on when shoppers view your auctions.*

FIGURE 11-1 Counters are usually placed at the bottom of a listing so they don't interfere with the description.

Letting Your Listings Build Your Brand

A "brand," in business terms, is something that represents the identity of a commercial entity. Brands are established by slogans or logos. Think about eBay itself: its own brand is built around its distinctive and colorful logo, and by catchphrases used in advertisements such as "Do it eBay."

One way to boost sales is to kick your sales descriptions up a notch. Instead of straightforward listings, turn them into advertisements that build your identity as an eBay seller. Reputation and professional appearance count for a great deal on eBay. Any time you can enhance your own identity as a reputable reliable seller, you should do it. Consider the standard description (shown in Figure 11-2) used by Lori Baboulis to advertise her own business, NYC Designs for Less.

As you can see from the figure, Lori created a logo with two photos and some distinctive type. She has a link to her eBay Store, and a button that enables high bidders or buyers to check out quickly using a system created by the auction service Andale (www.andale.com).

Beneath these features, Lori also includes a boxed selection of other items she is currently offering for sale. This, too, is provided as a service by Andale (see Figure 11-3). Beneath that box, there's another set of suggested items provided by eBay itself.

11

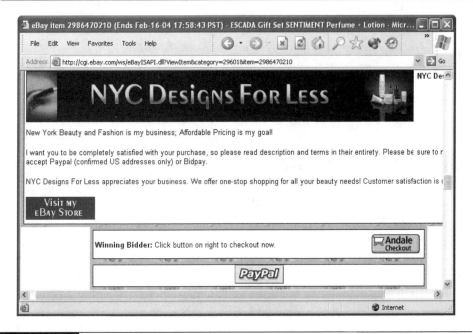

FIGURE 11-2   Sales descriptions can be used to build a business's brand.

FIGURE 11-3   Promote your eBay Store's inventory as part of your auction listings.

> **TIP** *Andale's "suggested items" feature is called the Gallery. You can add it to your auction listings for $2.95 per month, or as part of a $34.95-per-month package that includes counters, research on eBay sales, and image hosting. Find out more about Andale's features at www.andale.com/corp/products/ products.jsp.*

Automating Your Selling

The more merchandise you are able to sell within a given period, the greater your profits will be during that period. Rather than posting sales descriptions one by one and filling out the Sell Your Item form each time, you should devise an assembly-line approach. Manufacturers from Henry Ford to Hewlett-Packard know that it's not enough to have good products. You have to be able to turn out those products on an ongoing basis.

You do this by automating the tasks that are repetitive. By automating, you find time for the things that really make selling fun: shopping for bargains; making connections with customers and other sellers; and spending time with your family. The sections that follow describe ways to save time preparing sales, thus allowing you to focus on what's really important while boosting your bottom line.

Using Templates

Whenever you create a sales description for eBay and put it online, you are filling out a form with standard information. Some of the information is unique to the item, such as the description and photos. Much of the rest is information about you, your business if you have one, and the way you accept payments. This "boilerplate" content is the same from sale to sale.

If you already fill the Sell Your Item form with standard information, you can save yourself some work by creating a sales template. A template is a preformatted set of items that appears the same from issue to issue. A template saves time, and it lets readers know what to expect. If you get to the point where—like many of the sellers I profile in this book—you need to get 20, 30, or even more items online every day, a template can help you build volume with optimum efficiency.

Many eBay sellers create an auction template in the form of an HTML web page. The template contains the name of their business (if they have one), their shipping and payment policies, and any other phrases that apply to all of their auctions. I've taken the liberty of altering one of the auction listings of eBay seller Jill Featherston (User ID: bargain-hunters-dream), and showing it in Figure 11-4. The title, photo, and description are added in for each sale (as well as a graphic border that complements what's being sold). The standard information about payments is at the bottom and remains the same from sale to sale.

The beauty of a template is that your auction listing is actually half-complete before you even start. After you've taken your photos (see Chapter 8) and researched your item, simply paste the material that is unique to each sales item (the name, the description, and the links to images) into the template. You simply upload their pages, reopen their original template file, and paste in the descriptions that apply to the next sales item.

 eBay has a service called Seller's Assistant that streamlines the process of creating templates. See the section "Seller's Assistant" later in this chapter for more information.

Pasting Standard Information

In Figure 11-4, I've drawn a big X to mark the spots where the unique description and photos should appear in the template. Jill Featherston's template has another

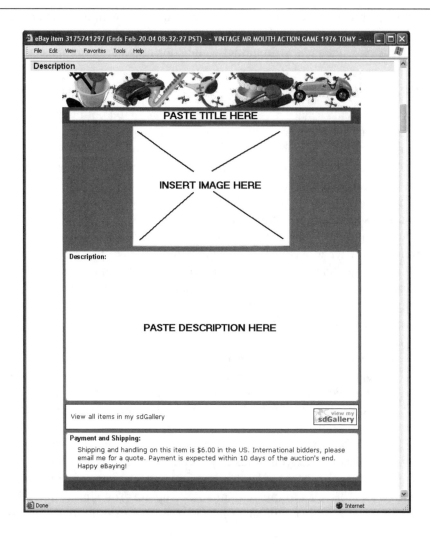

FIGURE 11-4   A template lets you create auctions quickly by saving standard information.

formatting trick: It's been formatted as a web page table, a container that allows web page contents to be arranged in the form of rows and columns. In this case, the table serves two functions. First, it keeps the auction listing at a fixed width so it's easier to read (it takes up a single column in the middle of the page), and second, the table has been divided into multiple rows. The first row includes the border, the second includes the title, and so on. Tables are useful ways to organize the contents of web pages and gain some control over how they turn out.

Once you have come up with a "look and feel" for your auction listings—one that might include a background, colors, graphics, and a logo—you need to add the parts of the template that you want identical from listing to listing. In the world of publishing, this sort of content is called "boilerplate." These elements might include the following:

- The name of your business

- Your shipping options

- Your payment options

- Your contact information

- Any additional statements about your policies, such as money-back guarantees, not selling to first-time bidders, not shipping overseas, and so on.

Create your listing and save it as a text document so you can simply copy and paste the contents from auction to auction. Your auction "boilerplate" might look like the following:

```
Beak Treats
Homemade Bird Treats for Feathered Friends
[REPLACE WITH AUCTION DESCRIPTION]
Buyer to pay $7.50 for shipping via USPS Priority Mail.
Ground shipping also available on request
International customers will pay extra air mail shipping charges.
Payment must be received within ten days of auction closing.
Money orders and personal checks accepted, but please note that checks take seven to
ten days to clear before item will ship.
We also accept Western Union Auction Payments and PayPal.
Illinois residents will be responsible for an additional 8.75% sales tax.
Feel free to e-mail us with questions. We will be happy to provide additional
information as needed.
```

You might also include HyperText Markup Language (HTML) formatting commands with your description to give your sale some graphic interest. To get some examples of simple HTML commands, click the HTML tips link just to the right of the Description box in the Sell Your Item form.

 *For more on formatting auction descriptions with HTML, see my book* How to Do Everything with Your HTML Business, *or* How to Do Everything with HTML *by James Pence. Both are published by Osborne/McGraw-Hill.*

Entering the Description

Once you have a template and boilerplate, you need to come up with what you might call the "silverplate" part of your listing: the actual description that applies to the merchandise itself. You do this by opening the Sell Your Item form:

1. From just about any part of the eBay site, click the Sell button in the navigation bar at the top of the page.

2. Sign in as a seller and create a seller account if you need to (see Chapter 7).

3. When the Sell Your Item form appears, fill it out. Paste your template into the Description box in the form (shown in Figure 11-5). Then add the details specific to the item you are listing, and put your sale online. You can use some tricks when you're creating the contents of your description to make your sale more attractive to bidders, such as imaginative words and good images, as described in the sections that follow.

TIP   *Auction listings don't have to be completely unique. While it's not a good idea to completely copy someone else's description and paste it into your own listing, you can use good descriptions as a "starting point" for creating your own if you are tired or in a hurry. Auction descriptions, like other web publications, are protected by copyright. However, the truth is that plenty of eBay sellers "reuse" one another's descriptions as a shortcut, or at least look at other descriptions for inspiration or tips on how to write their own listings.*

Using Auction Management Software

Many of the sellers who offer multiple sales listings each week make use of some sort of software to streamline the process of formatting their descriptions and

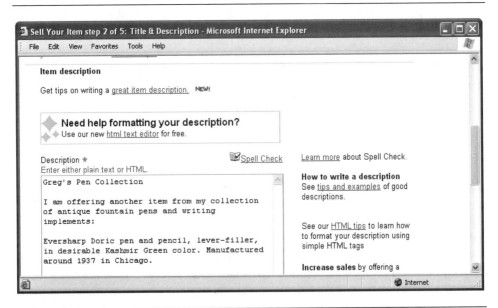

FIGURE 11-5 Paste your auction template into the Description box in the Sell Your Item form.

getting them online. The standard auction listing shown earlier in Figure 11-4 indicates that seller Jill Featherston uses software to create listings and add other features provided by SpareDollar Corporation. Others use similar software created by Andale (www.andale.com). eBay, too, offers several programs that help its members prepare and format multiple sales by means of a user-friendly interface. They're discussed in the sections that follow.

For a modest monthly fee of $4.95, SpareDollar (www.sparedollar.com) provides auction image hosting, auction listing software, and add-ons such as counters to its users.

Seller's Assistant

Seller's Assistant has two different levels. The Basic version, called Seller's Assistant Basic, provides you with 20 templates for designing sales listings and allows you to upload listings in bulk—you can upload, say, a dozen auction listings at one time. The Seller's Assistant Pro version enables you to create your own macros so you can repeat a sequence of steps and leave automated feedback in bulk with multiple User IDs. Both versions of the software are free for a 30-day trial period, but the monthly fee for the Pro ($24.99) is three times as much as for the Basic ($9.99).

TIP *To find out more about Seller's Assistant and to download a trial version, go to http://pages.ebay.com/sellers_assistant/index.html. Both programs require Windows 95 or later, a 200 MHz or faster processor, at least 64MB RAM, Microsoft Internet Explorer 5.01 or later, and 40MB free hard drive space. No Macintosh version is available, however.*

One important thing to keep in mind about Seller's Assistant is that it is software that you download and install on your computer. Like web browsers, word-processing applications, and other programs, it takes up disk space and consumes some of your computer's processing power. If new features are made available and updated versions are released, you have to download and install those new versions, too.

Other auction management applications (for example, Selling Manager, which is described in the following section) are made available as online services. You subscribe and pay a monthly fee to use the service, just as you do with your Internet service provider. You access the service with your web browser, and you don't have to install or learn to use a separate software application.

To get started with Seller's Assistant, go to the home page URL http://pages .ebay.com/sellers_assistant/index.html. Scroll down to the bottom of the page and click Feature Comparison to get an idea of the differences between the two versions of the software. Seller's Assistant Pro has the following features that Seller's Assistant Basic does not have:

- **The ability to schedule when sales go online**   This is important, because it enables you to control when sales end. You can arrange sales so they end on weekends when eBay gets the most traffic.

- **Bulk relisting**   Suppose you have 40 items up for sale in one week, and 20 of them go unsold. Bulk relisting lets you put all of that merchandise online at the same time.

- **Label printing**   You can print out mailing labels with the software using your buyer's contact information. Every bit of automation you can add saves you a few more minutes at shipping time.

■ **The ability to create sales reports and export them to another application such as Microsoft Excel**   If you depend on eBay for a substantial part of your income, such reports can be important. They can help you get business loans or streamline the process of doing your taxes.

> **NOTE**
>
> *On the other hand, Seller's Assistant Pro has some disadvantages for beginning-level users. It is a bigger file to download (20.5MB, compared with Basic's 17.3MB). Some of its advanced features, like the ability to create macros so you can prepare your own automated tasks, may be difficult to learn. If you are not familiar with computers and advanced applications, you may want to stick with Seller's Assistant Basic instead.*

When you have decided which version you want to try, click the Subscribe Now button. Follow the steps shown in succeeding pages to get started with the program.

Taking Charge with Selling Manager

If you are primarily interested in managing your ongoing sales and automating post-sales activities, consider eBay's online Selling Manager software. Selling Manager is similar to Seller's Assistant Pro, but there two very significant differences:

■ You cannot use Selling Manager to create or upload new sales descriptions. As the name implies, it's primarily a management program. (You can use Seller's Assistant or eBay's free program, Turbo Lister, which is described later in this chapter, to get your sales online and format them.)

■ Because you access Selling Manager online with your web browser rather than downloading an application, you can use it with a Windows or Macintosh computer.

Among the features are tools for tracking the status of sales; the ability to keep track of which post-auction e-mails you have sent to which customers; and the ability to quickly print invoices. There is also a feature that allows you to send preformatted e-mails. If you're a seller who has moved up to the big time (conducting dozens of sales a month), you're ready for a high-level tracker. By now, your time is worth money, and your profit is plenty big enough to handle the nominal monthly fee.

11

One of the best things about Selling Manager is the monthly fee, in fact: you can try out the software free for 30 days, and then pay $4.99 per month if you agree to keep using it. You can also get a package deal and use both Seller's Assistant Basic and Selling Manager for a combined $9.99 monthly fee. Selling Manager also has some features that eBay's other management tools don't provide, such as:

- The ability to create e-mail templates—standard e-mail programs that you send out at the end of an auction, as a sales reminder, or as a thank-you after payment is received. You only have to fill in the buyer's information and the item number of what you have sold.

- The ability to store your own favorite feedback comments and pick one to send to someone. It's not very personal, but it can save you time when you have lots of feedback to leave.

- Integration with your My eBay page. When you subscribe to Selling Manager, it appears as another tab on My eBay, so you can quickly manage sales you've bid on, feedback you've left, and other activities.

TIP   *You can find out more about Selling Manager's features by going to the program's home page, http://pages.ebay.com/selling_manager. Among other features, you can take a "guided tour" of the program that lets you see how it works with My eBay.*

Other Sales Management Software and Services

eBay isn't the only web site that provides software for managing auctions. In fact, if you pay attention to the various logos that appear at the bottom of the sales descriptions you see on eBay, you'll spot the names of other programs. Each icon indicates what auction management tool was used to format the sales listing and get it online. Before long, you're likely to spot programs like those listed in Table 11-1.

Why choose an outside service rather than eBay itself? Price is a big consideration: Some services are just less expensive than eBay's options. Another is the overall range of features that is made available to you when you subscribe to a service.

If you become a member of Inkfrog, for example, you get space to host your auction images, a program called eBay lister that you can use to format and upload sales descriptions, and management tools for relisting sales and printing invoices as well as exporting sales reports to spreadsheet applications. You would have to use two or more of eBay's applications to get all of those services (and you wouldn't get the image hosting space, either).

Service	URL	Description	Basic Membership Fee (Monthly)
Andale	www.andale.com	Each service requires separate download or subscription, though packages are available; research data is unique and of great benefit, however.	Varies depending on services used
Auctionworks	www.auctionworks.com	Good choice for existing businesses that want to expand to selling on eBay; provides inventory management and merchant account services.	$14.95
Channel Advisor	www.channeladvisor.com	Includes image hosting, auction-creation, software-inventory tracking, and fixed-price sales.	$29.95 for entry-level ChannelAdvisor Pro package
Inkfrog	www.inkfrog.com	Easy to use, with a particularly good range of features for beginning users.	$12.95 per month
SpareDollar	www.sparedollar.com	Includes image hosting, image editing, bulk uploading, counters, templates, inventory tracking, and more.	$4.95
Vendio	www.vendio.com	Includes image hosting, scheduled listings, templates, integrated UPS and USPS shipping, and more.	$12.95 to $39.95 for Sales Manager service

TABLE 11-1   Manager Software and Services

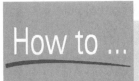

Sign Up for a Non-eBay Management Service

Each of the non-eBay auction management options involves a similar process: you sign up for a free trial if you wish, you register with a username and password, and then you either download software or begin to access services using your web browser. As an example of what to expect, here are the steps you would follow to use the least expensive of the services mentioned in Table 11-1: SpareDollar.

1. Go to the SpareDollar Corporation home page, and click the button labeled 30 Day Free Trial! Register.

2. When the Member Registration page appears, fill out the form, and then click Register.

3. Open your e-mail inbox and retrieve the e-mail message sent to you from SpareDollar. Click the hyperlink included in the body of the message.

4. When the Member Registration page appears, include your username and the password included in the e-mail from SpareDollar, and then click Activate.

5. When the page entitled SpareDollar - Powerful eBay Seller Solutions appears, click the sdLister tab so you can begin to work with SpareDollar's auction listing application.

6. When the Member Login page appears, enter your username and password, and then click Go.

7. In the sdLister Tasks column on the left-hand side of the page, click Create New Ad.

8. When the Create New Ad page appears, select the type of auction you want, and then click Next. The Create New Ad page refreshes, displaying a set of options that closely resembles eBay's own Sell Your Item form (see Figure 11-6). A Schedule section near the bottom of the page enables you to specify a starting time for your auction.

8. When you are done, click one of the buttons at the bottom of the form: Preview, Review Fees, Save Ad, or Save Ad & Launch. Save Ad lets you save the information you filled out in the form so that it remains in the form the next time you access it. You might want to do this if you want to reuse parts of the description, for instance.

By itself, sdLister doesn't represent much of an advantage over eBay's own Sell Your Item form, except in the ability to save listing information. But it's the add-on features included in the monthly fee—the counters, image-hosting tools, and other software—that make such non-eBay management solutions worth considering.

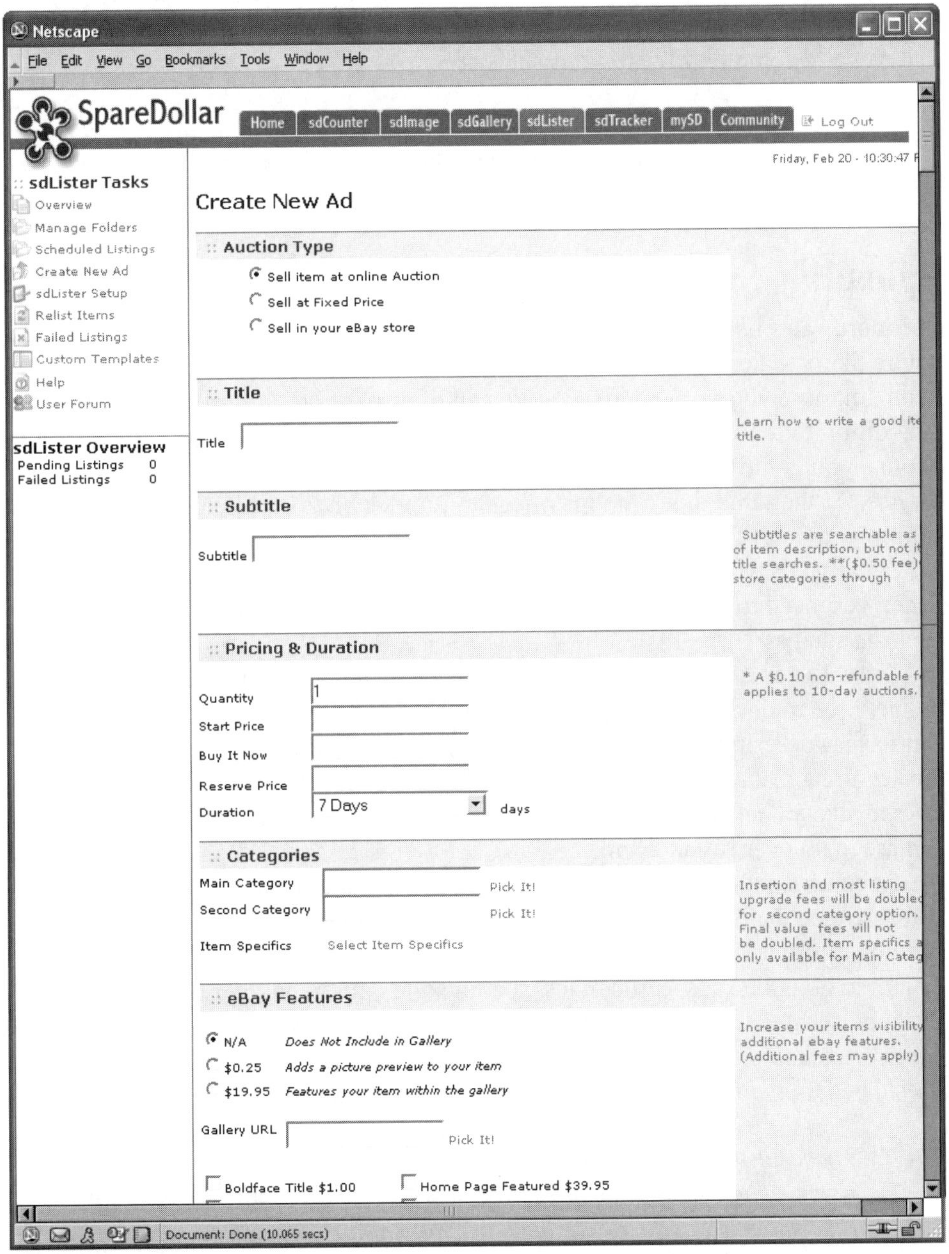

FIGURE 11-6   SpareDollar's eBay listing tool closely resembles eBay's Sell Your Item form.

If you choose Andale, you get access to the information that can help you research completed auctions on eBay, as well as hit counters and other features that can add some pizzazz to your sales.

TIP *Your own My eBay page contains some of the features mentioned in the "Sign Up for a Non-eBay Management Service" How to: box, and it's free and convenient to access. Find out more about My eBay in Chapter 2.*

Uploading Sales in Batches

The more sales listings you're able to include at any one time, the more income you're likely to generate. But the more sales you create, the more work you have to do. Suppose you open an eBay Store and offer a dozen or more items each week in addition to ten-to-twenty auction sales. If each of those sales has three or four photos, you could easily have 75 to 100 photos to upload to your photo hosting service. At the same time, you may need to remove photos of items that have been sold so you don't fill up your allocated web server space.

Luckily, eBay provides its members with a free tool for just such a purpose. When you need to get multiple photos and/or auction listings online, turn to a package such as Turbo Lister.

Turbo Lister is a smooth way to create groups of auction listings and get them online. Free to download and operate, it's all about the template. That means you can format descriptions without having to learn that nasty HTML. Scheduling is the key to its management capabilities, and the result is that you can schedule your sales to all start and end at a specified time or you can duplicate sales details so you can use them over if you want.

Turbo Lister, like Seller's Assistant, requires a fair amount of disk space and some software (see the Note that follows), but other than that it's free. Features include creating multiple listings and formatting them without using HTML, scheduling listings to go online at specific times, and tracking your remaining inventory. Turbo Lister presents you with a wizard-like interface (a wizard is a set of screens or web pages that leads you through a particular set of procedures). The Turbo Lister wizard should be familiar to anyone who has used the Sell Your Item form.

NOTE *Turbo Lister is free to download and use at http://pages.ebay.com/turbo_ lister/. The software requires Windows 98 or later, plus 20MB of hard disk space (Macintosh systems are not supported). If you'd rather use a CD-ROM to install the software rather than downloading the 18MB worth of files (perhaps you have a slow connection), you can obtain it for a $2.99 handling fee from eBay-o-Rama, eBay's online store, at www.ebayorama.com.*

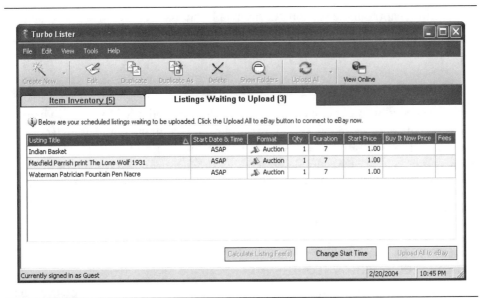

FIGURE 11-7 eBay's own Turbo Lister helps you upload groups of sales to eBay.

Like SpareDollar's auction listing program, sdLister, Turbo Lister presents you with a form that resembles eBay's own Sell Your Item form and enables you to prepare auctions. Unlike other programs, however, Turbo Lister maintains a list of all the sales you have prepared until you are ready to post them on eBay. You can scan the list (see Figure 11-7) and make sure the details are correct; then you can send them to eBay all at once.

Advertising Yourself and Your Sales

Every business needs to get the word out about its items for sale. Most eBay sellers depend on eBay's own popularity and the effectiveness of its search engines to point possible buyers to their sales descriptions. At any one time, however, there are as many as 16 million sales items on eBay, and a whopping two million new sales go online every day. Also keep in mind that there may be thousands or even millions of shoppers doing searches on eBay, and their auction searches won't turn up any of the items you have posted in your eBay Store. (eBay Stores use a different search utility than eBay's Basic Search or Advanced Search for auctions.)

One of the more obvious ways to drive prospective customers to your auctions and your eBay Store sales is through links you post on your web site (discussed later in this chapter in the section "Creating a Business Web Site"). Some other strategies for advertising yourself and your auction sales are described in the sections that follow.

Helping Searchers Find Your Sales

People who avidly collect one type of merchandise or another will look anywhere and everywhere for those few special items they need to round out their collections. But chances are, the first place they look, on eBay, is the Basic Search or Advanced Search page, or one of the simple search boxes that appear near the top of many pages on eBay's web site. Rather than waiting for shoppers to turn up one of your sales as a result of a search, you can take out advertisements just like many other commercial entities do, and place your sales directly before the eyes of prospective bidders.

Taking Out a Search Results Ad

There is a way you can literally purchase advertising space on eBay. You can even associate your ad with search keywords so that, when someone searches for one of the keywords you have specified, the search results page will turn up your ad. An example is shown in Figure 11-8. As you can see, the search for a particular type of Waterman pen did not turn up any results. But it did turn up an advertisement that refers specifically to this type of pen.

When I clicked the ad shown in the figure, my browser went not to an external web site, but to an eBay Store run by a PowerSeller with a feedback rating of more than 4000. The store's listings for pens were immediately listed on the page that appeared. How can you advertise your own wares in response to eBay searches? You don't have to have an eBay Store. You can advertise either your store's merchandise or individual auction sales by joining the eBay Keywords program.

Suppose you sell baseball trading cards. You could use the program to create an ad that appears when anyone does a search for the terms "baseball card" or "trading card." If someone clicks your ad, they go to your web site, and you pay eBay an advertising fee for this click (which, in advertising parlance, is called a *clickthrough*). You determine just how much you pay to eBay for each clickthrough; the suggested fee is 10 or 20 cents per click. The more you bid, the more likely your banner ad will appear, rather than other, similar banner ads set up by competing sellers.

NOTE   *You can find out more about eBay Keywords and sign up for a free demo at https://ebaykeywords.com/ebay/servlet/ebay/psp/stores.*

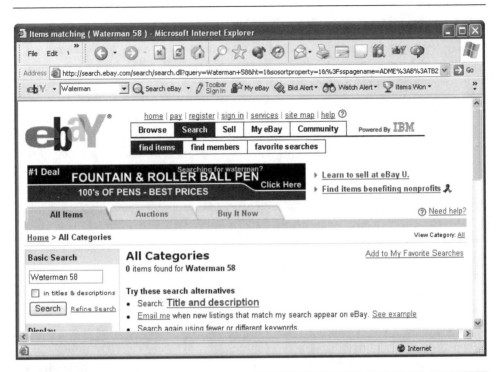

FIGURE 11-8   If you specialize in a type of item, you can advertise your sales or your web site on eBay.

Advertising Offline and Getting Reimbursed

If you become a PowerSeller (a seller with a high feedback rating and a large number of ongoing sales, as described in Chapter 12) or a Trading Assistant (someone who sells on eBay for other people), you are eligible to take out advertisements in offline media and get reimbursed by eBay. The eBay Co-Op Advertising Program will reimburse you for up to 25 percent of the cost of placing the ads, provided you meet the program's requirements. However, you must be a PowerSeller or Trading Assistant.

You also have to have an eBay Store and advertise the store and its URL in the ad, which must be placed in a printed newspaper, magazine, or catalog, not on a web site. Find out more at the program's web site, www.ebaycoopadvertising.com/Overview.aspx.

11

Creating a Business Web Site

In Chapter 7, you learned how to create an About Me web page to tell other eBay members about your buying and selling activities. When you make a commitment to increasing your profits on eBay, you should think about creating your own set of interconnected web pages—in other words, a web site.

A web site is a set of pages that exists outside of eBay. You (or someone you hire to design the pages) have complete control over how the site looks and the information contained in it. It makes sense to take this additional step if one of the following applies to you:

- You plan to sell not only through eBay but through a catalog you present on your web site, so all the income from the sale (less sales tax) comes to you and not to your web host.

- You operate a business related to the items you're selling.

- You plan to make auction sales a significant part of your income.

A business web site that is separate from your About Me page or eBay Store is an additional responsibility. Such resources are only truly effective if they are updated on a regular basis with new information: new items for sale, new promotions, links to new sales on eBay, or new information about you. Shoppers on the Web are always looking for something fresh and new, and if your site gets stale and doesn't contain anything new, they will stop visiting.

If you are ready to take on the additional responsibility of creating and maintaining your own web site, however, you open up a new way to make sales and make your business operations more successful. The following sections provide a brief overview of what you need to do to create your own web site.

> **TIP**　*At least one of the PowerSellers profiled in this book found another eBay member to design her own web site. If you see an eBay member with a web site you think is well designed, approach that person and ask if he or she will help you for a nominal charge. Or check eBay's own Professional Services area (http://pages.ebay.com/professional_services/index.html) for web designers who will be happy to create your site for a fee. When I checked, several web design companies were willing to create a simple web site with five to ten pages for less than $500.*

Finding a Host

Whether you attempt to create your own web site or want to hire someone to assemble it for you, one of your first steps is to find a service that will host your pages. A hosting service is a company that provides space on computers called web servers that are online all the time and are set up especially to make web content available online to anyone with a browser.

After you pick your host, you create your web pages, or work with the person or company you have hired to create the pages. If you do the work yourself, you have a choice of how to do it. If you are proficient with HyperText Markup Language (HTML), you can type the code yourself and build the pages from scratch. Most people, however, either make use of a user-friendly online tool such as a form you fill out to create the page, or purchase and install web page creation software and then design pages on their own computer.

Once you or your contractor have created your site, you get your pages online. Some web hosting services provide software that enables their customers to move their files to the web server where they can be seen by everyone. If you don't have access to a user-friendly way to move the files from your computer to the web server, you may need to install a special File Transfer Protocol (FTP) program to do the moving. Such programs aren't as user-friendly as filling out a web page form, but they aren't difficult to use and countless nonprogrammers like myself have learned to use them.

Where do you find a host for your web site? It's worth taking some time to find the right host because your page's location can affect how easily you create it and how it looks. You have three hosting options:

- **A free hosting service**   There aren't too many free web hosts left, but if you already have an account with America Online, you can set up your site easily. Or you can use Yahoo!GeoCities.

- **Your own ISP**   If you have an account with a company such as EarthLink, they'll usually give you space to create a simple web site as part of your monthly Internet access fee.

- **A full-time web site host**   This is a business that hosts web sites full-time and that provides lots of tools and help for creating sites that might come in handy.

Your choice of host also has an impact on how you create your web pages. Some examples are described next.

11

Free Web Hosting Services

If you aren't technically minded and have no interest in the technical aspects of designing web sites, you'll enjoy using the simple forms-based web site creators provided by AOL, Yahoo!GeoCities, and Tripod: you fill out a form, and your web pages are created and automatically placed online. If you are a member of Yahoo! already, you can sign up to set up a free web site with Yahoo! GeoCities and start creating pages in just a matter of minutes.

A variety of hosting packages is available. If you choose the free hosting option, you agree to display advertisements on your pages. You get access to a user-friendly tool called PageBuilder that creates pages by presenting you with forms that you fill out with your content (see Figure 11-9).

America Online is a wildly popular site for Internet access and, if you already have an account with AOL, you should certainly consider setting up a web page with them. If you have an account with AOL, you automatically gain 2MB of web server space where you can store your own web pages.

This might seem like only a small amount of room, but it's more than enough for a medium-sized web site, given that the typical web page only consumes 5K to 30K of disk space. Not only that, but each of the seven separate usernames you can create on AOL is entitled to 2MB of space, giving you a total of 14MB to work with.

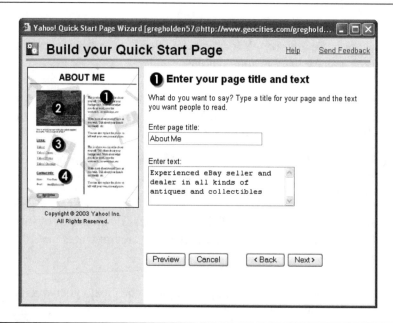

FIGURE 11-9   Free web hosts like Yahoo!GeoCities give you a user-friendly web page creation tool.

> ### TIP
> *If you don't want to show advertisements on your web pages, you can sign up for GeoCities' $4.95-per-month hosting option or the GeoCities Pro $8.95-per-month option. Find out more about Yahoo!GeoCities' hosting options at http://geocities.yahoo.com. Tripod (www.tripod.lycos.com) also offers a free, ad-supported hosting service. Other add-free hosting options are available, ranging from $4.95 to $8.95 per month. If you're looking for web space for nothing and you don't mind displaying ads on your web pages, consider Netfirms (www.netfirms.com), which gives you a whopping 25MB of server space plus the ability to create web page forms that are backed up by CGI (Common Gateway Interface) scripts.*

Your Own Internet Service Provider

The first place you should turn if you want to find a host for your own web site is the service that gives you access to the Internet: your Internet service provider (ISP). Along with Internet access, most ISPs also let users create personal home pages and publish them on a web server. The advantage of using an ISP as your host is that it's convenient and free, and you get the service anyway. Most ISP web servers are fast and reliable.

On the downside, you're pretty much on your own when it comes to obtaining software to create your web pages, and with publishing those pages by moving them from your computer to the ISP's web server. The process is hardly as user-friendly as it is on Yahoo!GeoCities or AOL, for instance.

Choose your ISP if you are satisfied with their service already and if you want to be in control and make everything look just the way you want. Be aware, though, that some ISPs discourage individual users setting up commercial web sites with the web space that comes with a personal account. If you want to set up a business site to supplement your auction sales, they want you to pay extra for a business web site account. Check with your own ISP to see what options are available.

> ### TIP
> *It's not hard to find ISPs. One of the best-known is EarthLink (www.earthlink.com). You can also peruse some lengthy and detailed lists of ISPs such as The List (http://thelist.internet.com) or Providers of Commercial Internet Access (http://celestin.com/pocia).*

I have some friends who have set up their web sites with EarthLink, and I have created a couple of web sites with my own ISP as well. EarthLink gives you a pretty good deal: at this writing, they offer unlimited dial-up access for $10.97 for the first six months and $21.95 per month thereafter. Users get 10MB of free web space and a web page creation tool called Click-n-Build, too.

11

When you use an ISP for web hosting, you don't need to necessarily use their free web editor, either. You can easily download and install the editor of your choice. By "web page editor," I mean software that lets you format web pages and then publish them on your web site.

The advantage of creating your own ISP-hosted web site is control: you can design your page by selecting your own colors and page layouts, and add as many images as you want. In contrast, a simple web page feature such as that offered by eBay lets you select a basic page layout that may or may not look the way you want.

On the other hand, the downside of creating your own web page and hosting it with an ISP is complexity: you're pretty much on your own when it comes to selecting web page software and learning how to publish your documents with the ISP. You'll probably be required to use a web page application like Macromedia Dreamweaver or Microsoft FrontPage and publish your page yourself with your ISP or a web-hosting service.

TIP   *Make sure your web host enables you to run a commercial (not just personal, but business-oriented) web site and that you can obtain an easy-to-remember domain name in the form of www.mysite.com. You can obtain such a domain name from a domain registrar such as Network Solutions (www.networksolutions.com).*

Including the Sales Content

Once you find a virtual home for your web site and you have chosen a way to create the pages, you next have to answer the question of what to put on those pages. Since your eBay sales are an important part of your business activities, you should say something about what you buy and sell on eBay. You should also talk about yourself and your products.

Keepsake Baby Bibs (www.keepsakebabybibs.com), a web site created by an eBay seller (User ID: owenandemma), has the basic information (see Figure 11-10). It also presents plenty of samples of the bib designs sold both on eBay and on the web site.

This simple, tasteful site includes the following must-have information you should consider including as well:

- An About Me page that presents a compelling story about who the seller is, what she sells, and how the business came about.

- A featured product: an item offered at a reduced price. The item changes every month.

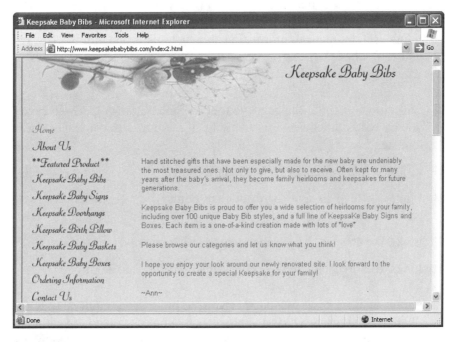

FIGURE 11-10   Promote yourself, your products, and your eBay sales on your own web site.

- A sales catalog divided into several separate categories—in this case, bibs, pillows, baskets, doorhangs, and boxes.

- An order page containing a form that customers can fill out to make purchases online. The site uses eBay's own PayPal payment system to accept credit card payments (see Chapter 9).

- A simple form enabling interested web surfers to contact the business, either by e-mail or phone.

In your own web site, as in your About Me page on eBay, you have the opportunity to provide background information about yourself. In both cases, you are able to tell visitors that you are a reputable person who can be trusted. The difference between a web site and an About Me page is the amount of detail you are able to provide.

On your web site, you can talk about yourself and then show people what you sell and explain why you sell it. You also have the chance to describe any honors, awards, or professional affiliations associated with your auction sales. You can explain, too, why you love what you do and why you're so good at it.

Providing useful, practical information about a topic is one of the best ways to market yourself online. You can provide general information about your area of interest as well as links to related resources, such as:

- Links to your About Me page, your eBay Store, or any other web pages you have; it's called *synergy*—making all of your sales components work together

- Links to your current eBay auctions, of course

- Links to eBay message boards or chat rooms where customers can meet you online

- Links to web sites or resources devoted to the item(s) you sell

- Links to sales conducted by other sellers you like and admire

Including such links is a two-edged sword. It builds community, but it also potentially leads visitors away from your web site—unless you point visitors back to your pages and your sales on eBay. You can use a program provided by eBay called the Editor Kit to include links to your current eBay auctions on one of your own web pages. Find out more at www.ebay.com/api/merchantkit.html.

Moving from Part-Time to Full-Time on eBay

Emily Baboulis made a big change right around the time she was interviewed for this book: she left her part-time job to work on eBay full-time at home while also caring for her new baby daughter. Taking the plunge was intimidating, but she gained courage from two important networks of support: a community of other sellers to call upon, and a solid base of repeat customers she had established through her web site, which is also her eBay Store. The fact that she's a Silver PowerSeller also helped give her the confidence to make the transition.

For Baboulis, the most important factor in the growth of her business, and her education as a businessperson, has been the eBay community. "The community is the crux of eBay, I believe, and what sets it apart from all other marketplaces. If it was not for the fantastic eBay community, I would not have been able to achieve the success I have," she says.

Baboulis confesses that prior to selling on eBay she had absolutely zero retail or sales experience. What's more, she describes her pre-eBay self as a computer illiterate. She was happy to discover, however, that she could find out what she needed to know by posting a question at any time of the day or night.

"From what to do about non-paying bidders to how to create a link, I'd always receive a knowledgeable answer from a fellow eBayer," she says. "I do not know of any other such forum of support anywhere. The participants in the Discussion Boards are some of the kindest, most helpful people that I have ever known. Their generosity in sharing their knowledge and experience continues to astound me. The eBay Groups are also an excellent source of information and support."

Baboulis continues the personal touch with the customer service she provides through her eBay Store. "An eBay Store does help your business and is worth the minimal ($9.95 per month) fee, I believe. Stores are excellent for sellers with multiple quantities of items, giving you a platform to showcase your entire inventory in one place. Stores encourage repeat buyers because they have one spot to search through all your items at their leisure. New buyers are great, but repeat buyers are free!" she says.

Having a lot of repeat customers was an important factor that enabled Baboulis to go from part-time to full-time selling. And what does she consider to be a primary factor in building such a strong base? Customer service is job number one. A secondary benefit of satisfying every customer within reason, she points out, is good feedback.

Communication is a simple way to increase your chances of getting favorable feedback and Baboulis touts the benefits of being in touch throughout the entire process. Among her recommendations: Answer every question honestly and in a timely manner. Post-sale, make sure you send a congratulatory winning bidder notice. A quick "payment has been received" e-mail is always appreciated. Once you ship an item, always send an "item has shipped, thank you for your order" e-mail.

Baboulis also has advice about auction management programs, which she thinks are a good idea for anyone doing eBay full-time. She points out that there are many, many available with all sorts of different features. Because most have free trials, you can look around until you find one that best suits your needs.

11

Where to Find It

Web Site	Address	What's There
eBay Verified Rights Owners program	http://pages.ebay.com/help/ confidence/vero-rights-owner.html	Information on how eBay members can help protect the rights of copyright and trademark holders
Seller's Assistant	http://pages.ebay.com/sellers_ assistant/index.html	Information about two versions of eBay's auction creation and management software you can download
Selling Manager	http://pages.ebay.com/selling_ manager	Information about two versions of eBay's auction management service. You subscribe here and use the service online.
Turbo Lister	http://pages.ebay.com/turbo_lister/	Software you download and install for free in order to get multiple sales online
eBay Keywords	https://ebaykeywords.com/ebay/ servlet/ebay/psp/stores	Advertising program in which you place an ad on eBay that appears in response to keyword searches
eBay Merchant Kit	www.ebay.com/api/ merchantkit.html	Free service that enables web site owners to link to their auction sales on eBay

Chapter 12

Running a Business on eBay

How to...

- Find merchandise you can resell for a profit on eBay

- Organize your sales activities in order to boost sales

- Increase sales by becoming a PowerSeller, Trading Assistant, or eBay Affiliate

- Practice accounting so you can save at tax time

All of the practices and techniques learned through selling on eBay lead many individuals to think about quitting their regular jobs, if they have them, and depending on eBay sales for all or part of their income. For a growing number of stay-at-home moms, antiques dealers, collectors, and entrepreneurs, eBay is an integral part of their daily lives as well as a primary source of revenue. Just how many full-time sellers are on eBay? The total is unknown, but in summer 2003, an eBay spokesman estimated in a general interview on eBay's operation (see the Tip that follows) that as many as 165,000 full-time "e-merchants" exist on the site.

Whether or not you want to "cut the cord" and turn your eBay sales activities into a full-time operation, you'll benefit from the extra steps needed to take your business to a new level. In this chapter, you'll get an overview of the things you need to do to make your eBay sales more systematic—and, as a result, more professional.

You can read or listen to the full interview with eBay's spokesman Kevin Pursglove on the Web Talk Guys site, www.webtalkguys.com/ article-ebay.shtml. Pursglove gives specifics on how many people use the site, how it has expanded internationally, and why eBay has become so popular.

Purchasing Inventory for Resale

After you have cleaned out your attic, basement, and garage, and raided the homes of your parents and other relatives and then sold all those items at auction, the question naturally arises: where do you find other treasures that you can resell for a profit on eBay? If you plan to turn your sales on eBay into a regular source of income, you'll quickly discover that finding items that shoppers want and that you can sell at a profit is one of your biggest challenges. The following general principles can help you develop a system for strategic purchasing:

- ■ **Come up with a focus**   You can be a generalist and sell all kinds of collectibles and merchandise if you are able to find them on a regular basis, but many sellers have found that by focusing on a particular area they know and love, they have better success. Most of the PowerSellers I've interviewed specialize in a particular type of merchandise: automotive memorabilia, cosmetics, clothing, and so on.

- ■ **Make friends with your suppliers**   If you get to know your resale shop managers or wholesalers, you stand a better chance of finding treasures before the competition does. You might even strike an agreement whereby a supplier actually calls you when a new shipment comes in.

- ■ **Buy out of season**   You are more likely to find winter merchandise in the summer and vice-versa, for instance.

- ■ **Advertise**   Some sellers place ads in local newspapers or post notices on supermarket bulletin boards offering their services, either as consignment sellers or as agents who buy up merchandise that people are cleaning out of their homes. Though you might have to buy a lot of things you don't want, you might find enough treasures in the bunch to make your efforts profitable.

Another tip that works in finding inventory, as well as other aspects of eBay selling, is this: don't try to do it all yourself. If you have one or two people to help you, you'll find much more than you could otherwise. You'll also have a ready source of help if you need to carry boxes from place to place.

Buying Cheaply at Government Auctions

Some of us would rather make love than war, but there are plenty of campers, students, and civilians who need sturdy, durable goods. In addition to surplus merchandise, there are always times that local governmental units need to offload items that have a rather sordid past. Your buyers need not know the product's history. If it's in good condition and the price is right, chances are you can resell it at a tidy profit.

While I was working on this book, in fact, a story appeared in the local Chicago TV news about a suburban police department that was planning to sell a 1933 Babe Ruth baseball card that had been seized as stolen property and whose owner could not be determined. The card was valued at $3,000. Not all of the property sold by municipalities and police departments is that valuable, of course, but often you can find items of value through such sales which can be resold online.

12

 *Check with your local city, county, or state to see if any auctions of surplus or unclaimed property are going to be held in your area. Also check eBay itself. A number of city and state departments sell surplus items on eBay: do a search for "surplus property" in either Basic Search or Advanced Search. Choose Exact Phrase from the drop-down list next to the search box to increase your chances of finding what you want.*

Visiting the Warehouse Stores

Costco, Sam's Club, and other warehouse stores deal in volume and only offer a limited selection. But if you can get name-brand merchandise or off-brand items that compare favorably to items sold at more well-known stores, you'll probably make a pretty good profit reselling it to someone who only wants to expend a few mouse clicks to get it.

Sometimes, the web sites operated by the warehouse stores offer desirable items like DVDs or computer games at two-for-one promotions. The Sam's Club's home page at www.samsclub.com contains a link that leads to the company's auction site (http://auctions.samsclub.com). The Sam's Club auction page, shown in Figure 12-1, is a great place to find bargains you can resell on eBay. (You can also shop online at Costco at www.costco.com).

FIGURE 12-1   Shop online at warehouse clubs to find bargains you can resell.

FIGURE 12-2 Goodwill reaches a nationwide audience through its own online auction site.

Dollar Stores, Resale Shops, and Consignment Outlets

Chances are, in your town, or in the nearest large metropolitan area, you can find a variety of outlets that sell merchandise at a deep discount. They go by a number of names—thrift shops, consignment stores, dollar stores, and so on—with specific stores being operated by Goodwill Industries, the Salvation Army, or similar organizations. By the way, you can shop Goodwill online by browsing through the organization's own online auction site (see Figure 12-2).

Don't overlook these stores, even if they don't sell antiques or collectibles. But keep in mind that the frequency with which you shop can have a bearing on what you find. For example:

■ **Look for off-season stock** Some resale shops put out Christmas items all year round, or Easter toys in the summer. You're more likely to find bargains among such seasonal items (as well as seasonal clothing) if you shop off-season.

■ **Revisit the store frequently** The resale store in my neighborhood has its employees put out new stock both at the beginning of the day and during the afternoon. Get to know when new selections are distributed. Go when the store first opens, and again later in the day after new items appear.

You might just find a batch of toys or household items that are in demand on eBay that you can purchase for a few dollars. You might even find a treasure among someone else's castoff possessions. Dollar stores are increasing in popularity, the names of which differ depending on where you live. They might be called Family Dollar in one area, or 99¢ Only in another, but the idea is the same: they sell merchandise at a dollar or less in cost, and they often sell in bulk, so you can get lots of merchandise cheaply if you have a discerning eye and can spot something that will be in demand on eBay.

Where Do You Find Merchandise to Resell?

The PowerSellers interviewed for this book have different ways of finding inventory they can resell on eBay. Some take the garage/estate sale route, while many others have struck up relationships with wholesale suppliers. They visit the same suppliers on a regular basis, saving themselves time and trouble.

"I find my own inventory primarily at yard sales and live auctions," says Jennifer Karpin-Hobbs of Morning Glorious Collectibles. "I have a few favorite second-hand shops that I haunt, looking for treasure. With retro things, what I buy and sell is different all the time. I have developed an eye for it, I look for vintage items that are collectible or beautiful and are in good condition. And I make sure I buy at a low enough price to get a strong profit margin."

In contrast, other sellers advocated working with regular suppliers, some of whom do drop-shipping—that is, delivering right to the purchaser's door. "I do deal with wholesale items, and those are delivered to me," says Jill Featherston. "However, after all these years, my favorite places to get inventory are still garage sales, flea markets, estate sales, and pawn shops. It's the thrill of the hunt. It is an amazing feeling to uncover a treasure, pay next to nothing for it, and watch the price soar on eBay!"

"I still do estate and 'vintage' pieces, but primarily I go to wholesalers and buy at wholesale shows," says Emily Sabako. "You have to be really careful and make sure there is a market for what you buy, though. I have had some great experiences and have had some total losers. You are competing with folks who get items directly from overseas; you have to be different and be able to have your merchandise found in a search of millions of items."

"My inventory is purchased in large bulk quantities from wholesalers around the nation," says Roni Neal. "Most all of these require a business license, and several of these require a minimum purchase of approximately $500 to $2000. The key here is the more you buy, the less it costs. I have made profits on all of my products. I am currently researching 'truckload inventory.'"

Obtain a Resale License

Buying wholesale can help you save money when obtaining merchandise to sell on eBay. But in order to buy directly from manufacturers or from wholesale distributors, in most cases you need to have some sort of license that identifies you as a business owner or manager. Manufacturers and wholesalers won't sell to the public. They need to know you're not buying from them just for yourself.

Call your city or county business agency to obtain the proper certificate, which might be described as a business license, tax resale license, Tax ID Certificate, or seller's permit. You will have to pay for such a permit, but on the other hand, you'll be able to make wholesale purchases without paying sales tax.

Wholesale distributors may have additional requirements. You may have to buy a minimum amount, and pay shipping and handling charges as well. Make sure you have done the research that lets you know for sure that your investment will pay off on eBay—in other words, that buyers will actually purchase what you've paid to obtain. In most cases, wholesalers don't allow you to return the merchandise if you are not satisfied.

12

TIP *eBay's own Wholesale Lots area (http://pages.ebay.com/catindex/ catwholesale.html) enables buyers and sellers to trade large quantities of items at bargain prices.*

Beating the Garage Sale Rush

Anyone who has headed out the door early in the morning and driven from one garage sale to another knows how much competition is out there for collectibles and bargains of all sorts. Professional antique dealers, collectors, and eBay sellers alike are out there, looking at the same sales you are and possibly hoping to purchase more or less the same sorts of merchandise.

Often, you have to wait in line just to have a chance at being one of the first when the sale opens. For estate sales in affluent suburbs, you might find the lines forming at 5 or 6 A.M., even if the sale opens at 9 A.M. Is it possible to find bargains without exhausting yourself? Frankly, it's getting more and more difficult to find valuable items at garage and estate sales, which is one reason why many eBay sellers turn to wholesale suppliers.

You might find a few suggestions that my mother, aunt, and other garage sale addicts I've known have tried over the years:

- **Don't go by yourself**   When the sale opens and eager buyers are combing tables, it helps to have two or three people shopping so you can visit different rooms or tables quickly.

- **Go before the sale starts**   This is a little devious, but experienced buyers do it all the time: go the night before the sale and try to talk your way into doing some shopping while the seller is still putting merchandise out for sale. Once in a while, it works.

- **Plan out your travels**   Scour the local papers as soon as they appear and plan your travels efficiently. Some sales start on Thursdays, some Fridays, and some only take place on the weekends. Plan a few sales each morning so you leave time and energy for other activities.

- **Become a dealer**   Some antiques dealers have branched out to running garage and estate sales for people who don't want to go through the work of organizing, labeling, advertising, and collecting money. The advantages of being a dealer should be obvious: you not only collect a fee based on what you are able to sell, but you see everything before it goes out on the tables and you can offer to purchase it yourself directly from the owner.

As I said, some of these strategies for finding collectibles are a little "crafty," but eBay itself is making everyone a possible dealer in secondhand merchandise, and you have to keep up with the competition.

TIP   *Many sellers are not above scouring alleys in their neighborhood the night before garbage is picked up. The art of "garbage-picking" and "dumpster-diving" is a popular activity, and those who have a discerning eye and some experience in what sells on eBay can sometimes turn up bargains.*

Becoming a Salvage Expert

The parts are equal to more than the sum when it comes to the salvage business. Whether it's a door, a light fixture, or a stained glass window, there's someone who can give new life to an old item. That someone could be you. Where I live, in a part of Chicago where many old homes are being remodeled, some local architectural detail companies and salvage companies are full of merchandise.

You, too, can scour your neighborhood for doors, doorknobs, fixtures, and architectural trim that you can resell. Be sure to give exact measurements and clear descriptions when you create your sales listings. That way, both you, the seller, and your buyer will end up happy.

You can also find bargains at going-out-of-business sales. You can't always predict why a seemingly perfectly good store fails. The owner may wish to retire, or may decide to relocate for any number of reasons. At any rate, they leave behind a smorgasbord of furnishings, shelving, or other store fixtures. Often, they're just happy to have you haul off what they can't use any more, permitting you to get some very nice stuff at really low prices.

Getting Organized

You've decided that it's time to take your auction sales to the next level. You need to turn what's currently an occasional thrill into a regular routine. If you are able to turn your eBay sales activities into a regular system, your sales will rise. In many ways, it's a matter of changing your perspective. The sections that follow describe some ways to organize your eBay selling, such as paying attention to "back office" functions like tracking customers, packing, and scheduling.

12

Keeping Track of Your Sales and Customers

You can boost sales if you're able to show people that you are professional in your manners and behavior. A professional demeanor, in turn, depends on how well you keep track of who your customers are and what stage of a transaction you are in with each person. Being professional doesn't mean you need to sell on eBay full-time, or that you need to run your own online business. Rather, it has to do with how you communicate—how quickly and completely you respond to questions from bidders, how well you deal with problems, and how promptly and carefully you pack and ship what you sell.

The easiest way to track your sales activities is through your My eBay page. It enables you to keep tabs on the items you currently have up for sale. The Items I've Sold section of the Selling page has a convenient list of all of your high bidders.

Simply clicking the User ID of each one lets you send the person an e-mail message. You can click Payment Reminder if you haven't heard from someone within three days of a sale's end.

It doesn't matter if you use My eBay, eBay's Selling Manager, or another management program, the software won't do you any good if you fail to check your sales regularly and contact the people you need to reach in a timely fashion. Draw up a calendar or use a personal planner, and pencil in specific times several days a week when you take stock of completed sales to see which customers have contacted you, which have paid, and which ones have failed to respond. Go down the list until every one has been contacted; remember that the reward for all this tedious labor is an increase in your PayPal account or bank account.

Coming Up with a Schedule

It's not easy to keep straight all the responsibilities that go with being an eBay seller. Come up with a plan for how you can get to 20 sales per week: you need to obtain merchandise by scouring flea markets, auctions, or garage sales; consider enlisting the help of friends and relatives who can assist you with packing and shipping; come up with a weekly schedule and stick to it.

Such a schedule would call for you to get your sales online, say, on Monday morning; end your sales on Monday night; get a new batch of sales online Tuesday; respond to bidders Tuesday night or Wednesday morning; ship out on Thursdays and Fridays; and so on. Also, remember to remind your customers, after they have received the goods, to leave a feedback comment. Otherwise, they might well forget to do so.

Table 12-1 tracks the sales activities of two of the most successful eBay sellers I interviewed, Shannon Miller and Suzanne Ziesche of Venus Rising Limited. They complete as many as a dozen or more sales per day. Not all of the sales attract bids. Sometimes, only one or two sales a day are completed with a high bidder or buyer. But nearly every day, some sort of sale is completed. Those items that don't sell the first time around can go up for sale on their eBay Store or be relisted.

CAUTION *Be sure not to end the sale at a time when eBay is down for maintenance. Frequently, eBay goes offline around 3 A.M. PST on Friday mornings. (You'll find announcements of such system shutdowns at http://www2.ebay.com/aw/ announce.shtml.) If you attempt to end your sale at that time (this is more likely for overseas users than those in the U.S.), you should get a notice from eBay advising you to pick another time. Just the same, it's better to be aware of the occasional maintenance and avoid Friday morning endings.*

Date	Sales Completed that Day	Sales with No Bids
1/24/04	2	0
1/25/04	2	1
1/26/04	1	0
1/27/04	24	22
1/28/04	2	0
1/29/04	15	13

TABLE 12-1   Venus Rising Limited's Weekly Sales Activity on eBay

Finding Employees to Help You

One way to turn a part-time eBay sales activity into a full-time business is to work with other people rather than operating as a "lone wolf." Most auction sellers who turn around dozens of sales each week have friends, relatives, or employees to help them. (In some cases, the friends and relatives are paid employees.) It's ideal for two people to divide up the weekly tasks: the carrying, the photography, the publishing, the shipping, and the bookkeeping.

Look first to your family: enlist your kids, your brothers and sisters, anyone who has time and is willing to help. Some sellers even find college students to carry boxes or to stand in line at estate sales. The students wait in line before the sun is up and get a number, which they turn over to the actual seller at a more reasonable hour, just before the frenzied shopping begins. The point is that you shouldn't try to do it all yourself. Distributing your workload will allow you to ship purchased items out quickly, and enable you to remain courteous with your customers.

Build a Professional Sales Reputation

Buyers on eBay are looking for bargains. And bargains are seldom hard to find. Often, among the millions of sales items that go online every day, shoppers find five, six, or more items that are similar and that they desire. The item they choose often has to do with you and your reputation and experience. They want to feel they can trust you, and they want to get what they pay for quickly.

With this in mind, you can control how much trust your bidders place in you. In many professions, service providers go to school to add some significant letters to their names, such as Ph.D., M.D., J.D., C.P.A., and so on. You can do the same in auction sales. Bob Kopcynski, who's profiled in my previous book *How to Do*

Everything with Your eBay Business, went to school and became a licensed auctioneer. You don't have to do that, yourself, but you *can* demonstrate that you know something about what you're selling. For instance, you can do the following:

- Operate a web site or online store devoted to your area of interest, as described in Chapter 11.

- Moderate a discussion group (popularly called a newsgroup) or an eBay Group devoted to what you buy or sell.

- Answer questions on eBay's message boards.

- Answer questions in Internet newsgroups about your area of interest.

If you have written any essays or books about the type of merchandise you typically sell, so much the better. Each one of Venus Rising Limited's auction sales includes the reminder that the company is the "only gold PowerSeller fine linen specialist on eBay," and mentions the article in *Newsweek* magazine in which Venus Rising was featured. Even if you don't do any of the foregoing, you can still create an About Me web page that tells visitors something about you and what you do, and about your commitment to customer service as well.

Also, when offering items for sale, you should let buyers know about any defects or flaws your merchandise has before they even bid, so they won't get any nasty surprises when they receive the item. Being accurate and honest shows your customers that you are trustworthy and that you are making every effort to be up-front with them. The description shown in Figure 12-3 is straightforward about defects, but plays up the parts of the package that are in exceptionally good condition, too.

> **TIP** *You can build credibility by advertising yourself offline as well as on. Consider creating a nametag that displays your eBay User ID instead of your "real" name. Wear it to sales events such as auctions or flea markets. You just might meet fellow eBayers with whom you can share tips and experiences.*

Opening Up New Sales Channels

As stated earlier, any professional titles or honors you can cite in your auction sales or your About Me page will encourage buyers to have faith in you and bid on what you are selling. In the world of eBay, one of the most valuable icons a seller can have is the PowerSeller icon, which eBay bestows on sellers who have

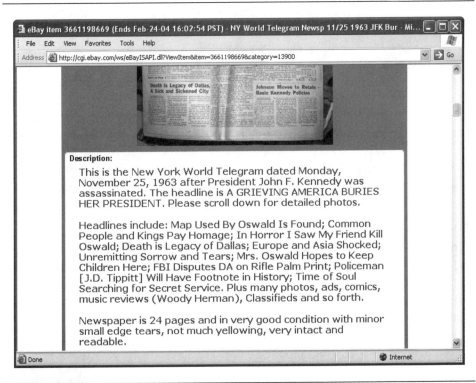

12

FIGURE 12-3   Be straightforward about your item's defects so customers won't be disappointed.

demonstrated high volume and consistently good customer service. The feedback star that accompanies your User ID and feedback rating is also important, as is designation as one of eBay's Trading Assistants.

Striving for Good Feedback

According to some sellers I have interviewed, something changes when your feedback rating gets into the 1000–1200 range. There's nothing wrong if your feedback is in the range of 200–1000. You're certainly doing well, and customers can have confidence that you will treat them fairly. But when you crack 1000, people see you as a businessperson, a professional. "When my feedback rating went over 1000, I started getting more bids and higher prices for what I was selling. It was like people recognized me as a retail businessperson, not just a part-time seller," one seller told me when I was writing *How to Do Everything with Your eBay Business*.

If, however, you want to make all or part of your regular income through selling on eBay, you need to set your sights higher—the higher, the wider your perspective will be, and the better your chances of success.

Try to establish a long-term "numbers goal" for your eBay sales. The moment you declare to yourself, "I'm going to have an 800 feedback rating by the end of the year," or "I want to be making $1000 a month on eBay by the end of the year," or, "I'm going to be a PowerSeller by the end of the year," your perspective changes. Individual sales become less important than your cumulative sales figures. Turning sales around quickly and keeping your customers satisfied becomes the top priority. Rather than focusing on this or that individual sale, you start thinking of coming up with a system, and building volume, with the ultimate goal of building profits.

Striving for PowerSeller Status

A PowerSeller is someone who has achieved a 98 percent or higher feedback rating and who has maintained at least $1000 in gross monthly sales for at least three months. You don't apply to be a PowerSeller; eBay invites you to join the program based on your sales record. Once you are a PowerSeller, the goal is to increase your monthly sales so you can move from one "tier" to another.

- **Bronze** $1000 gross monthly sales
- **Silver** $3000 gross monthly sales
- **Gold** $10,000 gross monthly sales
- **Platinum** $25,000 gross monthly sales
- **Titanium** $150,000 gross monthly sales

Besides the status of being a PowerSeller, you get one huge benefit: group health insurance through eBay, which is invaluable for people who are self-employed. How do you build a good feedback rating and become a PowerSeller? It might not take years, but it does take time, effort, and commitment.

A system for completing transactions and shipping out merchandise is essential. Do everything you can to build your feedback by putting up lots of no-reserve sales and shipping them out promptly to your high bidders or buyers. Suppose you sell 20 items a week: you'll get to a feedback rating of 1000 in a year, provided all your responses are positive.

TIP *You can find out more about the eBay PowerSeller program by clicking the PowerSeller icon when you see one next to a member's User ID.*

Becoming a Trading Assistant

As described in Chapter 7, when you are just starting out as an eBay seller and you only have a few items to sell, it's worth considering the services of a consignment seller—someone who puts items up for sale on your behalf and manages the transaction in exchange for a consignment fee. By the same token, when you turn eBay selling into a business, you should consider increasing your income by doing consignment sales.

As stated earlier in this chapter, one of a seller's biggest long-term challenges is finding a steady source of merchandise to resell. Consignment selling can help solve this problem, because people come to you with items for sale. Selling for others is a great way to boost your feedback rating quickly. The merchandise is sold under your User ID, and buyers never have to know that their objects belonged to someone other than you.

Of course, consignment selling isn't without its downsides. For one thing, it takes a lot of consignment sales to make a decent living. Some sellers charge 20 to 30 percent of an item's final sale price. Others charge a listing fee of $10 per sale, or a fee to the buyer (called a "buyer's premium") of 15 percent of the sales price. But if the item does not sell and no listing fee is charged, the seller makes nothing.

And then there is the challenge of dealing with people who may or may not understand how eBay works and who need to have the system explained by you. You may also have disagreements with owners who want to make suggestions on how you should sell their merchandise, about whether or not you should specify reserve prices, or whether or not you should relist items that don't sell the first time around.

You can take two paths toward becoming a consignment seller. One way is to sell for friends, family members, or neighbors. Another way is to become an officially designated Trading Assistant. You need to have a feedback score of more than 50, at least 97 percent positive feedback comments, and have sold at least four items in the past 30 days to join the program. Once you are a Trading Assistant, you can create a profile about yourself and your area of interest, which is then included in a searchable database of such sellers (see Figure 12-4).

To find out more about the program and how to become an assistant, go to the Trading Assistants Program page (http://contact.ebay.com/aw-cgi/eBayISAPI.dll?GetTAHubPage).

12

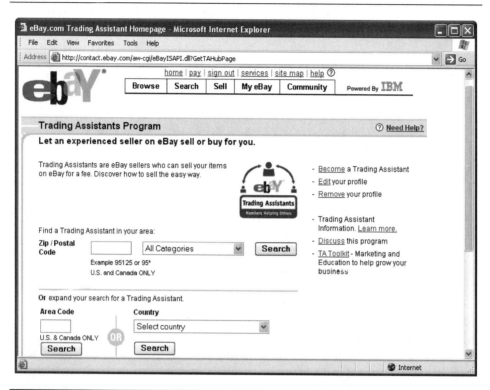

FIGURE 12-4   Trading Assistants can advertise their services in this searchable database.

Streamlining Your Accounting Practices

When you start collecting on eBay sales, you've got to start thinking about subjects that many people love to avoid: taxes and accounting. The income you receive from your eBay business is subject to tax just like any other income, even if you don't have that income documented by W-2 or 1099 forms.

I know what you're thinking: who's to know how much I make from eBay? Well, eBay certainly knows, and if the Internal Revenue Service tries to get income statements from eBay, do you think eBay is going to say no? Don't take chances. And remember that the income from your eBay business is deductible as a business expense. You can actually realize some substantial benefits from that income when it is compared to the expenses of doing business: the supplies, the mileage, the Final Value Fees, the cost of purchasing stock, the computer equipment you use, and so on. It's all a matter of keeping good records.

Just what kinds of financial things do you need to do differently when you run an eBay business? Here are a few examples:

- You may have to pay estimated taxes on a quarterly basis; self-employed people like myself don't have taxes deducted by our employers. We have to pay it to Uncle Sam four times a year.

- When tax time comes, you'll probably have to report income and expenses on Schedule C of Form 1040, Profit or Loss from Business.

- You'll need to keep all of your receipts, including the mileage spent driving to garage sales, wholesalers, and other places where you find objects to sell.

It pays to be meticulous about keeping financial records. After all, the better your records, the more accurate your estimated tax payments will be, and the more deductions you'll be able to take. Besides keeping records of your expenses, record how much income you make from eBay sales. Just how should you keep those records? That's described in the following section.

Accounting for Your eBay Business

Accountants, whether they are professional financial experts or eBay sellers who are only keeping books because they have to, choose one of two general methods to account for income and expenses:

- **Cash-basis accounting**   You report income when you actually receive it and write off expenses when you pay them. This is the easy way to report income and expenses, and probably the way most new small businesses do it.

- **Accrual-basis accounting**   This method is more complicated than the cash-basis method, but if your online business maintains an inventory, you must use the accrual method. For instance, suppose your eBay business sells an inventory of surplus items. You report income when you actually receive the payment; you write down expenses *when services are rendered* (even though you may not have made the cash payment yet). For example, suppose 25 of your eBay sales are completed on June 31, and you ask your customers to get their payments to you by July 8. The payments don't all arrive, however, until July 15. You still record the income as having been received on July 8, when the payment was originally due. Accrual-basis accounting creates a more accurate picture of a business's financial situation. If a company is having cash flow problems and is extending payment on some of its bills, cash-basis accounting provides an unduly rosy financial picture, whereas the accrual-basis method would be more accurate.

12

Because eBay businesses aren't likely to have a steady inventory, chances are the cash-based method is the one to use. Either way, this activity is called accounting because it makes use of a few standard types of business accounts:

- **Bank Account**   This is your income from sales—the good stuff.
- **Accounts Receivable**   This is the amount that people owe you and that you expect to receive at some point—those checks that are in the mail, that money in your PayPal account that hasn't yet been transferred to the bank.
- **Asset Account**   This is the value of your business assets—your inventory, your equipment, the items you currently have up for sale.
- **Expense Account**   This is the amount you have allocated for expenses.

Your eBay business consists of different financial accounts. Every time a financial event occurs, an account's balance either decreases or increases. When someone purchases one of your auction items and you deposit the payment, your bank account increases and the money people owe you decreases. The dual activity—one account goes up while another goes down—is known as *double-entry accounting*.

> TIP   *To find out more about what you need to track while you run your eBay business and what you have to pay at tax time, consult the Internal Revenue Service's Publication 334, Tax Guide for Small Businesses, www.irs.gov/pub/irs-pdf/p334.pdf.*

Voices from the Community

Debits and Credits and Bids Add Up to Success

Emily Sabako is well acquainted with the financial side of selling on eBay. She worked as a corporate Chief Financial Officer before the birth of her daughter, and as a consultant after that, but gave up this $50- to $100-per hour job for eBay when her son was born in 2001.

"I have a husband with a good job and great benefits," she explains. Most female eBayers aren't the primary breadwinner, I have found, especially if they have kids. "When I started selling my dolls and made $2000.00 for Christmas in 2001 I was hooked. The following year, I bought and sold using the 'throwing dart' method and had some great successes and great failures. I decided to focus on selling new, wholesale items in early 2003 and got my business license, resale license, etc. After around ten months of this I had my best month ever."

Sabako, who lives in San Marcos, California, only charges sales tax for transactions conducted with buyers who are California residents. She obtained her resale certificate with the State of California's Board of Equalization, which requires such permits of individuals and businesses engaged in business in California with intent "to sell or lease tangible personal property that would ordinarily be subject to sales tax if sold at retail."

At tax time, she does file Schedule C, Profit and Loss from Business. "The first year I did have a loss which, according to my accountant, is fine for a few years as 'start up' costs. She uses eBay's auction management software Seller's Assistant Pro, which uses the accrual-based rather than the cash-based accounting method. "The software calls an event a sale even if you don't have the cash in. Conversely, it does not account for all goods purchased unless they are sold."

Despite her financial background, she doesn't do the bookkeeping herself. "I don't do windows and I don't do taxes," she jokes. "Tax is a specialty and even when I was a CFO I didn't do them. We have a very seasoned tax accountant who we take all our info to and who does our taxes in about three hours. I do use Seller's Assistant Pro and I think my background in accounting and computer programs has made it pretty easy for me to use. It does a pretty good job and I also have supplementary Microsoft Excel spreadsheets that I use to supplement it for inventory management, and profit-and-loss tracking. I am still working on doing this and enhancing my tracking information.

"One of the things I think you really have to do is to apply basic business principles, including tracking and accounting procedures, to your eBay business. I have recently developed a Daily tracking sheet where I am accumulating summary daily data to use for comparison purposes. I don't know if eBay will ever get around to better info, so I am going to build my own."

eBay isn't all business for Emily. She enjoys the discussion boards, and she made many personal connections at the annual eBay Live conference in 2003, where she met eBay CEO Meg Whitman. Emily is on the left and Whitman is on the right in the image shown next.

12

Using an Accounting Program

What's the best way to record the income and expenses mentioned in the aforementioned accounts? For each item, write down a brief, informal statement. This is a personal record that you may make on a slip of paper or even on the back of a canceled check. Be sure to record the following:

- The date of the transaction

- The type of payment (PayPal, credit card, or check)

- The amount you were paid

- The name of your high bidder or buyer

You can write these figures in an old-fashioned account book using an old-fashioned pen, of course. But since you're already familiar with computers, you might want to use an accounting program to record your records.

The cost of purchasing accounting software counts as a deductible business expense, of course. Other deductible equipment includes the following:

- Your computer

- Your digital camera and/or scanner

- Modems, hubs, cables, speakers, printers, and other computer-related equipment

- Packing materials: boxes, tape, packing peanuts, and the like

- Postage machines

You might have to *expense* (in other words, spread out) the original cost of the equipment that is expected to help you generate income over its useful life. Expensing the cost of an asset over the period of its "life span" is called *depreciation*. In order to depreciate an item, you estimate how many years you're going to use it and then divide the original cost by the number of years. The result is the amount that you report in any given year. For example, if you purchase a digital camera that costs $1000 and you expect to use it in your business for five years, you expense $200 of the cost each year. Be sure to keep records of each device's name, model number, description, and purchase date.

A good software package can help save time when it comes to accounting and tax preparation for small businesses. All let you record income and expenses and prepare business reports. The well-known packages described in the list that follows have plenty of features and add-ons. Each year, it seems, Microsoft, Intuit, Quicken, and MYOB come out with new, souped-up editions of their software, each designed to have more features than the last. On top of that, most of the products come in several versions, each with a different set of features:

- **QuickBooks Basic (www.quickbooks.com)**   A good program for small businesses that lets you track inventory as well as record income and sales. Users have access to an online Help & Support Center.

- **QuickBooks Online Edition (http://oe.quickbooks.com)**   You can try the service for free for 30 days, and then subscribe for $14.95 per month. You keep all of your books online. On the plus side, you don't have to install and keep updating the software. On the minus side, you place a lot of trust in the manufacturer, Intuit, to handle your financial information securely and maintain your privacy.

- **Quicken Premier Home & Business (www.quicken.com)**   Software oriented toward home and personal finance needs; it helps you track mileage and receivables as well as a merchant account service that enables you to receive credit card payments.

- **Peachtree First Accounting (www.peachtree.com)**   This program integrates well with Microsoft Office products and helps you handle payroll, taxes, and bill payments.

- **Microsoft Money Deluxe & Business (www.microsoft.com/money/info)** This program lets you do online banking as well as prepare taxes. It integrates your financial information with Microsoft Outlook.

In addition, Microsoft Money and Quicken let you create customizable home pages that you can configure to provide up-to-the minute reports on your stock holdings. They also help you with financial planning.

> **TIP**   *A shareware program called OWL Small Business Accounting gives you a simple way to create accounts and enter income and expenses. You can then generate financial reports that you can use to prepare your taxes.*

12

Becoming an Inc. and Reducing the Red Ink

You might think the word "corporation" is for multinational companies. But when you think about it, you, too, are a multinational business concern when you buy and sell on eBay. Some eBay businesspeople incorporate in order to shield themselves from liability. The process isn't straightforward, and you'll need a lawyer to help you through the process of incorporation. But if you incorporate and manage the corporation properly, you gain some protection from liability in case of lawsuits.

Once you decide to incorporate, you next have to pick one of three options: a chapter C corporation, a chapter S corporation, or a Limited Liability Corporation. The latter is the most likely choice for small businesses, whether they are auction concerns or not. C corporations are for big-time businesses rather than small-time auction operations. They tend to be large and have lots of shareholders. S corporations are intended for businesses with fewer than 75 shareholders, and the income the S corporation gains is subject only to personal tax, not corporate tax. Unfortunately, S corporations are still fairly complex and can take weeks to set up. Consider the Limited Liability Corporation (LLC), which combines aspects of both S and C corporations. Advantages include the following:

- Income and losses are shared by the individual investors, who are known as *members.*

- Members are subject to limited liability for debts and obligations of the LLC.

- LLCs receive favorable tax treatment.

The responsibilities of LLC members are spelled out in an operating agreement, an often complex document that you'll need a knowledgeable attorney to prepare. If you don't want to incorporate, you can run your business as a sole proprietorship. All you do is pay a small fee to your county clerk, and you're in charge. You don't need an accountant or lawyer to help you form the business (though it helps), and you certainly don't have to answer to partners or stockholders.

Paying the Piper: Sales Tax

The question "Should I charge sales tax?" is asked all the time by people who conduct business online. There's no simple answer—not yet, at least. The question of whether sales tax should be assessed on out-of-state sales that occur online is continually being debated by legislators. But at this writing, things are moving in the direction of collecting sales tax for transactions conducted on the Internet.

On November 1, 2003, the U.S. Congress allowed the Internet Tax Freedom Act to expire. The act called for a freeze on new taxes related to Internet access and e-commerce. The question of whether Congress will enact any new laws relating to online sales tax is still pending. But the Streamlined Sales Tax Project, a model law that would standardize a single sales-tax rate for goods traded across state lines, has been ratified by more than 20 states and is supported by bills proposed in both the U.S. Senate and the House. The initiative would nullify the central argument for not requiring online merchants to collect sales tax—that keeping track of all the tax laws of all state and local jurisdictions would be overly burdensome—thus, opening the door for collection of the taxes.

At this writing, you are required to add sales tax only to in-state transactions—unless, of course, you hang your hat in one of the five states that doesn't collect sales tax at all: Montana, Alaska, Delaware, New Hampshire, and Oregon. If you live in one of the states that does require you to collect sales tax, you need to collect only from your customers who live in the same state where you reside. But this could quite possibly change later in 2004. Keep track of the news, and prepare to add sales tax to the statements you send to your buyers.

> **TIP** *Most states require their merchants to charge sales tax not only on the purchase price but on shipping and handling charges as well. Check with your state to make sure. You'll find a list of links to state tax agencies at www.tannedfeet.com/state_tax_agencies.htm.*

Where to Find It

Web Site	Address	What's There
Wholesale Lots	http://pages.ebay.com/catindex/catwholesale.html	Categories of surplus, discontinued, or discounted merchandise sold in quantity
System Status Announcement Board	http://www2.ebay.com/aw/announce.shtml	Announcements of technical problems or scheduled maintenance affecting areas of eBay
Trading Assistants program	http://contact.ebay.com/aw-cgi/eBayISAPI.dll?GetTAHubPage	A searchable database of Trading Assistants and information on how to join the program
PowerSeller page	http://pages.ebay.com/services/buyandsell/welcome.html	Information about who PowerSellers are and how to become one yourself

Index

Sound Off!

Visit us at **www.osborne.com/bookregistration** and let us know what you thought of this book. While you're online you'll have the opportunity to register for newsletters and special offers from McGraw-Hill/Osborne.

We want to hear from you!

Sneak Peek

Visit us today at **www.betabooks.com** and see what's coming from McGraw-Hill/Osborne tomorrow!

Based on the successful software paradigm, Bet@Books™ allows computing professionals to view partial and sometimes complete text versions of selected titles online. Bet@Books™ viewing is free, invites comments and feedback, and allows you to "test drive" books in progress on the subjects that interest you the most.

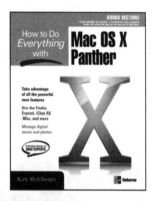
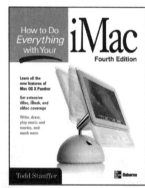

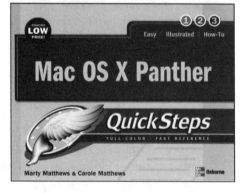